Lissa McCullough is an independent scholar who has taught religious studies at Muhlenberg College, Hanover College, and New York University. Previous books she has edited are *Thinking Through the Death of God: A Critical Companion to Thomas J. J. Altizer* (with Brian Schroeder), *The Call to Radical Theology,* and *Conversations with Paolo Soleri.*

"The Religious Philosophy of Simone Weil is a beautifully written exposé of one of the most spiritually intense thinkers of the twentieth century. Shunning the cult of personality, McCullough delves deeply into Weil's thought, offering the reader a lucid exposition of a spiritual path sustained by profound philosophical wisdom. The writing of this book, and the reading it demands, are exemplary of the kenosis that is at the core of Weil's mystical vocation. We are all indebted to the author for this labor of love."

—Elliot R. Wolfson, Judge Abraham Lieberman Professor of
Judaic Studies, New York University

"This book is a page-turner. It is totally compelling in the service of making available a religious thinking on the border between Judaism and Christianity, and also on the border between Platonism and Christianity; a thinking of God that continually troubles Christian orthodoxy while embracing it passionately; a thinking of God beyond the idolatries of divine presence. This is an extraordinarily readable text. The author's meticulously close attention to Weil's own texts makes for the appearance of the stark beauty of Weil's thought."

—Cyril O'Regan, Huisking Professor of Theology,
University of Notre Dame

THE RELIGIOUS PHILOSOPHY OF SIMONE WEIL

An Introduction

LISSA MCCULLOUGH

I.B. TAURIS

LONDON · NEW YORK

Published in 2014 by I.B.Tauris & Co Ltd
6 Salem Road, London W2 4BU
175 Fifth Avenue, New York NY 10010
www.ibtauris.com

ISBN: 978 1 78076 795 6 (HB)
    978 1 78076 796 3 (PB)

A full CIP record for this book is available from the British Library
A full CIP record is available from the Library of Congress

Library of Congress Catalog Card Number: available

Typeset in Garamond Three by OKS Prepress Services, Chennai, India

Contents

ABBREVIATIONS AND TEXTUAL NOTES

FLN	*First and Last Notebooks*
GG	*Gravity and Grace*
IC	*Intimations of Christianity among the Ancient Greeks*
LP	*Lectures on Philosophy*
N	*The Notebooks of Simone Weil*
NR	*The Need for Roots*
OC	*Oeuvres complètes*
OL	*Oppression and Liberty*
PSO	*Pensées sans ordre concernant l'amour de Dieu*
SE	*Selected Essays*
SL	*Seventy Letters*
SNL	*On Science, Necessity, and the Love of God*
SWL	Simone Pétrement, *Simone Weil: A Life*
SWR	*The Simone Weil Reader*
RM	Miklos Vetö, *The Religious Metaphysics of Simone Weil*
WG	*Waiting for God*

The bibliography contains full details for all references. An equal sign ("=") in parenthetic citations indicates that the same passage appears in two texts available in English. At points I have slightly altered the English translations for accuracy or readability. Italicization is always in the original text unless otherwise indicated. Citations of the *Oeuvres complètes* are by tome, volume, and page (for example, OC

6.4.184), or tome and page (OC 1.72) for one-volume tomes; all unpublished translations from the French are mine. Since the generic masculine is present in Weil's own French usage, I have allowed it to stand as historical and have not attempted to avoid it in my commentary. All biblical quotations are taken from the Revised Standard Version (RSV) of the Bible.

Weil's extensive notebooks are the major primary source for her religious thinking. The *Oeuvres complètes* published in 16 volumes by Gallimard (1988–2006) has made them available in the original French in a superb critical edition (*Cahiers*, tome 6, vols. 1–4). In English, the closest parallel we have is *The Notebooks of Simone Weil* (2 vols., Routledge, 1956), which spans 1940–2, combined with *First and Last Notebooks* (Routledge, 1970), which made Weil's pre-war notebooks (1933–9) and final New York and London notebooks (1942–3) available in English for the first time many years later.

Portions of Chapters 2 and 5 of this book were integrated into a presentation at the University of Amsterdam in March 2005 and published as "The Void: Simone Weil's Naming of Evil," in *Wrestling with God and with Evil: Philosophical Reflections*, ed. Hendrik M. Vroom (Amsterdam: Rodopi, 2007), 25–42.

INTRODUCTION

Where does religious feeling come from? From the fact that
there is a world. (OC 1.402)

Since her death in 1943, acute interest in Simone Weil's maverick
personality and intensely lived short life has tended to deflect
attention away from sustained consideration of her thought, or at
least has diluted the quality of attention directed to it as something
standing in its own right. As Palle Yourgrau noted recently,
"hagiography of Simone has provided a convenient excuse not to take
her *ideas* seriously."[1] Serious exposition of her philosophical and
religious thinking has in effect been in competition with her
biography. There is reason to believe that Weil herself would have
been intensely displeased with this, since she maintained that every
human being embodies a unique perspective on the world, and it is
the distinctive world-perspective, not the "personality," that
embodies a precious and irreplaceable value. "To recount the lives
of great figures in separation from the oeuvre itself," she observed,
"necessarily ends up revealing their pettiness above all, because it is
in their work that they have put the best of themselves" (OC
2.1.351). Weil felt that her perspective on the world was embodied
most essentially in her writings, not in her actions, and certainly not
in her personal biography. In life she would tolerate no attention to
her person, for the personality (*la personne*), the natural self, "that

which says I," has a strictly negative value as something to be "decreated" and rendered transparent, in her view, the better to refract the love of God in the world without egoistic distortion.

Yet the world is not—any more than the self who says "I"—an end in itself, in Weil's thinking. Although it is to be loved with all possible loyalty, the world is but a sign or metaphor of a reality that is more ultimately sacred: "The order of the world is providential [. . .]. The world is God's language to us" (N 480). If we learn how to read the world as a sign or metaphor, having freed it from the distortion of all self-centered attachments, what the world signifies to us is an anonymous presence of love. The name "God" is only a convenience for speaking about this fundamental insight concerning reality. In Weil's thought, God is never a reified concept of dogmatic religion, but a naming of reality that becomes increasingly all-pervasive and experientially certain as the dogmatic idea of "God" is dissolved as unreal. Only when all idolatrous preconceptions and illusions concerning "God" are revealed to be false does the hidden God emerge, the God encountered in the void.

Indeed, the void is Weil's primary image of God as the inexistent ground of all existence. Precisely because God is God, God does not exist (N 139, 127). If God existed as things in the world exist, God would be a creature. Everything that does exist is destined to travel into the nothingness of the void: the nothingness of the nonexistent God (FLN 310). Not only is it "God who fills the void" (N 491), but conversely also "the void is God" (N 82). Any image of God, therefore, that protects us from the truth of the void—suffering, loss, and death—is idolatrous and illusory, for "to love truth signifies to endure the void, and consequently to accept death" (N 161). But for the one who seeks it out, there is *love* in the void, a love that is the one true value, the supreme good.

This anonymous God, encountered in the void, was to become the consuming center of Simone Weil's thought from the time of her late twenties until her early death in 1943 at the age of 34. Earlier in her life she had professed agnosticism, and the subject of God was only infrequently and rather abstractly an issue for her. When she did refer to God in her early writings, it was the God of the philosophers—of

Descartes, Spinoza, and Kant in particular—who was meant, not the gracious God about whom she was later to write with passionate firsthand knowledge: "When the guest is drunk, it is then that Christ gives him the best wine" (FLN 113). As a young lycée professor with Rousseau in her intellectual background, Weil noted that "God does not teach us anything about conscience; it is the conscience (liberty) that teaches us something about God" (OC 1.402, see LP 171). Later, with her religious turn, she would come to emphasize precisely the reverse order of determination: that supernatural grace is the prevenient source of all conscience, most often "secretly" or anonymously, because it is the sole source of all authentic and pure good (FLN 122).

Biographical Groundings

It was contact with the world—actually, a passion for the *real*—that effectively turned Weil to God. Earlier in her life, Weil wrote, "my only faith had been the Stoic *amor fati* as Marcus Aurelius understood it, and I had always faithfully practised it—to love the universe as one's city, one's native country, the beloved fatherland of every soul" (SL 140). At first glance Weil's turn to God seems to be a *metanoia,* a change of mind marking a conversion from strict agnosticism. From a deeper standpoint, though, this change exhibited such underlying continuity as hardly to constitute a disjuncture at all. Weil's commitment to *amor fati* simply deepened to take on a more all-encompassing and sacred cast, and as it did she turned to language of God and grace to articulate a *love for the real*—and for *truth* as the shining forth of the real—which could no longer be adequately expressed in secular or nonreligious terms.

But at no point did Weil believe that overt religious language or "religious belief" are necessary to authentic faith or salvation. Even the name of God is dispensable. Everything that religious symbolism seeks to express is anonymously embodied in a pure, non-illusory love for the world, embraced in full awareness of its ambiguous good and evil: "Not to believe in God, but to love the universe, always, even in the throes of anguish, as a home—there lies the road toward faith by way of atheism. This is the same faith as that which shines resplendent in religious symbols. But when it is reached by this road, such symbols are of no practical use at all" (N 469).

Weil recounted in an autobiographical letter, written near the end of her life in 1942, that she grew up "in the Christian inspiration" (making no mention of the secular Jewish background of both her parents, from which she sought to dissociate herself), and that she adopted a Christian attitude with regard to the problems of life, even though the name of God had no part in her thoughts. She had decided that the problem of God was one for which the data (*les données*) are lacking here below, and in order to avoid reaching a wrong solution she resolved to remain agnostic. She recounts, "I thought that being in this world our business was to adopt the best attitude with regard to the problems of this world and that this attitude did not depend on the solution of the problem of God" (WG 62).

Yet a thirst for purity and the quest for truth had already emerged as keynotes of her vocation. At the age of 16, the "idea of purity, with all that this word can imply for a Christian" (WG 65) took possession of her in a sort of contemplative thrall as she was absorbed in a mountain landscape. She writes that the idea was "imposed" on her in an "irresistible" manner. Thus in Weil's youth there was some precedent for the several overwhelming experiences of grace, culminating in 1938, that impelled her to begin using the name of God.[2] In the year 1942 she recalled this change: "the word God had no place at all in my thoughts [. . .] until the day—about three and a half years ago—when I could no longer keep it out." Something wholly unexpected had occurred; while in a condition of intense pain from one of her chronic headaches, she had felt "a presence more personal, more certain, and more real than that of a human being" (SL 140). In the wake of this palpable experience of grace, the names of God and Christ began to occupy her thoughts. She began not only using religious language, but also directing sustained attention toward the very problem of God that she had long avoided, since apparently it was not possible to make sense of her experience without exploring it intellectually and critically.

Initially Weil resisted lending this mystical occurrence the full credence of her intellect, however, believing that "one can never wrestle enough with God if one does so out of pure regard for truth." In her reasonings about the insolubility of the problem of God, she had never foreseen the possibility of "a real contact, person to person, here below, between a human being and God" (WG 69). But after this contact, in the light of this experience, her writings began to invoke supernatural grace (*grâce surnaturelle*), by which she means specifically: a principle of thought and action not derived from the web of determinations governing natural phenomena. The supernatural is wholly other than the natural, categorically.

By referring to the supernatural, Weil does not mean to invoke an occult or superstitious belief in divine intervention, magic, or "miracle" in the commonly understood sense, but rather a certitude concerning the illuminating and transformative power of pure love wherever it occurs. Wherever love achieves a pure, unmixed presence in thought or action—and she insists that such purity is extraordinarily rare in human life—it is "supernatural" (beyond the principles of nature) in Weil's sense of the word. Love that manifests this degree of purity is not explicable by the mechanisms and energies of the natural order: it is "in" the world but not "of" the world. This love is radically contrary to the fundamental principle of nature, which is "gravity" (*pesanteur*) as she employs the term. Supernatural love is unconditioned by nature; wherever it exists within nature (meaning in the purest part of the soul) it is an inspiration directly from God.

Thus Weil's religious turn came as a surprise not only to those closest to her, but most overwhelmingly to Weil herself. As a consequence of the love of Christ that descended and "took possession" of her (*m'a prise*), Weil became a religious thinker (WG 69). Her writings record the metamorphosis of a secular and agnostic consciousness into a deeply religious consciousness as the necessary movement of a mind and sensibility coming into greater consistency with its experience. She revised her earlier materialist outlook without repudiating it in any way, but rather retaining it in a new light. Weil maintained even more stridently after these experiences that nothing is more intellectually corrupting than to harbor a "will to believe" in God or supernatural truth that has not been attested—even forced on the mind—through actual experience of grace. She continued to hold that skepticism and agnosticism are preferable to idolatry and bad faith: "Among those in whom the supernatural part of themselves has not been awakened, the atheists are right and the believers wrong" (N 238).

Where faith is absent, Weil considered it appropriate to maintain an attitude of undogmatic, provisional skepticism concerning the question of God, pending a change in the nature of one's data. Although to speak of "contact" with God seems to contradict ordinary language, derived as it is from relations between tangible objects, grace is a *datum* in the sense that it comes from outside the bounds of our own volition, hence outside the givenness of our existing nature. It is not part of us and not in our power, therefore it is something we receive by contact. Experience of the transcendent seems a contradiction in terms, she admits, and yet the transcendent "can only be known through contact, since our faculties are unable to construct it" (N 242–3).

Our faculties cannot construct the effects of grace. What our imaginative and intellectual faculties construct are religious symbols, ideas, and beliefs. The latter are our means of approaching God through the intentionality of intellect and feeling, whereas the former are God's means of inspiring and acting through us. Although the two are routinely equated, Weil distinguishes them absolutely. The latter is usually derived from the former—that is, actual experiences of grace form the bases of appropriate religious concepts—but the two are distinct movements that ought not to be confused: "It is not for man to go towards God, it is for God to go towards man. Man has only to watch and wait" (N 272). Religious concepts are a constructive means of watching and waiting for God, a means of hoping and asking for grace, but they in themselves do not attain the object. Fulfillment is *sola gratia*, by grace alone.

As we will see, loving God, for Weil, is an indirect route to loving the world and its creatures exactly as God loves them, with God's own love. While Weil frequently employs otherworldly language of "heaven" and images of transcending this world "here below" (*ici-bas*), this otherworldliness is only one side of a dialectical movement; the other side entails our return to the world as our true home and the proper object of our most sacred calling as human beings. Weil writes of our duty to love the world as our homeland— the whole world inclusively in all its particularity—as the embodiment of the providential will of God. Her term for this love is *amor fati*. We prove that we belong to God by refracting God's love into the world, sacrificially and sacramentally, through our action and our work. Love of the world is finally the whole point of talking about God, since loving God is simply a means of radically transcending ourselves and our attachment to lesser goods in order to return to the world, detached, purified, and transfigured by supernatural love—which is God's love for the world active in us.

Through this process of detachment and purification, which Weil calls *decreation*, the end to be realized is a perfect poverty of spirit— "becoming nothing"—achieving a nakedness that is not only a condition of love of God, "it is an all-sufficient condition; it is love of God" (N 282). Pure love for the world thus becomes the *criterion* of pure love of God. In fact, when it is perfectly pure, as we shall see, love of the world is a participation in the absolute love of God for God. When we become transparent to the love of God, it is God who loves the world *through us* as if through a transparent pane of glass.

Reading Simone Weil

Our focus will be on the last few years of Weil's reflections (1939–43), when language of God and religious faith becomes prominent, even dominant, in her writings. The theological ideas she recorded during these years occurred as a result of intensive contemplation of her own experience in light of what she knew or began to learn of Christian symbolism, scripture, and doctrine—as well as of non-Christian religious traditions and texts, in which she had an avid and active interest.[3] Beginning from a largely incidental knowledge of Christianity, she launched into experimental reflection on those symbols and concepts that had resonance for her, forging a highly individual—some have said heterodox and idiosyncratic—theological language as she went along. Brilliantly educated in philosophy, she tended to view whatever theology she did read from a philosophical point of view (in the tradition of the French moralists), believing that the only important difference between philosophy and theology is that philosophy is accessible to few, whereas religion—at least in the best of circumstances—becomes incarnate in an entire society. At no point did Weil study theological traditions systematically, and though this may imply "willful neglect" on her part, it was perhaps this disregard that allowed Weil to record and theorize her experience of faith spontaneously, free of doctrinal preconceptions, with uninhibited forging of theological meaning as her sole concern. Precisely this gives her religious thinking its atmosphere of immediacy, directness, and realism.

Weil did not write books but was a prolific author of thematic essays, philosophical and political articles, occasional reviews, and some 2,000 pages of meditative notebook entries. Only a few essays were published in her lifetime. Her most stunning and original religious thinking is scattered in her disparate notebook entries and passages of certain essays. This state of the texts left for posterity would seem to belie the nearly unanimous claim among her dedicated interpreters that Weil's religious thinking forms a "coherent whole" (Springsted) or "consistent whole" (McLellan), a "powerfully comprehensive vision" (Williams), a sort of "system" despite the absence of any attempt to systematize (Milosz); one having a "profound internal logic" and "organic connections" (Vetö), such that "her treatments of apparently disparate topics do hang together and frequently cannot be adequately grasped or evaluated without a view of the relation between them" (Winch). Moreover, she has "that marvellous ability, found only in the greatest thinkers, to reflect the whole of her work in each of its parts" (Rosenthal).[4]

In the realm of thinking, coherence is power, and Weil's thought undeniably manifests this kind of power despite the fragmented form of its expression. Here the aphoristic writings of Nietzsche are perhaps the nearest analog, notwithstanding that Weil could not abide reading Nietzsche, whom she detested with an "almost physical" repulsion (SL 122): "he makes me sick" (*il me rend malade*).[5] Nevertheless, what Erich Heller has written of Nietzsche also holds for Weil: "His is the brilliance of sudden illuminations, often the wisdom of deeply pondered paradoxes; and sometimes, of course, the shrill foolishness of the fool." Like Nietzsche, Weil is "the very opposite of a 'systematizer,'" yet both exemplify the power of coherent thinking, a coherence achieved through the deep pondering of paradox.[6]

The coherence that is actually there in Weil's fragmentary work must be patiently reconstructed. Though such a reconstruction is by its nature not perfectible, this matters little as long as the rough whole is brought forth with its most important insights intact. Weil's restless activity and the cataclysmic historical events of the mid-twentieth century were at least partly to blame for the fragmentary and occasional nature of her writing. She was a refugee from Nazi-occupied France in 1942 when she wrote to Jean Wahl:

> I cannot detach myself sufficiently from what is going on to make the effort of drafting, composing, etc.; and yet a part of my mind is continuously occupied with matters absolutely remote from current events (though current problems are indirectly related to them). My solution is to fill notebook after notebook with thoughts hastily set down, in no order or sequence. (SL 159)

But even setting aside the tumult in which she lived, the fragmentary expression of Weil's thought may have reflected her peculiar difficulties as a holistic thinker, however counterintuitive that may sound. For her, all thought originates in a unitary feeling, and thinking advances by distinguishing and isolating definite elements from an aggregate. Thus, ideas come about by a process of dissociation, proceeding from a feeling of the whole to a conceptual breakdown of its component elements in their interrelationship (LP 63). Weil betrayed in a letter to her mother that this effort to dissociate ideas—to pry apart the "felt" whole—was the most exhausting and agonizing aspect of thinking for her. Referring to her thought, she wrote: "It's a dense mass. What gets added to it is of a piece with the rest. As the mass grows it becomes more and more dense. I can't parcel it out into little pieces" (LP 1 = SL 196). This analytic effort on the part of the thinker calls for a reciprocal synthetic effort from the reader. Whereas the writer must manage to break down the aggregate truth into communicable thoughts, the reader must manage to "reconstitute" it, with the goal of arriving at a unitary synthetic insight.

In general, Weil has not been well treated by commentators in this regard. Her work, as David McLellan points out, has "too frequently been used to reflect personal preoccupations or points of view" and has been "more often quoted piecemeal than studied at length" (*Utopian Pessimist*, 2). Before her death, Weil herself was already pained by an awareness that readers were accepting and rejecting bits and pieces of her work, failing to grasp its unitive inspiration:

> They listen to me or read me with the same fleeting attention they give everything else, taking each little fragment of an idea as it comes along and making a definitive mental decision: "I agree with this", "I don't agree with that", "this is brilliant", "that is completely mad" [...]. They conclude: "It's very interesting", and then go on to something else. They haven't tired themselves. (SL 196–7 = LP 1–2)

Clearly, although Weil recorded her thinking piecemeal, she did not want to be read or understood piecemeal. She wanted her readers to discern the "indivisible dense mass" that ever more overwhelmingly inspired and tired her genius, even unto death. The mortal exhaustion of which she died in her early thirties was a consequence of the inescapable responsibility that came with her gift; our less onerous responsibility, if we are inclined to accept it, is to make an effort to receive it.

For all the lucidity of her style, Weil's predilection for bold, unqualified statements poses a challenge. The point of view from which she presents her thoughts can shift radically from sentence to sentence, and she rarely qualifies her statements to clarify the shift. This proves especially confounding in her dialectical language about

God: whenever she writes of God we must ask *which* God she means—or rather, which aspect of God as viewed from what point of view? Careful attention to the dialectical perspective of each statement is crucial if the structure that orders Weil's "immoderate affirmations" is to be elucidated.[7] When elucidated, Weil's affirmations remain immoderate, to be sure, but remarkably coherent and cohesive. The principal aim of this study is to elicit the dialectical structure that unifies the contradictions and paradoxes of Weil's religious thinking, the better to demonstrate how much consistent and thoughtful method lurks in her "madness." Her beyond-the-edge radicality is not mere accident or appearance but is the direct expression of a stark, unsentimental, disenchanted, and nonetheless profoundly joyful late modern religiosity, bringing light to bear on the darkest of times.

In the case of Weil's religious thinking there is a need in some sense to *establish a text*, given that we do not have a sustained treatment from her, but a mass of disconnected notes and a handful of more cohesive essays. The present exposition therefore offers a close reading that quotes heavily from her writings, and when not literally quoting often paraphrases her words. The heavy citation of sources is a necessary distraction, since the ability to locate specific thoughts and concepts is crucial for building a fuller critical understanding of her work. The purpose is to characterize Weil's theological ideas as tenably as possible from within her own perspective, using her own wording as an ever-present touchstone. This expository effort emphasizes the most coherent and holistic reading possible rather than looking for inconsistencies and logical holes, but with the conviction that, as a result of seeing the basic whole, the problems and inconsistencies will become more visible.

Frequent interpretive extrapolation on my part—a certain amount of speaking "for" her—may create the cumulative impression that I agree with everything Weil thought. That would be incorrect and, anyway, beside the point. The task at hand is simply to establish what Weil actually did think as accurately and sympathetically as possible, since only then can her thought be critiqued with justice. To date, more than a few commentators have tossed off hasty readings of Weil based on randomly emphasized fragments, only to reject summarily what she is imagined to have thought or to judge her ideas ad hominem. As McLellan notes, "facile judgements of her character have often led to equally facile judgements of her work" (*Utopian Pessimist*, 269).

To avoid this regrettable pattern, I have distinguished the secondary task of critical interpretation from the primary project of exposition, deferring it until Chapter 6. This concluding chapter contextualizes Weil vis-à-vis the key intellectual traditions and thinkers that formed and influenced her and draws out core aspects of her dialectical theology in a critical light. It finishes with suggestions as to how Weil's conception of a truly "catholic" and anonymous Christianity can help us to envision "a new religion" as Weil thought the times required—one that is of Christian inspiration while also being in some sense both post-Christian and post-Western in outlook. The predominant task of this study is expository, however, since seven decades after Weil's death we are still working on how to read her religious thinking with full attention and in one piece.

Weil's insistence that "real contact" with supernatural love is the only authentic source of religious faith must inform the way we read her work, understanding that her religious affirmations do not have their source in scriptural, dogmatic, or abstract conceptual grounds, but in her direct experience of faith and grace as refracted in the light of her critical intelligence. Because this is their source, they cannot easily—or hastily—be judged on other, extraneous grounds. Reading Weil's notebooks, one senses the ad hoc nature of her observations: sudden dawnings of insight recorded as they occur, expressed spontaneously, often in condensed gnomic phrases that are difficult to decode. There is nothing final or definitive in the form of expression—the writing is often tentative and questioning—but a deep deliberation is attested in the dedication to the inquiry itself, the restive seeking embodied in this painstaking record. If we learn from Weil only how to seek in this way, when ultimate matters are at stake, we will have received her gift.

CHAPTER 1

REALITY AND CONTRADICTION

To love truth signifies to endure the void, and consequently to accept death. Truth is on the side of death. To love truth with all one's soul is something that cannot be done without a wrenching. (N 161)

Religion could have been defined by Simone Weil as it was more recently by the Buddhist philosopher Keiji Nishitani as the "real self-awareness of reality."[1] Weil claimed that nothing is so important as to be able to define reality (N 480), and although nowhere in her writings does she make a definitive effort to do so, she does provide clues here and there toward a definition, and indeed the problem of ascertaining reality arises in her work passim. Her thinking is continually in quest of the *real*, understood as that which cannot be reduced, disciplined, or purified away; that which, when tested—not abstractly but experimentally, existentially, and especially under conditions of extreme suffering— cannot be found to be *unreal* and in this sense cannot be denied or doubted, cannot be an illusion. The real for Weil is finally the true, for "truth is the radiant manifestation of reality," and to desire truth is to desire direct contact with a piece of reality (NR 253). This makes the need for truth the most sacred need of the human soul (NR 37).

Reality: The Irreducible

Only the real has value precisely because it is real, nonillusory. The real is real by virtue of being irreducible, and its virtue is precisely its irreducibility. It is that which remains when all else has, through the discipline of necessity and the expiation of suffering, been accounted as nothing. Ultimately, what is real cannot be lost; it is inalienable. By this strict criterion, only God is maximally real for Weil. Only God is eternal, uncreated, without beginning or end, and as such can never perish or be lost. Weil acknowledges differing "degrees" of reality, reflecting a traditional Western metaphysics of being, according to which the more perfect has more reality than the less perfect.[2] God therefore has absolutely maximal reality. But her concept of creation gives this traditional "chain of Being" metaphysics a strong dialectical and existential twist: it presses the continuum of "degrees" toward a comprehensive ontological dialectic.

The world exists; God does not exist—at least not in an equivalent sense. God is transcendently real. The essential being of God resides in the fact that he is not a being or thing to whom good is attached as an attribute, but is absolutely pure good in itself (N 383, FLN 316). Following a Platonic logic at this point, Weil posits that pure good eludes all particular relationships (FLN 285). Whereas all things that exist have properties, making them a mixture (*mélange*) of good and evil, the good itself, because it is transcendent, is without properties and therefore is not representable in itself. It has no property at all except the fact of being good. The good cannot "exist" for this reason. Or rather, it "exists" or "has reality" in such a radically different sense than do things of the world that "it makes no sense to say the good exists or the good does not exist; one can only say: the good" (FLN 316).

We can only approach the good itself by analogy, tending toward the nonapprehensible (N 252). We can only represent it indexically by making an architecture of the goods that can be represented:

All goods in this world, all beauties, all truths, are diverse and partial aspects of one unique good. Therefore they are goods that need to be ranged in order [...]. Taken all together, viewed from the right point and rightly related, they make an architecture. Through this architecture the unique good, which cannot be grasped, becomes apprehensible [...]. The entire universe is nothing but a great metaphor. (FLN 98)

While God is essentially a good that does not exist, *necessity* (*nécessité*) is the essence of the reality of the things of this world. Weil uses the word necessity to invoke all reality that is essentially determinate, conditional, and contingent. Their essence lies in not being goods or ends in themselves: "Just as God is a good that is nothing else but a good, so matter is nothing else but a non-good" (N 496).

It is the creation of the world that inaugurates this dialectical relationship between two incompatible, contradictory realities—God and world—which then gets expressed in many correlative oppositions, such as necessary versus good; immanent versus transcendent; created versus uncreated; and temporal versus eternal. These oppositions derive from the primordial contradiction that originates in the will of God as creator, for creation itself is a contradiction of the infinite being of God: "It is contradictory that God, who is infinite, who is all, to whom nothing is lacking, should do something that is outside himself, that is not himself, while at the same time proceeding from himself" (N 386). The supreme contradiction, Weil writes, is the creator–creature contradiction.

There is an absolute contradiction between the nonexistential reality of God and the existence of the world. God and world are posited in inverse relationship: "Full reality for God lies outside this world, but full reality for a man lies within this world, even should he happen to be perfect" (N 374). To be grasped by the full import of this contradiction is to live in the fullest possible contact with reality. The human being as a thinking creature in the world participates existentially in the dialectic of this contradiction. Far from being an intellectual abstraction, this contradiction is undergone in all rigor by the existing creature:

God has created a whole range, an infinitely varied scale of beings. And the lowest limit of this scale in the category of thinking creatures is *the most wretched one that is capable of loving him*. The love of the most wretched one is the most precious love of all; for when such a creature has become transparent, something by way of which God can love himself, the creative act has been completed. (N 333) / God has left in the world the minimum amount of good that is indispensable for enabling a thinking and carnal creature to conceive good—the strict minimum. He has placed the greatest possible distance between his creation and Himself, who is pure good. Thus creation by itself forms a harmony, a union of opposites. (N 486)

Creation is completed only when the furthest extreme of the dialectic is reached: when the maximal goodness of God, who does not exist, is correlated with the maximal wretchedness of the creature, who does exist, across the greatest possible distance, an infinite distance. This infinite distance itself constitutes the crucifixion (N 429).

So the creator–creature contradiction that is posited in creation lays the foundation for a dialectical faith in God who is, as pure good, a totally transcendent reality.

To believe that nothing of what we are able to grasp is God. Negative faith. But also, to believe that what we are unable to grasp is more real than what we are able to grasp; that our power to grasp is not the criterion of reality, but on the contrary is deceptive. To believe, finally, that what lies beyond our grasp appears nevertheless—hidden. (N 220)

Weil's religious thought is structured at its core by a dialectical opposition between the "full reality" of God and the "full reality" of creation, two full realities that are portrayed not as in a continuum of being, but as in ontological contradiction. This fundamental framework bears closer structural resemblance to modern Christian dialectical thinkers like Hegel or Kierkegaard than to Plato or Platonic traditions. God and the world not only belong to two disparate orders of being, as in Plato, but to mutually contradicting realities, as a consequence of creation *ex nihilo*, and this contradiction defines the most elemental structure of Weil's theology. This supreme contradiction is not one that can be "solved" in the sense of eliminated or done away with: it does not admit of being denied, avoided, or evaded. It must be recognized, consented to, and lived as an "impossible" reality for as long as we exist (N 311, SNL 197). To do this is to resort to dialectical faith, a mode of existing that recognizes and contemplates the contradiction without removing it. Faith is what reconciles the *nonexistence of the good* (God) with the *existence of the nongood* (the order of the world), as we shall see in some detail.

Real contact with the reality of the world—in all its paradoxical existence-and-nonexistence—is achieved through love of the world, for to *believe* in the reality of the outside world, fully and truly, and to *love* it are one and the same thing. In the last resort, Weil claims, supernatural love is the "organ of belief" not only with regard to God, but even with regard to earthly things (N 299).

> The mind is not forced to believe in the existence of anything [...]. That is why the only organ of contact with existence is acceptance, love. That is why beauty and reality are identical. That is why pure joy and the feeling of reality are identical. Everything that is grasped by the natural faculties is hypothetical. It is only supernatural love that posits. In this way we become co-creators. (N 309)

Because of an illusion of perspective, being seems to us less and less concentrated the more remote it is from us (WG 159); therefore only love teaches us truly to believe in an external reality (N 198). Love accepts any and every event because it exists, and by this acceptance loves God through and beyond it, for nothing happens unless God wills it (FLN 136). Acceptance is none other than the full recognition that something *is* (N 293). To *recognize* reality and to *accept* it are always achieved in the same stroke of consciousness: "To accept that it should exist, because it does exist, what exactly does this mean? Is it not simply to recognize that it *is*?" (N 288).

The human faculty most effective in denying and evading reality is the imagination, which fabricates an "ersatz form of reality" for itself (N 313) as a way of escaping the inconveniences, disappointments, and sufferings inevitably caused by the contradictions in which the finite creature must live. Even in petty matters, we hate people who try to bring us to form connections we do not wish to form (N 349). The powerful falsifications and illusions put in place by imagination can be overcome only by recognizing and unveiling them as such: *"The imagination is something real*. In a sense the chief reality. But *in so far as* it is imagination" (N 125). A crucial aspect of contending with reality as we actually encounter it is contending with the ersatz reality that human imagination produces, both in individual perceptions and in collective consciousness at all levels of society.

For Weil, time is a ubiquitous component of imaginary reality, just as it is (in rather different senses) for Spinoza and Kant, who are her philosophical forebears in this judgment. Although time is not real, strictly speaking, *humanly* speaking it is the most ominous and imperious of realities; it always occupies the forefront (N 70). The illusory veil of time is woven of past and future; that is, memorializing imaginings of the past and fantasizing imaginings of what might occur in the future are the actual stuff of which a human life is composed. Both are nonexistent projections of imagination. As such they compose the real-qua-imaginary substance of all human suffering: "Suffering is nothing outside the relationship between past and future, but what is there more real for man than this relationship? It is reality itself" (N 157). Time is all too real qua imaginary; it is the stuff of which the world is woven (N 26). Time does us violence; it rends the soul (N 28). "Hell would be pure time" (FLN 198).

Because of the imperious grip of time on us, and only because of it, Weil insists, we must believe in the reality of time, otherwise we are just dreaming (N 305). But this is nonetheless to believe in the ersatz reality of time as an illusory product of human imagination, for human beings are really bound by unreal chains:

Time, strictly speaking, does not exist (except the present, as a limit), and yet it is that to which we are subjected. Such is our condition. *We are subjected to that which does not exist.* Whether it be a question of duration passively endured—physical pain, waiting, regret, remorse, fear; or of time actively handled—order, method, necessity—in either case, that to which we are subjected does not in fact exist. But our subjection exists. Really bound by unreal chains. Time, itself unreal, covers everything, ourselves included, with a veil of unreality. (N 71)

So, even though space and time are in a sense only thoughts, they constitute that which fetters thinking being beyond any possibility of liberation (N 23).

But under certain circumstances, suffering can also penetrate the unreality of time's illusions, enabling one to distinguish between real and unreal. Finally human desire must find something to love that is not unreal, even if it means that what we love is strictly speaking nonexistent, either nonactual or purely transcendent.

> Love is in need of reality. What could be more appalling than to love through a corporal appearance some imaginary being, when the day comes that one realizes the fact? Far more appalling than death, for death cannot prevent the loved one from having existed. It is the punishment for the crime of having fed love with imagination. (N 273)

Because the distinction between illusion and reality can be profoundly elusive to pin down (N 327), the danger of idolatry, or faith in a false God, is especially worrisome, for "nothing is easier than to fall into an imaginary love of God" (N 326). Even in the case of what she calls "real love of God," she asks, is it not simply a second-rate form of the imaginary revalued into a first-rate form? She finds this a "horrible thought" (N 326), for it implies that ersatz reality produced by imagination is inescapably part of irreducible reality—even in the truest and purest possible faith.

Although there is no possibility in human life to escape the effects of imagination, the principal criterion for distinguishing its falsifying illusions and projections from perception of reality is contact with *necessity*. Necessity is the criterion of reality always, in all orders of reality (N 361), because it is the obstacle that persists in contradiction to our will and its arbitrary desires.

> Reality for the human mind is contact with necessity. There is a contradiction here, for necessity is intelligible, not tangible [...]. We convince ourselves of the reality of an object by going around it, an operation successively producing varied appearances that are determined by the immobility of a form [...]. By this operation we know that the object is a thing and not an apparition, that it has a body. (IC 178)

Weil scholar J. P. Little remarks on the Weilian paradox that access to knowledge of the real begins only with the recognition of the impossibility of such access.[3] Reality represents essentially contradiction, for "reality is the obstacle," and the obstacle for a thinking being is contradiction (N 387). Necessity is that which defies our will and thereby convinces us that we are contending with a set of conditions extraneous to and independent of our desires, independent of our imaginative construal of things.

Truth and Affliction

Knowledge of the existence of something other than oneself is especially irreducible and inescapable in suffering, when the negation of good by evil is most acutely felt. This uniquely privileges suffering as a mode of relation to the supernatural. If beauty gives joy through a sense of perfect *finality*, suffering imposes a sense of perfect *emptiness of finality*, absence of significance, futility, meaninglessness, nothingness, void; whereas joy increases the feeling of reality, pain diminishes it. To find transcendent joy in suffering is a question of recognizing the same fullness of reality in the case of pain as in that of joy. In suffering, "the sensibility says: 'That is not possible.' One must reply: That *is*" (N 288). The beauty of the real then shines through suffering more purely than it can ever do through joy.

Our lives are lived in constructs and distortions of perspective that refuse reality to people and things outside the orbit of our interests. We do this systematically, according to Weil, and it is the predictable, systematic quality of the distortion that constitutes the "false reality." Because imagination is prone to uphold a false reality, acceptance of what *is* is never simply necessitated for the mind. A commitment must be made by the mind that it is preferable to be in contact with reality than with fantasy, falsehood, and illusion. This entails a commitment to the inescapable relation between truth and necessity. At this point a cognizance of the ontological poverty and perishability of the human condition is indispensable for grasping the inexorable subjection of everything to necessity: "Reality only becomes perceptible for the man who accepts death [. . .]. It is death alone that teaches us we have no existence except as a thing among a lot of other things" (FLN 285). Consciously and unconsciously, we resist awareness of reality because it entails a death-dealing immersion in the void to be seized by the realization that we are "nothing," that we are creatures constituted by radical want (IC 129), that ultimately we have no resource against the conditions that rule our existence, and that time is ineluctably carrying us where we would not go (N 28, 131).[4]

Truth is more than simply thought about reality, it is a spirit in which reality is encountered: it is a critically self-purifying relationship of thought to reality. Truth is the work that results from thought that is pure, not the expression of things themselves (LP 195). Truth is not an object, therefore it cannot be the object of love; only reality can be: "The acquisition of knowledge causes us to approach truth when it is a question of knowledge about something we love, and not in any other case" (NR 253). We desire truth in order to know the truth about what we love. Rather than talking about "love of truth," then, it is more accurate to evoke the *spirit of truth in love* (FLN 349–50). Inasmuch as truth is the thought of a purified thinker, the real value of truth is that it transforms the one who proves capable of it. When Weil writes of truth, she nearly always has in mind its power to effect salvation, for truth is the means to salvation, and because "only death is true" (NR 249), nothing apart from salvation ultimately matters in human existence.

Thus Weil writes of a purity that is achieved only through death, and that purity is *truth*. To realize that death is the truth of the human condition is to accept it, and one who does not accept it will never truly or fully *realize* it. What is to be realized is that the individual life is destined to be overruled by annihilation and negation; that from the time of birth, life is saturated with the destiny of death; that finally human life is a "nothingness."[5] Life posits a contradiction for which death is the only resolution. Weil considers this the starting point for contemplating truth as against illusion. Life is a lie, she writes: an impossible, untenable attachment (NR 249). Life must be purified of this lie if truth is to be attained (RM 183n17). Death—or rather, the in-life equivalent of death, a state of absolute detachment—is the only purification. "Total humility means consent to death, which turns us into inert nothingness. The saints are those who have really consented to death while they were still alive" (FLN 353). We must die—be killed—not literally but virtually so, undergoing in our flesh and soul the equivalent of death (N 60, 78–9).

A life that achieves detachment is lived in acceptance of the truth of death, which detaches one from the conditions of life, and this is a liberation of both energy and perspective. When one's energy and perspective are no longer devoted to serving the illusory "end" of life, which is inherently nonteleological (N 493–5), they are freed up for dedication to the real and the true. But we do not have to go out in search of reality, as though it were something rare or inaccessible. Reality is that which is ever impinging on us, contradicting our needs and desires. Yet despite the ubiquity of reality, we succeed in staving it off by denying it our attention, for "to become conscious of even the simplest realities one needs to pay attention" (SE 150). Where reality causes suffering or self-diminishment, we turn away, refusing to see, much less accept and contemplate it. Contact with reality entails a confrontation with finitude, death, perishability, irreparable loss: "There is nothing like misfortune for giving the sense of existence. Except when it gives the sense of unreality. It may give the one or the other; or even both of them" (SL 159). But precisely to submit to this contact is to learn that the world exists, that there is a real world subsisting beyond the self-orbiting perspective of the "I." Reality forces the "I" to recognize that the self-centered world-construct of the "I" must perish.

What is gained with this perishing is the world's *reality*. An abnegation of false reality and the correlative acceptance of death is the only means of receiving the joy of the real qua real. "Reality has, in a sense, need of our adherence" (N 293), and it is love—love of necessity, not necessity per se—that brings about this adherence. One comes to "believe in" reality through the voluntary reception of what is. "Love: teaches one to believe in an *external* reality [. . .]. One places the centre outside oneself. But still in something finite" (N 198). This abnegation is not natural but supernatural; when reality is encountered, it is the work of supernatural love, for as we have noted, supernatural love is the organ of belief not only with regard to God, but even to earthly things (N 299). The world's reality is such that good is intermixed with evil, and is therefore at least partially unlovable, repugnant, impossible to love. "The world is neither purely good nor purely evil, but good and evil together: in a relative sense, *mixed*; in an absolute sense, *dialectical*" (N 343). This presents the deepest of problems: how is one to love the unlovable, that is, a reality that contains every known evil, a reality encountered in terms of necessity rather than the good, though the good is "secretly present" in it?

Like death, extreme suffering, or what Weil calls "affliction" (*malheur*), impels us to question all the suppositions that support life: that life is a good, that it is worth living, an end in itself, that life can be thought of as a pursuit of happiness. "Human life is *impossible*. But affliction alone causes this to be felt" (N 311). When life's underside of wretchedness and horror is exposed, the first impulse is to close one's eyes and turn away—to deny its reality. But to close one's eyes does not take the reality away; all such denial does is break faith with the real, veiling it with a "falsified" point of view. Whereas a movement of *love* grants it full reality—however painful it may be—because it *is* real.[6]

To be dedicated to truth is to look on existence as real, contemplate it as such, and seek out the full truth of it: "Since affliction causes everything to be called in question, let us call everything in question in our own consciousness" (N 191). This is the one source of hope in the midst of human misery, for "knowledge of our misery is the only thing in us that is not miserable" (N 235, see 232). The vast majority of the time, however, we do not let reality touch us and instead live in an "I"-centered reality, filtering the world through a falsifying and distorting perspective. The most formidable obstacle to truth is this falsification inherent in the "I"-centered perspective.

Life, which is essentially attachment to the conditions of life, thrives on the basis of illusions and distortions and prefers its false reality as a survival tactic: "It is attachment that produces in us that *false reality* (ersatz form of reality) connected with the outside world. We must destroy that ersatz form of reality in ourselves in order to attain to the true reality. No doubt extreme affliction produces this far more surely than any religious practices" (N 313, see 318). The value of affliction is that it is a touchstone for reality. Affliction destroys our ersatz reality, exposing us instead to a reality outside our imaginations and illusions. Suffering offers knowledge of the real as nothing else can: knowledge of that which, because it is irreducibly real, transcends the limits of our creaturely perspective, and contact with which offers us the hope of transcending ourselves.

One dimension of Christianity that Weil unconditionally embraced is its elevation of suffering, symbolized in the cross, as the principal means of entering truth. Yet Wiel also wanted to disabuse Christianity of the criticism that it indulges in a kind of perverse delectation of suffering: "People often reproach Christianity for a morbid preoccupation with suffering and grief. This is an error" (SNL 192 = SWR 462). Christianity is concerned with real suffering—in the form of affliction—not with psychological states, she insists. No one, however perverse, could possibly find genuine affliction attractive or "choose" to become afflicted. Not even Christ was fully able to choose it, she points out, but prayed in dread that the cup be removed from him (see Mark 14:36).

Weil distinguishes between suffering, *souffrance*, and the phenomenon of affliction, *malheur*, an "admirable word" without equivalent in other languages ("we haven't got all we could out of it," N 3). The passage of her writings in which she elaborates most fully what she means by *malheur* was recorded in 1943, a historical period during which millions of human beings experienced it firsthand:

> Human thought is unable to acknowledge the reality of affliction. To acknowledge the reality of affliction means saying to oneself: "I may lose at any moment, through the play of circumstance over which I have no control, anything whatsoever that I possess, including those things that are so intimately mine that I consider them as being myself. There is nothing that I might not lose. It could happen at any moment that what I am might be abolished and replaced by anything whatsoever of the filthiest and most contemptible sort. (SE 27 = SWR 332)

Affliction is a condition of utter degradation and abject humiliation, an extreme nakedness both interior (bereft of consoling illusion) and exterior (bereft of material and social protection), that destroys forever the aspiration to natural joy (IC 180) and induces in the onlooker not pity but revulsion and contempt. The afflicted are the unburied, breathing dead; those who, while still alive, have despaired completely of life's goodness. "Affliction," Weil writes, "deprives its victims of their personality and makes them into things. It is indifferent; and it is the coldness of this indifference—a metallic coldness—that freezes all those it touches right to the depths of their souls. They will never find warmth again. They will never believe anymore that they are anyone" (WG 125). There is not real affliction unless the uprooted life is attacked in all its parts—social, psychological, and physical (WG 119)—for social degradation is an essential aspect of this abjection.

The afflicted live in a quasi-hell due to their complete uprooting in affliction. They have lost all the clothing of social standing, prestige, dignity, character; their humanity has been annihilated, and all the usual attachments have been replaced by the one of survival. Affliction under this aspect is hideous, as life in its nakedness always is, like an amputated limb or the swarming of insects (N 223). "Human injustice generally produces not martyrs but quasi-damned souls [...]. The greatest suffering that allows some roots to remain intact is still infinitely removed from this quasi-hell" (N 252). While everyone suffers misery in a metaphysical sense, only a portion of humanity at some point enters the condition that Weil calls "real misery" or affliction:

> Misery is always metaphysical; but it can be merely so, or it can be brought home to the soul through the pain and humiliation suffered by the body. That I call real misery. It was not till Christ had known the physical agony of crucifixion, the shame of blows and mockery, that he uttered his immortal cry, a question that shall remain unanswered through all times on this earth "My God, why hast thou forsaken me?" (SL 103)

The principal emotion we feel when we are the object of ill treatment is one of astonishment: Why are we being treated like that? (N 154).

All creatures suffer, but it is a matter of chance, historical circumstance, and disposition which individuals and peoples suffer most piteously in the course of time. The protective guises of society only mask the general misery of the human condition; it is in the afflicted that the truth of that condition is made visible: "Human misery is not created by the extreme affliction that falls upon some human beings, it is only revealed by it" (N 262). Those who receive the blows of necessity most nakedly in the form of affliction are least able to deceive themselves about the creaturely condition, as they are severed from their most cherished attachments and every illusion of protection is shattered.

> There is a class of people in this world who have fallen into the lowest degree of humiliation, far below beggary, and who are deprived not only of all social consideration but also, in everybody's opinion, of the specific human dignity, reason itself—and these are the only people who, in fact, are able to tell the truth. All the others lie. (SL 200)

All creatures qua creatures are essentially equal in the face of necessity, notwithstanding that all do not suffer equally. Death and the threat of affliction, taken in tandem, are the supreme equalizer, the inexorable judge of every pretension to power, autonomy, capability, or merit. Because suffering is an irreducible quantity in everyone, "every man is identical with every other man" (N 237). Social illusion persuades us that there are important differences between human beings, but this is because we manage not to see and accept the human misery to which all are equally subject. To see through social illusion, penetrating to this essential misery, is to begin to question everything, to distinguish real conditions of human existence from illusory appearances. Weil writes that helplessness, utter lack of material force, is better for the soul than triumph and power because there is truth in it; it is not poisoned with delusion and lies (SL 104). It is imperative that one contemplate affliction as a way to break the imperious grip of illusion.

Despite her reputation for rigorous asceticism, Weil does not discount the value of natural joy; it is "good, healthy and precious" (IC 180) when illuminated by a pure sense of the beauty of the world. She recommends that we "seize upon every delectation offered by pure pleasure," while thrusting aside the merely mechanical and pleasureless following of our inclinations (N 462). All desires are precious for the energy they contain (N 175), and we may legitimately respond to the things of this world with pleasure and pain, only not with willful desire and repulsion (FLN 136, 159). Natural joy does not compete with or exclude supernatural joy, nor does supernatural joy blot out natural joy: "The experience of, and the desire for, supernatural joys do not destroy the soul's aspiration to natural happiness, they confer a fullness and a significance upon it" (IC 180). But for the afflicted, the aspiration to natural joy is destroyed forever. Spiritual death takes it away irredeemably, and the only joy possible for one in such a condition is transcendent joy—a joy not of this world but from beyond the world, outside it—an incommensurate joy that passes understanding, like the affirmation that occurs to Job in the furthest depths of his suffering: "For I know that my Redeemer lives, and at last he will stand upon the earth; and after my skin has been thus destroyed, then without my flesh I shall see God" (Job 19:25–7).

Job's testimony poses a question concerning the level of love. Is love situated on the level of sheep, fields of corn, numerous children, Weil asks, or is it situated deeper down, farther back, in the third dimension, behind? The book of Job attests to a transcendent joy that becomes possible only when earthly hope is slain and a final breaking point, a point of no return, is reached—an affliction wrenching the finite toward the infinite, making the love of the soul for God *transcendent in the soul* (N 261), and this is the *death* of the soul. Joy in reality, in beauty, is felt right through the keen bitterness of abandonment and affliction, for the joy of Easter is the joy that soars above pain and perfects it: "Pain is the contrary of joy; but joy is not the contrary of pain" (FLN 69). In order to find reality in suffering, the revelation of reality must have come to one through joy, "otherwise life is nothing but a more or less evil dream" (N 291). It is through a transcendent joy in the midst of suffering that we learn that the good does not exist in this world; that human life is impossible; that "the world is necessity not purpose" (SNL 197 = SWR 466); that only death is true; hence the only life possible for us is a life that has undergone and passed through death. Because affliction alone causes the impossibility of life to be felt, "when one understands the nature of affliction, one loves it" (N 311). Thus impossibility is the sole gateway leading to God (N 341).

The Role of Attention

Reality has need of our adherence—whether it be the reality of God, the world, or another finite being. We adhere to reality by means of attention. It is attention that *real*-izes the real. Weil brings this point home by asserting, somewhat figuratively, that "God is attention without distraction" (FLN 141). Just as we deny a thing's reality by denying it our attention, so we lend a thing reality by lending it attention. "Attention is what seizes hold of reality, so that the greater the attention on the part of the mind, the greater the amount of real being in the object" (N 527). The attention we pay with our intellect

actually "gives birth" to reality in this sense, because intellect reads
necessity into relations where it would be just as possible to read
imaginary relations.

Weil embraces a Kantian position that mind is what orders reality,
since reality has no intrinsic order in itself:

> The necessary connections that constitute the very reality of the
> world have no reality in themselves except as the object of
> intellectual attention in action [...]. This virtue of intellectual
> attention makes it an image of the Wisdom of God. God creates
> by the act of thinking. We, by intellectual attention, do not
> indeed create, we produce no object, yet in our sphere we do in a
> certain way give birth to reality. (IC 188)

But Weil models the intellectual attention that gives birth to reality
more on Spinoza's "adequate ideas" than on Kant. Under the
influence of Spinoza, she posits that differing degrees of attention
confer different degrees of reality. There is a limited intellectual
attention that is capable of recognizing conditional relationships in
the order of the world, but this attention produces only a "half-
reality" (IC 188); as merely half-reality, it is a false reality—part real,
part illusion—and the source of the illusion is attachment. We must
destroy this ersatz reality to attain the true (N 313). Like Spinoza,
Weil saw the arbitrary associations of imagination, rather than
cognizance of necessary relations, as the predominant determinant of
social life and the dynamics of history, for "the social domain is
unreservedly that of the Prince of this World" (N 296). Few
individuals are ever sufficiently liberated from the spell of
imagination to attain knowledge of Spinoza's third (deductive,
rational) kind, much less of the fourth (intuitive, essential) kind.[7]
"The influence of real needs and compulsions, of real interests and
materials, is indirect because the crowd is never conscious of it. To
become conscious of even the simplest realities one needs to pay
attention" (SE 150–1).

Only extreme attention is able to grasp the full reality of the real,
and Weil calls that maximal attention *love*: "We confer upon objects

and upon persons around us all that we have of the fullness of reality when to this intellectual attention we add that attention of still higher degree which is acceptance, consent, love" (IC 188). Love (consent) produces reality (FLN 90). Extreme attention is perfectly "patient" in the etymological sense of the word, derived from the Latin *pati*, to endure: it "suffers" the reality of the object with detachment and consent, regardless whether that reality causes joy or suffering. What is attention, that it can achieve genuine contact with the real? In her most explicit description of the phenomenon, Weil characterizes it in this way: "Attention consists of suspending our thought, leaving it detached, empty, and ready to be penetrated by the object [. . .]. Above all our thought should be empty, waiting, not seeking anything, but ready to receive in its naked truth the object that is to penetrate it" (WG 111–2). Attention is an activity of desire, not will; the quality of attention is as pure and receptive as the desire that motivates it. An open, docile, detached desire is a perfectly receptive desire. It is prepared to receive that which is "other," to spontaneously respond to what comes to it from outside the domain of the will.

The act of paying attention is a supremely active passivity: "Attention is an effort, the greatest of all efforts perhaps, but it is a negative effort. Of itself, it does not involve tiredness" (WG 111). Weil's appreciation for the saying of Aeschylus, "there is no effort in what is divine" (WG 195) underscores that, for her, attention exercised purely is a grace, which is to say a supernatural rather than a natural gift, capable of attaining what a "muscular" effort of the will cannot (N 205). When attention is pure, its motivating energy is pure love. "Attention, taken to its highest degree, is the same thing as prayer. It presupposes faith and love. Another form of freedom than that of choice is bound up with it, [. . .] namely, grace" (N 205). Conversely, as well, supernatural love and prayer are nothing else but the highest form of attention (N 311).

Pure and unmixed attention is indistinguishable from prayer. Indeed, attention is in effect a prayer for truth, a receptive waiting for truth in a condition of humility. The virtue of humility in the domain of the intelligence is nothing other than pure detached attention (N 245, see 274). Since truth is the manifestation of reality to the mind, it comes to us as something extraneous to ourselves, and attention is the faculty in us capable of receiving the things given, the "data" from outside the limits of our perspectival predisposition. The way to seek the truth is by "setting our hearts on it, yet not allowing ourselves to go out in search of it" (WG 113), since searching remains a function of the will.

It follows that the wrong way of seeking is by fixing attention on a problem and, in doing so, premanding a result. We are inclined by nature to seek in the wrong way because whenever we invest our efforts, we are averse to having them wasted; this is a dread of the void, in which our energies are consumed and turned to naught. Hence, we are predisposed to depend on a reward in the form of attainment of fruits. But it is only effort not thus attached to an object that infallibly contains a reward of a higher order, for "we do not obtain the most precious gifts by going in search of them but by waiting for them" (WG 112). In intellectual endeavors, error creeps in when thought seizes on an idea too hastily, becoming prematurely blocked so that it is not open to truth; everything from poor translations to faulty arguments and awkward style is the consequence of such blockage (WG 112). Weil contends that this principle applies in all the realms of human creativity, intellectual and artistic as well as spiritual:

Active searching is prejudicial, not only to love, but also to the intelligence, whose laws are the same as those of love. We just have to wait for the solution of a geometrical problem or the meaning of a Latin or Greek sentence to come into our mind. Still more must we wait for any new scientific truth or for a beautiful line of poetry. Seeking leads us astray. This is the case with every form of what is truly good. Man should do nothing but wait for the good and keep evil away. (WG 197, see N 301)

Effort has its essential place, of course; medieval France was not "given" a Chartres cathedral by the builders' waiting for it, but Weil's point is that higher orders of achievement are attained only when a transcendent inspiration informs the labor.

A lack of objectivity, or what Weil calls "impersonality," is evident in our errors of thought and judgment. When we apply our will to attain an object, the result is inevitably a piece of ourselves; it is "pre-judicial" because the motive impulse has a preconditioning effect on the result, forefending the action of grace. Alternatively, when attention waits for what is desired without this insistence on winning a result, any result that comes is gathered from outside the demands of the will. This is the essential difference between will and attention: will keeps us bound within the determinations of ourselves, whereas attention is a grace that releases us from those bounds. This is why, Weil maintains, the greatest achievements of human creativity are arrived at indirectly. "To draw back before the object we are pursuing. *Only what is indirect is effective.* We do not accomplish anything if we have not first drawn back" (N 169). The human effort that occasions creative work is never a "mastery," properly speaking, but always actually a form of obedience; even technical power derives from obedience to a complex set of conditions. Weil was fond of quoting Francis Bacon's idea that "man can only gain control over nature by obeying it" (LP 214).

Weil defends a strict individualism of the intelligence (WG 79), yet when it is regarded and exercised properly, one's intelligence—however individual—is not one's own. "I myself cannot utilize my own intelligence," Weil wrote near the end of her life, "It is my intelligence that utilizes me, and it obeys—at least I hope that it's so—what seems to be the light of truth" (SWL 530). Any intellect consecrated and surrendered to truth cannot be utilized by any human being, not even by the person in whom it resides. The role of the intelligence is solely one of submission to truth (N 238). "Attention alone—that attention which is so full that the 'I' disappears—is required of me" (N 179).

In intellectual, technical, and artistic pursuits, then, a detached, patient, waiting mind or sensibility is the most productive because it most effectively transcends the limits of the "I" and is most receptive to what does not already belong to it. This is why we must keep our desire "tense and undirected" (N 593), for attention is nonactive action of the divine part of the soul upon the rest of the soul (N 262). "The pure and authentic values—truth, beauty, and goodness—in a human being's activity are the result of one single and self-same act, a certain application of the attention at its fullest to the object" (N 449). Contact with these pure values brings joy, and Weil insists that the intelligence can function only in joy, as the absence of joy asphyxiates it; it is perhaps the only one of our faculties "to which joy is indispensable" (IC 123). Desire for beauty, when it reaches a certain degree of intensity and purity, is the same thing as genius. It is a barely disguised desire for God—or rather, for the incarnation of God in the world—since the beauty of the world is God's own beauty (IC 150). "The highest ecstasy is the attention at its fullest. It is by desiring God that one becomes capable of attention" (N 515).

Attention is a kind of obedience; it is the virtue of humility in the domain of the intelligence (N 245). In fact, pure attention as such is a species of genius, and the virtue of attention is in every respect similar to artistic creation (N 417). The great artist and the saint are practitioners, in different ways, of the genius of attention; both callings entail keeping the attention oriented purely to the transcendent. All true novelty in science and art is the work of genius, and true genius, unlike talent, is supernatural (IC 171). "That to which authentic genius has access, to the exclusion of the common run of mankind, is purely and simply the transcendent, which is also the object of sainthood" (N 260, SE 26–7 = SWR 329).

Weil does accept the existence of a spiritual elite; she distinguishes "the elect" from the "common run of mankind" in a quasi-Jansenist fashion.[8] But it is crucial to note that for Weil the essential nature of this spiritual gift is such that it banishes any taint of "elitism" among the few who have it:

> Genius is distinct from talent, to my mind, by its deep regard and intelligence for the common life of common people—I mean people without talent. The most beautiful poetry is the poetry that can best express, in its truth, the life of people who can't write poetry. Outside of that, there is only clever poetry;

and mankind can do very well without clever poetry. Cleverness makes the aristocracy of intelligence; the soul of genius is *caritas*, in the Christian signification of the word; the sense that every human being is all-important. (SL 104–5)

The least indulgence of elitism would bar one from the cadre of those geniuses and saints whose lives are governed by *caritas*, since the virtue of humility is incompatible with the sense of belonging to a social group chosen by God (FLN 297).

The Negative Role of Will

Everything that is grasped by the natural faculties is only hypothetical. The motive that breaks through this de-realizing tendency is love, for love is in need of reality (N 273). Love must have a real object to love, in its truth, as it really is (FLN 350); therefore love, in the form of attention, teaches us to believe in an external reality. Only supernatural love posits the reality of things, thereby making us co-creators (N 309). It places the center outside oneself (N 198) and makes the attention creative of reality. But just as in the case of God, for whom creation is a *renunciation* of power and being (as we shall see in Chapter 3), this co-creative act of paying attention on our part is a renunciation, a self-abdication:

> The attention is creative. But at the moment when it is engaged it is a renunciation. This is true, at least, if it is pure. Man accepts to be diminished by concentrating on an expenditure of energy, which will not extend his own power but will only give existence to a being other than himself, who will exist independently of him. (WG 147)

Attention is a self-abnegating discipline of the mind, grounded in the supernatural humility and generosity of love. Because this is so, it is a movement of grace contrary to our "nature," our will, and for this reason, something in our natural faculties has a far more violent repugnance to it than the flesh has for bodily fatigue. This repugnance toward paying attention, Weil maintains, is much more closely connected with evil than is the flesh as such (WG 111) because it reinforces ersatz reality, giving license to evil.

It is the will that resists, since in itself it has no desire to renounce its own illusory claim to being in order to give reality to other beings, except those on which it substantially depends; it has no incentive to recognize beings that are "unusable" and only diminish its own power to say "I." This is the reason, as David McLellan paraphrases Weil's idea, "it is granted to very few minds to discover that things and people exist" (*Utopian Pessimist*, 181). When we do truly give attention to things and people, this constitutes our consent to their existence (N 527) and a corresponding renunciation of our will. And precisely to know that others veritably exist—to know this with one's whole soul—constitutes what is most precious and most desirable (N 51).

An effective way of pursuing this negation of the will without inadvertently reinforcing willfulness is to shift the will's desire away from *something*—whatever supports its substantial being—to *nothing*. This is to say, if one succeeds in training one's will to desire the void, the will as such is debilitated and transcended.

> In all our acts of willing, whatever they may be, over and beyond the particular object, we must want gratuitously, want the void. For this good that we can neither visualize nor define represents for us a void. But this void means more to us than all plenitudes put together. If we manage to reach this point, we are out of trouble, for it is God who fills the void. (N 491)

When we enter the void and electively remain there, the will is denied and succumbs to a grace that lies outside it, for "if one finds the fullness of joy in the thought that God *is*, one must find the same fullness in the knowledge that oneself is not, for it is the same thought" (N 291).

Attention is intimately related to desire, not to will (N 527). Will by its very nature is a barrier to true attention. Just as we are not able to take a single step "toward heaven" (WG 194), we cannot take a single step outside our "I"-saying perspective by means of the will. "The effort that brings a soul to salvation is like the effort of looking or of listening [...]. It is an act of attention and consent; whereas what language designates as will is something suggestive of muscular effort" (WG 193). Will is on the level of the natural part of the soul, whereas pure attention is supernatural; it is love, and all pure love descends from God. The good begins at a point beyond the reach of will, just as truth begins at a point beyond the reach of intelligence (FLN 262).

Weil's thinking on the will is consonant with that of the later Augustine. In consequence of the Fall (conceived radically differently by each), the will is in bondage and can do only evil. "When our actions only depend on earthly energies, subject to the necessity of this world, we are incapable of thinking and doing anything but evil" (WG 221–2). Even "good works" are evil when they are motivated out of will rather than obedience to supernatural love, that is, to grace: "Whatever the 'I' does is bad, without any exception, including good, because the 'I' itself is bad" (N 361, 417). Nevertheless, the will does play a subordinate role in salvation. The will may be used for one thing that is "good" due to its negative, deconstructive, decreative effect: it may pursue the task of uprooting and removing itself (N 298). The only good use for the will is a negative one (N 404): "The right use of the will is a condition of salvation, necessary no doubt but remote, inferior, very subordinate and purely negative. The weeds are pulled up by the muscular effort of the peasant, but only sun and water can make the corn grow. The will cannot produce any good in the soul" (WG 193). Though it cannot produce any good, the will can be employed negatively in a way that is good. To overcome our faults we must not turn to the will for help because the will is impotent to produce good; instead we must try to cure faults by cultivating a purer capacity for paying attention (N 265).

The Value of Contradiction

Weil embraces contradiction as the thinking creature's avenue to truth. To lack a sense of ultimate contradiction or paradox is to lack truth on two fundamental levels. First, it is to lack a legitimate concept of eternity, transcendence, or the supernatural. For her, as for the Danish religious thinker Søren Kierkegaard, the supernatural must be adequately heteronomous or "alien" (N 248) from a creaturely point of view to have the power to transform the creature through its otherness, through the enticement of calling and conversion. This culminates in "decreation" (*décréation*)—a key Weilian concept that is fully elaborated in Chapter 5. To implore God is to attempt to cause the divine values to pass into one's own soul, and any such attempt produces an interior void that is a self-voiding: "One desires to become other than one is; one is thus turned toward the outside" (N 188). At a second level, also, to lack contradiction or paradox is to lack an adequate grasp of the nature of created existence as such. Just as "contradiction is our path leading toward God because we are creatures, and because creation is itself a contradiction" (N 385–6), Weil equally maintains that contradiction is our path to the reality of the world because it is only through contradiction that thought comes in contact with necessity:

> Reality represents essentially contradiction. For reality is the obstacle, and the obstacle for a thinking being is contradiction. (N 387–8) / *The contradictions that the mind is brought up against form the only realities, the only means of judging what is real. There is no contradiction in what is imaginary. Contradiction is the test on the part of necessity.* (N 329) / Only necessity is an object of knowledge. Nothing else can be grasped by thought. Necessity is known through exploration, experiment, experience [...]. Necessity is the thing with which human thought has contact. (FLN 143)

Contradiction is what evokes thought, for wherever there is contradiction there is a relation, a *ratio*, a correlation of contraries. When the intelligence is brought up against a contradiction, it is obliged to conceive a relation that transforms the contradiction into a correlation, and this exercise "draws the soul upward" (SNL 113).

The exercise of reason works to make things transparent to the mind, but Weil's point is that we do not see what is transparent. What we cannot help but see and struggle with, butt our minds against without ever arriving at transparence, is what cannot be pierced by thought: the *incomprehensible*. And so, that which is merely "non-understood" must be eliminated by the work of reason, if only because it hides from view the properly incomprehensible—that which is incomprehensible or mysterious by its essential nature: "The intelligence exercises itself in obedience by coming up against the unintelligible" (N 617). Thus to know what is impossible for us by nature is the first opening to supernatural possibility, and she considered it an urgent and essential task to formulate a logic of the absurd, that is, "to define so far as possible the criterion of truth and falsehood in the transcendent sphere, wherein contradiction is not out of place" (FLN 182). Cognizance of impossibility constitutes the basis of ascending movement: the transcendental movement of mind and spirit that is in opposition to gravity (N 547). This is the movement of grace.

Reason, applying itself in a spirit of truth, must work through and resolve whatever contradictions it possibly can in order to encounter and contemplate the authentic paradoxes, where contradiction is "the lever of transcendence" (FLN 134). This makes contradiction, for Weil as for Kierkegaard, "a bulwark against pantheism" (N 329) since the eternal and the temporal, the supernatural and the natural, are kept infinitely distant from one another in paradox. Yet precisely the extreme and irreconcilable tension of paradox makes it an inherently synthetic movement of thought. Weil reaches for a synthesis of Hegelian and Kierkegaardian dialectics: genuine contradiction is irreconcilable, yet precisely through the extremity of its irreconcilability, "contradiction is mediation" (IC 166).[9]

Weil saw a need to elucidate the "way that opposites have of being true" (N 121), but her notes toward such elucidation are scattered and sketchy. She maintained that "truth manifests itself as a result of the contact made between two propositions, neither of which is true; it is their relation that is true" (N 406). In themselves, thoughts are essentially separate; for example, the "thought that one exists, and the thought that one doesn't exist" (N 458). In relationship to each other, both thoughts are true at different levels in different senses, but they cannot be thought at the same time at the same level. The resistance, the tension, the express contradiction between them is what makes each "true" when both are viewed in tandem. They need each other to be true because their truth is correlative and cooperative.

Truth is lost when rendered static, when "stated" in univocal language. The isolated "stating" of a truth kills its tensional relation to other truths and makes of it an object or idol. Only an active *contra-diction*—a speaking against the static "state" in statement—can keep truth alive as a thought process occurring at different levels simultaneously, thus protecting against the idolization of truths.

> Beliefs at different levels. E.g. belief that God exists, in me, at such—such—and such a level; that he does not exist, at such—and such a level, etc.— There has not to be any choice made from among the opinions (except in certain cases); they should all be entertained, but arranged vertically and lodged at suitable levels. Thus chance, destiny, Providence. (N 139)

Appropriate use of contradiction prevents misappropriation of the relative truths we capture in the framework of language. Contradiction always resurrects precisely the relativity of truths, the mutually qualifying relationships among the "states" expressed in statements. The truth is in the relativity as such—the different levels of correlation for the thinking mind—it is not "contained" in the statements per se. Consistent with this, Weil proposes the following method of investigation: as soon as we have thought upon a certain matter, to discover in what sense the contrary is true (N 121 = GG 102).

One can make an error either by denying a truth or by affirming it in a sense in which it is not true (N 152). Some truths cannot be true when held affirmatively because by affirming them on such-and-such a plane one destroys them (N 163). Resolution of a genuine contradiction by the "happy mean" compromises the opposition of truths in the poles of the contradiction, and this is just what is most contrary to the union of opposites (N 494). To weaken one of the terms of the contradiction is to weaken the contradiction itself, and consequently the use to be made of the contradiction (N 342). If truth is to be attained, the contradiction as such must be thought, not simply submitted to unthinkingly as if it were not a contradiction at all: "The identity of opposites unconsciously submitted to constitutes evil. This identity properly understood as such constitutes good" (N 486).

In the case of the natural–supernatural contradiction, mediation by thought produces what Weil refers to as the supernatural harmony of opposites. Just as the unity of relative contraries (light–dark, high–low, true–false, good–evil) produces a natural harmony, the unity of absolute contradictories (temporal–eternal, world–God, necessity–good) issues in a supernatural harmony. Among the supernatural contradictories that serve as the basis of ascending movement by the intellect, according to Weil, are the doctrines of God both One and Three; Christ both God and man; the Eucharist both earthly matter and the body of God. The fact that it is impossible to conceive together, by means of a relation, the two ideas that make up these contradictories results in precisely the point aimed at: God, the object of contemplation, is transported beyond the infinite: "If the unified conception is impossible, and yet the whole of the attention is brought to bear on it, it is a transcendent harmony" (N 341).

We must employ natural–supernatural contradictories as "pincers" in order for the mind to approach the transcendent. What the relation of relative contraries can do to touch the reality of natural existence, the relation of absolute contradictories conceived together—but really conceived together, despite their radical irreconcilability—can do to touch God (N 363). Correlations of contraries are like a ladder: when reflected on, they raise thought to a higher level where the connection that unifies the contraries resides. When we reach the last rung of the ladder, a spot where we are denied access to the level at which they are linked together, we can climb no further: "We have only to look up, wait and love," she writes, "and God descends" (N 412).

Legitimate contradictories, for Weil, include the central mysteries recognized as dogmas by the Roman Catholic Church, but also ones that would be anathema to it, such as the contradictory thought that God exists *and* does not exist:

> Cases of true contradictories: God exists; God doesn't exist. Where lies the problem? No uncertainty whatever. I am absolutely certain that there is a God in the sense that I am absolutely certain that my love is not illusory. I am absolutely certain that there is not a God in the sense that I am absolutely certain that there is nothing real that bears a resemblance to what I am able to conceive when I pronounce that name, since I am unable to conceive God—But that thing, which I am unable to conceive, is not an illusion—This impossibility is more immediately present to me than is the feeling of my own personal existence. (N 127, see 150–1, 421)

The poles of such a contradiction—that God exists *and* does not exist—occupy different levels. There is no need for a choice to be made between the ideas except in particular moments or contexts; "they should all be entertained, but arranged vertically and lodged at suitable levels" (N 139).

The essentially *alogos* quality of ultimate truth—its transcendence of positive affirmation and denial—stymies not only language, but reason and sense (N 306). Only what Weil calls intuition—with Spinoza's fourth kind of knowledge in mind—can sustain the thinking of ultimate contradiction.[10] Transcendent things have to be thought according to a transcendental logic of their own because "with regard to the transcendent, one can only deny, and affirmations are in their true sense negations" (N 254). A specific form of attention is required for this, an attention that desires absolute good more than life itself and is willing to pass through a "dark night of reason" in order to seek contact with the truth. *"Intuition, being immediate, can only be preceded by a* 'dark night', contrariwise to discursive thought" (N 125).

Every act of the intelligence is a manifestation of intuition (N 118), but not all acts of intelligence use intuition transcendentally.

The discursive intelligence, which grasps relationships and presides over mathematical knowledge, lies on the boundary between matter and spirit; "it is the intuition alone that is purely spiritual" (N 509). We must apply discursive reason with all due rigor in order to arrive at the point where intuition is able to transcend those limits. *Dialectics* is the work of pure intuition beyond the univocal range of discursive thought (N 45). Weil thought it crucial that the transcendent be recognized as the *sole* source of inspiration for the natural world, and that natural reason be recognized as "a degraded form of faith" (FLN 117–8), or rather the same thing as faith but in a lesser degree of illumination.

It will become ever clearer as we proceed that for Weil the ultimate contradiction—indeed, the originary ground of all contradiction—is the one that pertains between necessity and good. Weil draws the terms of this opposition from Plato's *Republic* (6.493c) and *Timaeus* (47e–48a), but her metaphysical and Christian conceptualization of them moves far afield of their meaning in Plato. This essential contradiction is centered in God himself as creator and redeemer, as we shall see in full detail in Chapter 3, and the crucifixion is its symbolic name: "God and creation are one; God and creation are infinitely distant from each other: this fundamental contradiction is reflected in that between the necessary and the good. To feel this distance means a spiritual quartering, it means crucifixion" (N 400).

This most fundamental contradiction, deriving from the infinite distance between the Creator and creation, serves as a primary criterion of truth. If this painful contradiction is compromised by a "happy mean"—that is, if God is not thought to be absolutely good (the opposite of necessity) or if the world is not seen as entirely in the grip of necessity (the opposite of good)—the result is idolatry, an increase of evil. Yet the very same contradiction consented to while cognized in the full extremity of its contradiction reveals the transcendent harmony between necessity and good. "It is through knowing what a difference there is between them that their unity can be grasped [...]. Only supernatural love is able to contemplate stark necessity. It ceases then to be an evil" (N 480, see 493).

Correct Use of Dogma

The intellect requires perfect freedom in spiritual matters, Weil insists, because "the intelligence is a specifically and rigorously individual thing" (WG 78), and every mind must remain free to think in and through error on the way to truth. To remove the liberty to err is therefore to remove the means of access to truth. The freedom to try out the range of conceptual positions and to discover error in the process is integral to intellectual pursuit; without it truth cannot be sought and tested experimentally, and without testing, cannot be attained. Similarly, on a higher and parallel plane, prayer and contemplation exercise the individual faculties capable of responding to supernatural love. Indeed, faith is enacted precisely through this multilevel process of searching, asking, praying, contemplating, and obeying.

In this light, Weil viewed the Roman Catholic Church's use of *anathema sit* as an authoritarian proscription of the free operation of intellect that is essential to genuine faith. She writes of the consequent need to restore spiritual liberty since "the Church wrongly separated liberty and spirituality" (N 227).[11] The Catholic Church, due to its own lack of faith, has abrogated liberty of thought vis-à-vis the mysteries of Christianity:

> Lack of faith, as shown in the totalitarian orthodoxy of the Church. Whosoever asks bread of God will not receive a stone. He who desires truth, if an error appears to him, it is because it represents for him a stage along the road to truth, and if he continues his way he will see it as an error. He who does not desire truth deceives himself, but he also deceives himself when reciting the creed. The condemnation of errors was in itself good; but not *anathema sit*. How do we know that such and such an error is not necessary for such and such a spirit at a stage in development? It was sufficient to say: Whosoever declares that ... has not reached the goal. (N 228)

Weil affirms that the Church has the prerogative to condemn errors, thereby attesting publicly that they are errors; but to forbid and anathematize them, condemning the very thinking of them as damaging to faith, is an abuse of power, a totalitarian usage that she considers an "absolutely insurmountable obstacle" to the incarnation of Christianity (WG 77).

Attempts to instill faith through authoritarianism—whether by the extreme tactics of Inquisition or by mildly coercive catechism—can only produce adherence to a false God and an ersatz salvation. That is why Weil maintains that "a society with divine pretensions like the Church" is more dangerous on account of the ersatz form of good it contains than on account of the evil that sullies it (N 296). The great danger of Christian education is that the "lower parts of the soul" become attached to the mysteries of the faith when they have no right to do so (N 238). Weil contrasts the use of indoctrination in Christianity with what she sees as Plato's discretion toward the divine:

> [In Plato] there is no question of God so long as real contact has not been established by mystical experience, and not even then except by allusion. This is the opposite of the Christian way, in which one speaks of God long before having the least suspicion of what that word signifies. The advantage is that this word by itself has a power, the disadvantage is that the authenticity is lessened. (IC 148)

When indoctrination encourages unreflective attachment in the form of "belief," thus preempting the free workings of grace and illumination of the intellect, religion becomes religiously disguised idolatry. Indeed, Weil contends that the majority of the pious are idolaters who adhere to a false or illusory idea of God (FLN 308). "Everywhere, always, in everything, the social feeling produces a perfect imitation of faith, that is to say perfectly deceptive" (WG 198).

Weil criticizes Roman Catholicism for positively affirming as *tenets* those religious mysteries that should be contemplated wholly without attachment, without a yes-or-no judgment.[12] For her, as for Kierkegaard, much of what has been taken for Christianity is a kind of pseudo-Christian paganism characterized by attachment to a set of beliefs having no relation at all to authentic faith, and this gives rise to the evangelizing problem—posed in its full irony by Kierkegaard—of "how to introduce Christianity into Christendom" (see *Practice in Christianity* and *Attack Upon Christendom*). Weil espied the spell of such idolatry in the most authoritative fathers and doctors of the Church, foremost among them Augustine and Aquinas: "The unconditional and total adherence to everything the Church teaches, has taught, and will teach, which St. Thomas calls faith, is not faith but social idolatry" (FLN 133, 117, 145). In her judgment the Church has been a totalitarian "great beast" dedicated to aggrandizement of its own existence, meddling with the whole of human history (*le tripatouillage de toute l'histoire de l'humanité*) for purposes of apologetics (N 620).

Intellectual attachment to what one imagines to be the dogmatic truth about God displaces the freedom, the interior void, that invites the genuine workings of grace. Nothing is easier than to fall into an imaginary love of God, and this imaginary love "occupies a place, which is not an empty one, where true love cannot enter" (N 326). Weil sees grist for conflict, then, in the fact that a collective body (the Church) is the guardian of dogma, when the dogmatic mysteries are properly objects of free contemplation by love, faith, and intelligence—all strictly individual faculties. "Almost since the beginning," Weil writes, "the individual has been ill at ease in Christianity, and this uneasiness has been notably one of the intelligence" (WG 79).

Intellectual attachment and social coercion are opposed to grace not only because they fail as a conduit, but because they stand as an obstacle. In its proper role as a guardian of dogma, the Church should act as a beacon, directing its seekers toward worthy objects of contemplation. The authority of the Church has a rightful claim to *attention* only, not adherence. Acceptance of dogmatic truths should proceed by the interior illumination of intelligence and love (FLN 133). Here we see the quasi-Protestant side of Weil inasmuch as the collectivity of the Church and its episcopal authority, in her view, should never be permitted to stand between the individual and direct dispensation of grace by God. The Church can legitimately foster the birth of this direct relationship, but cannot dispense, control, or deny grace. It is not able to mediate grace charismatically, but only to help occasion it through teaching, ministry, and sacramental functions.

At the core of Weil's Protestantesque understanding of the proper role of the Church is her distinction between faith and belief: she insists that "faith is not belief" (FLN 207). The mysteries of the Catholic faith—like those of other religious and metaphysical traditions—are not designed to be believed in the way that one believes in empirical facts or rational deductions. The presence of Christ in the host, for example, is not a fact in the same way that the presence of one's friend Paul in his body is a fact. The Eucharist should not be an object of belief for the part of the soul that apprehends facts (N 238). Only that part of the soul that is made for the supernatural should adhere to the mysteries of faith, and this adherence is a matter of love rather than belief.

> Belief. Very different meanings attached. $2 + 2 = 4$, or: I am holding this pen. Belief is here the feeling of evidence. I cannot, by definition, believe in mysteries in this fashion. But I believe that the mysteries of the Catholic religion are an inexhaustible source of truths concerning the human condition. (In addition to which, they are for me an object of love.) Only nothing prevents me from believing the same thing with regard to other mysteries, or from believing that some of these truths have been directly revealed elsewhere. Spiritual adhesion similar to the kind obtained by a work of art (the very greatest art). (N 190)

Such an openness to truth, wherever it is found, constitutes an irenic principle. Religious intolerance proceeds, Weil thinks, from a confusion between ways of believing. Religious mysteries are true when regarded and contemplated in a certain way; the very same mysteries are *not* true when held in the wrong way, as tenets, by means of affirmation or adherence that leads to attachment. "By saying that the Catholic religion is true and the other religions false,

one does an injustice not only to the other religious traditions but to
the Catholic faith itself, by placing it on the level of those things that
can be affirmed or denied" (N 242).

Weil's critique of the Catholic Church denies it the status of a
divinely inspired institution protected from fallibility by the Holy
Spirit, therefore from the corruptibility of human institutions in
general. For Weil it is a social organism like any social organism, but
one with a special propensity to idolize itself owing to its "divine
pretensions." The only unconditioned thing in the Church is the
presence of Christ in the Eucharist; in every other way "the Church as
a society pronouncing opinions is a phenomenon of this world,
conditioned" (FLN 130). Indeed, Weil was a severe critic of all types
of collectivity because of their corrupting social dynamic: their
propensity to vaunt the quantitative force of the collective "we" over
the individual capacity to discern, deliberate, and judge. This disdain
for the social organism in Weil is not—as it often seems in Nietzsche,
for example—an expression of contempt for common humanity;
rather, it is a realism concerning the human tendency, under powerful
pressures of social influence, to obey socially determined inclinations
instead of supernatural inspiration. In the Church considered as a
social organism, the mysteries "inevitably degenerate into beliefs,"
Weil warns, making it problematic for a person of authentic faith to
enter this social organism honestly (N 284).

Those who do develop an idolatrous attachment to the mysteries
or to the Church as a collective society need to undergo purification
by means of atheism and incredulity: that is, by doubting their
beliefs. Since faith is not belief, doubt is not incompatible with faith
(FLN 207). Far rather, deep experience of doubt is conducive to faith
in that it shatters the complacence of one's belief in God, opening the
way to an infinitely superior faith. Although certain forms of atheism
constitute a lack of faith, other forms effect a salutary purification of
the notion of God (N 126). Atheism is a means of purifying the
religious inclination of its attachment to a God of consolation: "For
religious feeling to emanate from the spirit of truth, one should be
absolutely prepared to abandon one's religion [. . .]. God ought not to
be for a human heart a reason for living like treasure is for a miser"

(NR 250). When religion is embraced as a consolation for the anguish of finitude, as an illusory solace that fills the emptiness and desolation of the void, then the truth of the cross, the very heart of Christian faith, is regarded in vain. The vocation of the cross calls for an acceptance of pain and bitterness unbuffered by consoling illusion.

A dark night of atheism, then, is necessary so that one's attachment to God be severed. "To the real God we are not attached, and that is why there is no cord that can be cut. He enters into us" (N 326 = GG 64). The dark night burns away the illusions of belief. Faith is as much a consent to the realization that "God" as we conceive him does not exist, as it is a perception that, when every conceivable "God" is exposed as a construct of the desire to be empowered and consoled, there is still in our interior emptiness, in the midst of the darkness and void, something irreducible that is susceptible to being experienced as grace. "The man who places his life in faith in God can lose his faith. But the man who places his life in God himself—he will never lose it" (N 493–4). This is the hidden God, the inconceivable and ineffable God, the God of sudden unanticipated gift and revelation. The hidden God is the one actually encountered through the void, in the midst of the dark night of faith. God is most truly known through void, for when illusion is burned away there is nothing in the void but nothingness, and within that nothingness emerges the "nothingness" of God, who is the "fullest possible fullness" (N 492).

Balanced against the Protestant-leaning side of Weil is her firmly Catholic side, which emerges whenever it is necessary to defend the mysteries central to Christianity from interpretation as "mere symbols"—for example, making the Son an only half-divine being, or modifying the divinity and humanity in Christ so as to reconcile them, or reducing the bread and wine of the Eucharist to a mere symbol. "The mysteries then cease to be an object of contemplation; they are no longer of any use" (FLN 132–3). She affirms that the Church's authority has been legitimately exercised when it has warded off attempts to *mitigate the absurdity* of the authentic mysteries (FLN 133). The virtue of the dogma of the real presence lies in its very absurdity (WG 187); yet it is not absurdity per se that is a virtue, but rather the contemplation of the apparent absurdities (of the God–man, the Trinity, the real presence, and so on), which illumine the intellectual faculties on the plane of natural reason with the light of supernatural inspiration (FLN 110). Contemplation of these super-rational absurdities draws one upward if they are contemplated *as absurd*—but they must not then be defended, because any such defense would put them on the plane of natural reason where their virtue no longer obtains (N 243). Their absurdity is such as to illuminate the mind and cause it to produce in abundance truths that are clear to the intelligence (NR 279). They are not in any *natural* sense true; they are true only in a supernatural sense: they are true only for the faith that is able to grasp them as true.

The intelligence requires a complete liberty to take the mysteries of faith as, at one level, absurd and nonsensical, and even to deny God altogether—since religion is related to supernatural love and not to rational affirmation or denial (N 242). For just as the intelligence finds nothing in the music of J. S. Bach or Gregorian melody to affirm or to deny, but something to feed on, should not faith, Weil asks, be an adherence of this kind? "The mysteries of faith are degraded if they are made a subject of affirmation and negation, when in reality they should be a subject of contemplation" (N 245). This means a prayer-like adherence of attention.

Weil assigns to intellect the role of guarding against irrationalism disguised as religious faith. The intelligence is that part in us that affirms and denies, formulates opinions; its role is solely one of submission (N 238). Yet the intelligence must recognize, by means that are proper to it, to what it should submit itself, and it should only submit itself when it knows in a perfectly clear and precise manner *why*, otherwise submission is an error (N 240); it might be a submission to social influence, for example. It is for the intelligence to discern what constitutes the proper object of supernatural love. Discrimination on the part of intelligence is essential to distinguish supernatural love from attachment, intelligible truth from that which is below it (N 241). Operating as it does in the realm of natural reason, the intelligence cannot control mystery itself, but it does control the roads that lead to mystery and those that lead down from it. While remaining absolutely loyal to itself as discerning, judging intelligence, it can recognize the existence within the soul of "a faculty superior to itself and which conducts thought on to a higher plane than its own" (FLN 131). This faculty is supernatural love. Thus we know through the intelligence that what the intelligence does not apprehend is more real than what it does apprehend (N 24). Supernatural love constitutes a fuller apprehension of reality, and this is known through the intelligence itself (N 238–40).

There is, then, a legitimate and an illegitimate notion of mystery. An illegitimate mystery is one the intelligence has not put in a thorough effort to "demystify" on the grounds of natural reason. A legitimate mystery is one that inherently transcends the logic of contradiction because the contradiction itself is transcendent, when the most logical and rigorous use of the intelligence leads to impasse, to a contradiction that is inescapable. "But to arrive beyond the domain of the intelligence one must have traveled through it to the end, and by a path traced with unimpeachable rigour" (FLN 131). There is a need to distinguish between those absurdities that project light (such as the Trinity, the Incarnation) and those that project darkness (N 454). The latter should be resolved by appropriate distinctions of reason and assigned to sundry levels of understanding rather than being embraced as avenues to transcendence, for theirs is an imitation of transcendence, a bad infinite, a false God.

Just as the world is for us a barrier, a closed door, and at the same time the only passageway (N 492), so all the symbolic languages at our disposal are walls that imprison, yet the only keys we have to open to supernatural truth. And just as God transcends every *divine* manifestation, he transcends all human language and symbolization as well. We must bear these limits ever in mind when we say "God" or we necessarily utter idolatries.

CHAPTER 2

THE PARADOX OF DESIRE

All created things in this world, myself included, refuse to become ends for me. Such is God's extreme mercy toward me. But this itself constitutes evil. Evil is the form that God's mercy takes in this world. (N 495)

"Our love is our very being, which nothing can eradicate from us" (FLN 324). Weil views the human being as fundamentally a desiring creature, which is to say, a valuing creature actively seeking out what it considers good, whatever that good may be. Seeking of any kind implies valuation; all searching for something, for anything whatever, is implicitly a quest for a value, a good. Whatever else we may not know about ourselves, we know for certain that we desire, we *want*. Weil takes this principle as the beginning of all truth about human existence. The radical poverty of finitude makes us essentially reducible to the irreducibility of our desire: "There cannot be a want more radical than that of being other than God. This is the poverty of every creature" (IC 129).

We Desire the Good

It is through our desire for good that the reality of the world and our own existence gain a real and ineluctable grip on us. If not for our radical want for things outside ourselves, of which we constantly stand in need, we would not be compelled to accept anything whatever as real. We might bask in a seemingly timeless existence, in pointless and purposeless fantasy, all without harm to ourselves or others. It is vulnerability to harm that forces the distinction between fantasy and reality. Need, destitution, suffering, desperate lack—this is what fuels desire, and desire searches out an object to answer it.

Desire is first directed to the primary conditions of existence, but when primary needs are satisfied, always only temporarily, our desire remains and the object of desire transmutes. Satisfaction of material needs—for air, water, food, protection—is never experienced as an end in itself, but as a means to that for which it seems to hold out the promise. Life is desired as the means to fulfillment, happiness, that unnamable x for which we long when we strive to sustain life by obtaining its necessities. Why would life seem desirable if something more than mere survival per se were not promised? Although the object of our desire continually changes, the unabating quest for a greater good than the one we now possess is intrinsic to our existence.

We might refer to this ever-changing object that we long for when we long for the fulfillment of our desire as an x, or we might coin a term to represent this longed-for x toward which our particular desires tend. Weil calls it *the good*. The good is what is desired, by definition: "To say that what we really want is always and only the good is like saying that what we desire is the desired. It is a purely grammatical statement [. . .]. The good is nothing else but the object of our will" (N 290). In speaking of the good, she has in mind not a hypostatic Platonic form but the constantly metamorphosing object of actual human desire, the protean "good" we inexorably pursue, whatever the specific object may be in which we see it embodied for the moment. Desire decides and defines the good, not good desire. Here Weil is closer to the nominalism of Hobbes and Spinoza than to the idealism of Plato; or more precisely she is reaching for a transcendental realism that synthesizes the Hobbesian idea of good with the Platonic.[1]

A perpetual, insatiable longing for good, then, is the deepest center of the human being:

The aspiration for good exists in all men—for every man desires, and all desire is desire for good—and this aspiration for good, which is the very being of every man, is the one good that is always unconditionally present in every human being. (FLN 284) / At the bottom of the heart of every human being, from earliest infancy until the tomb, there is something that goes on indomitably expecting, in the teeth of all experience of crimes committed, suffered, and witnessed, that good and not evil will be done to him. It is this above all that is sacred in every human being. (SE 10 = SWR 315)

Why this longing for good is the most sacred element of the human being is perhaps not immediately obvious: it is because it is the only purely *impersonal* part of the person. It is equal and irreducible in everyone because, rather than being a quality of "personality" or "character," it is the core element of the creature qua creature. Contact with injustice through pain, then, provokes a cry of anguished protest from this core element, which is always an "impersonal" protest (SE 12 = SWR 317).

The irreducible reality and urgency of longing for good is grasped first and most immediately within oneself, in the fervency of one's own desire for the good that life seems to hold out. "The poor wretch who kneels and begs for life is saying, unknown to himself: Leave me more time in which to become perfect. Do not put an end to me while I have had so small a part in the good" (FLN 125). Weil identifies this longing for a greater part in the good in every human being as the foundation of all compassion in the human mind and heart, the interior wellsprings of justice.

This is where the good has a grip on us: it is embodied in lack, in infinite desire for a good we do not and cannot possess. Ceaseless desire for good is the action of love in us, however narrowly, selfishly, or demonically it may be directed. "We need not ask ourselves how to have love, it is in us from birth to death, imperious as hunger. We need only to know in what direction to direct it" (IC 109). Our thirst or passion for good as we experience it can be extended to others by an analogical transference. It is such transference that transmutes our interior passion for good into an outreaching *com*-passion, a longing for good on behalf of others. Weil maintains that love is only real when it is directed toward a particular object; the sole exception to this is love of God, which is love without an object. Hence love "becomes universal without ceasing to be real only as a result of analogy and transference" (WG 184).[2] We transfer our longing for good to another by analogy with ourselves.

> The compassion one feels for the afflicted is the compassion felt, in affliction, by the impassible part of one's own soul for the part of it that feels. The compassion Christ felt for himself when he said: "Father, if thou be willing, remove this cup from me [...]. My God, why hast thou forsaken me?" The silent compassion of the Father for Christ. This self-compassion is what a pure soul feels in affliction. A pure soul feels the same compassion for the affliction of others. (FLN 94)

Compassion is universalized by this process of transference, for "compassion is the recognition of one's own misery in another" (FLN 209). The transference of our desire for good to others is the sole basis of a genuinely universal love for others—a real, concrete love for the anonymous neighbor, the stranger—as contrasted with the abstract and indiscriminate notion of "universal love" lambasted by Freud and Nietzsche.[3] To love our neighbor as ourselves, she clarifies, does not mean we should love all other persons *equally*—for we love different elements of ourselves differentially—but we should have with each person the relationship of one conception of the universe to another conception of the universe, thus respecting the person's unique value (N 23–4).

Weil acknowledges that human beings are radically unequal in their relations with the things of this world; that it is impossible to feel equal respect for things that are in fact unequal unless the respect is given to something that is identical in all of them (SE 220). What possible ground is there, then, for claiming an essential equality among human beings? The foundational basis of universal respect and love in Weil's thought is not that all human beings *are* good, or lovable, or "deserve" love, but that all equally and without exception *long* for good, and this longing for good—which is the impersonal, transcendental element actually embodied in every person—is what is universally to be honored as sacred. The commonality of desire for good among creatures becomes the foundation of all sacrality, equality, and justice in human relations. Universal desire for good is the primary coordinate that orders human existence, both individually and communally.

Weil is concerned to identify the root source of *moral interest*—that interest which supplies the indispensable motive for acts of justice and love. The serious limitation of an ethical system such as Kant's, for example, as laid out in *Groundwork of the Metaphysic of Morals* (1785), is that the basis for equality and mutuality among human beings lies in their potential rationality. Kant himself acknowledges that rationality is an insufficient condition for moral acts if the unconditional moral interest that is presupposed (*voraussetzungslose moralische Interesse*) is lacking.[4] Without the motive of moral interest, the categorical imperative is, to employ one of Weil's metaphors, like "a motorcar with an empty gas tank" (NR 190).

For Weil, equality among human beings and the root source of moral interest are grounded in one and the same creaturely condition: that "all human beings are absolutely identical in so far as they can be thought of as consisting of a centre, which is an unquenchable desire for good, surrounded by an accretion of psychical and bodily matter" (SE 220).[5] Because suffering, the default of good, is an irreducible quantity in every human being, "every man is identical with every other man" (N 237). The deep-seated and powerful influence of social prestige, which gives rise to every kind of illusion, causes us to think there are differences between human beings, Weil writes, but this is only because we manage not to know and accept human misery.

As we have noted, one's longing for good is itself the immanent presence of good in a human being: it is that being's sacred core. This is a core that exists even in vicious and hardened criminals who commit heinous acts, injuring or destroying hope for good in others—though not desire for it. Because a deep estrangement from the good is manifested in such extreme criminality, it is the role of rehabilitative punishment, Weil posits, to reawaken the interior point in the offender that feels pain, thereby stimulating a thirst for the good: "Punishment is solely a method of procuring pure good for men who do not desire it. The art of punishing is the art of awakening in a criminal, by pain or even death, the desire for pure good" (SE 31 = SWR 336). Individuals who are so estranged from the good that they are prone to spread evil everywhere can only be reintegrated with the good by having harm inflicted on them; this must be done until the completely innocent part of their souls awakens with the surprised cry, "Why am I being hurt?" (SE 31 = SWR 335).

Weil's point is that we have to feel nakedly what it is to suffer in order to desire not to cause suffering, and also to mitigate and prevent suffering whenever we are able. Without consciousness of the passion for good in oneself, there can be no transference of it to others as a basis for *com*-passion. "All suffering is caused by unsatisfied desire. Love that adheres to the desire of another is compassion" (FLN 284). Self-compassion is the purest and most immediate basis of every form of other-directed compassion (FLN 94). "Compassion makes love equal for everybody" (FLN 96), including equalizing it between self and other.

Purposely to injure a human being is to injure the sacred center of that being—the center that desires and expects the good, the center that is that being's lifeline to love and compassion. Sacred desire for good is thus the unique basis of morality for Weil; morality is for her essentially a religious, or to use her term, a *supernatural* matter (N 487). All genuine morality is essentially grounded in the supernatural because it is motivated by supernatural love. There is no such thing as a secular morality because it is not possible for us to "do good" or "be good" except insofar as we receive that good from outside ourselves, seeking it from a transcendent source. It is never the product of our rational mind, our will, or our natural being, but always and only the fruit of that impersonal core that is sacred in us: our infinite desire, which is an implicit and unceasing prayer for good. Desire for the good is the only positive, impersonal, universal basis for moral conduct: "It is because the will has no power to bring about salvation that the idea of secular morality is an absurdity. What is called morality only depends on the will in its most muscular aspect. Religion on the contrary corresponds to desire, and it is desire that saves" (WG 195; see SE 220).

The Good Is Absent

The contradiction that rules human existence, as Weil analyzes it, is that our unlimited desire for good is invested in the limited objects at hand in the world, and by virtue of this attachment our desire for good suffers evil and is turned to evil effects. There is always some form of illimitability in desire: "To conquer only the terrestrial globe? To live only a hundred years? To make only 40% profit on the money one has invested?" Desire is illimitable by nature, and this is contrary to nature, since nature is defined by limit (N 88). All human relations that have something infinite about them are unjust and become the cause of harm (N 34). This outcome is virtually inevitable because our desire for good seeks to gratify itself with objects that cannot contain the degree of good that is asked of them:

> What we really want in an object is not the whole of it, but the good in it. The good in [things we desire] becomes exhausted, whereas our hunger for good is never exhausted. When I have eaten a certain quantity of bread, what is left over no longer contains any good for me. But I can never have enough good— never, at any moment; so I go in search of another kind of good. The good was not, therefore, in the bread, but in the appropriate relation existing between the bread and my hunger. (N 490–1)

We seek satisfaction in such "appropriate relations" not only with objects but with other human beings as well, never fully recognizing that desire for another human being, when it exists on this level of necessity, is "ghoulish" (FLN 285). There is the example of Don Juan (N 494, 547), but even a love characterized by a permanent bond of fidelity must dread the loss of its object—a loss of the vital "food" that the loved one's existence supplies. "Instead of loving a human being for his hunger, we love him as food for ourselves. We love like cannibals. To love purely is to love the hunger in a human being. Then, since all men are always hungry, one always loves all men" (FLN 284).

The threat of depletion or loss applies to every particular object of desire without exception, actually or potentially—hence to all objects taken in totality. Because of death, human affections are all irremediably doomed and futureless; what we love barely exists (N 582). We too, like the objects of our desire, barely exist. "Everything here below is the slave of death. The horror of death is the iron law that determines all our thoughts and all our actions" (FLN 112). Because our existence is inherently limited, absolutely conditioned by death, we cannot regard our existence as a good in itself, much as we try to transform it into one. We invariably seek more than simply to exist; we seek the means to secure and aggrandize our existence, which is to say, we crave power after power in a Hobbesian sense.[6]

> We seek after everything that increases our power. But power is only a means. We love things for ourselves. But we do not satisfy ourselves with what is us. Desire continually makes us go outside ourselves [...]. This world—the domain of necessity—has absolutely nothing to offer us except a series of means. Relative good represents the means. Our volition is incessantly shot back and forth from one means to another as a billiard ball. (N 493)

Since we are constitutionally disposed to regard the conditions of our existence as our good (N 491), we "find it difficult to conceive that what is necessary to us is not automatically good" (N 492). But having existence, upon reflection, cannot be thought of as the possession of good if it is constituted by an incessant longing and striving for good. The irony of desire is that in desiring the means to our existence, we treat as an end an existence that is not good, but merely the means to a good. "By placing all our desire for good in an object, we turn that object, for ourselves, into a condition of existence. But it doesn't mean that we thereby turn it into a good, for our existence is not a good. We always want something else than simply to exist" (N 494). In desiring unlimited good as our end, we are actually, paradoxically, desiring the end of our existence. We ourselves cannot become the end of our desire. Rather, we ourselves are but means to pursuing what we desire.

Precisely because we are only means, and all objects we encounter are likewise means, "any end whatever is like a stick to a drowning man" (N 546). We grasp at sticks when we set our heart on this or that good; we fasten onto anything and everything that provides our vital instinct with support (N 223). We look on everything that aggrandizes our power and increases our energy as a good, attempting to create an end where none can exist, for desire continually makes us go outside ourselves (N 493). Means as such are something altogether different from forms of good (N 551), and when separated from their function as means, they are still further removed from being forms of good: "gold is not good to eat, neither is a gold spoon any good for stirring soup" (N 489). Good resides in the movement of our desire, not in the thing desired. When we find that every "stick" we reach for sinks under the weight of our desire, we discover that we are surrounded by lack, loss, powerlessness, evil—all manifestations of death and nihility. To experience this is to experience "the void" (le vide) as Weil uses the term. The void is the absolute deprivation of an end: the realization that there is simply no end in the world. To refuse to accept this, to take means as ends, to pervert means into ends, is the root of untruth and therefore of inevitable evil: "The inversion of means and ends, which is the very essence of all the evil in society, is inevitable for the very good reason that there isn't any end" (N 495).

Here we observe the emergence of what Weil calls the "infinite distance" between the necessary and the good (N 343, 350, 363, 379, 400, 410, 480, 493), wherein lies "the root of the supreme secret" (N 365). Our unabating longing for good is a testimony to the absence of good and the presence of necessity, its actual contrary. The pressures of necessity enslave us to "goods" that can be good only under certain conditions of desire, and those conditions are ever changing. Our goods are always relative and temporary, intrinsically correlated with evils. What we want is absolute good; what is within our reach is the good that is correlated with evil: we mistakenly take it for what we want (N 592). Attachment of our desire is what actually creates, invests, or implants the good and evil qualities in things. "One may call it an evil to have one's desire attached to the things of this world, because so long as desire is attached in this way one has the illusion of a pair of contraries: good–evil" (FLN 318; see N 78).

We want the good in things alone, but the good that we are capable of finding in things is governed by conditions, both in them and in ourselves, that continually change; in changing, they cause the good vis-à-vis ourselves to retract. The retraction of good is experienced as evil. Good and evil are intrinsically correlated in human experience, just as light and shadow are intrinsically correlated for the human eye. They define one another experientially. "Good as the contrary of evil is the equivalent of it, in a sense, as is the case with all pairs of contraries" (N 108). Relative good thus inescapably delivers us into evil; only absolute good can deliver us from evil.

Often only a desolating loss or crushing failure unveils the insubstantiality of the "ends" we live for—"ends" that cannot serve as ends at all because our desire is infinitely incommensurate with the limited good in them. Temporal things are filled with finitude, mortality, and are destined to perish. This means that by their nature things refuse to be ends for us. The essence of created things is to be intermediaries (N 496): they mediate relative aspects of good without being good per se, and likewise they mediate relative aspects of evil without being evil per se. Everything in nature is both good and evil together; in a relative sense, mixed, in an absolute sense, dialectical (N 343).

Our life is "nothing but impossibility, absurdity," for each thing we desire is in contradiction with the conditions or the consequences attached to that thing (N 411). Pure good is the only possible finality, and that finality is absent from the world. Really to experience this knowledge through suffering is to undergo a death more encompassing than a merely personal or bodily death:

> Every human being has probably had some lucid moments in his life when he has definitely acknowledged to himself that there is no final good here below [. . .]. Men feel that there is a

mortal danger in facing this truth squarely for any length of time. That is true. Such knowledge strikes more surely than a sword; it inflicts a death more frightening than that of the body. After a time it kills everything within us that constitutes our ego. In order to bear it we have to love truth more than life itself [...]. It is for [those who do] to remain motionless, without averting their eyes, listening ceaselessly, and waiting, they know not for what. (WG 211)

The bereavement effected by this death is total. But the very darkness of total death brings the first inkling of an absolutely ulterior basis for life. Because everything here below is the slave of death, acceptance of death is the only liberation (FLN 112). A new liberated life becomes possible in and through the realization and acceptance of death. Death is the root source of all untruth *and* all truth for human beings (N 166).

We exist as an incarnation of the creator–creature contradiction, which is a contradiction between the good and the necessary: we are finite creatures, ruled by necessity, whose desire for infinite good is bereft of its object by the very fact of our being finite creatures. According to Weil, the sooner we are able to grasp this paradox at the core of our existence, the sooner we can recognize our unsatisfied desire itself as a mercy. "All created things in this world, myself included, refuse to become ends for me. Such is God's extreme mercy toward me" (N 495). This absence of an end, which in itself constitutes evil, is the form that God's mercy takes in this world. Each desire is a road leading to nonsatiety, since the impossibility of satiating desire is the ultimate truth about it (N 60). Desire is abandoned in this night of evil, in absence and darkness, reaching out for a good that is nowhere to be found in the world. The only *good* strictly speaking is supernatural good (N 410).

Good Is a Nothingness

The unlimited, insatiable desire for good that constitutes the core of the human being can be commensurate only when directed toward a good that is unlimited, absolute, unconditioned (FLN 143)—and therefore toward a good that is absolutely absent, that is a "nothingness." Nothing we touch, hear, or see, nothing that we visualize to ourselves, nothing that we think of is the good. "If we think of God, that is not the good either" (N 491). All that we conceive in the mind is as imperfect as we are, and what is imperfect is not the good.

> The good represents for us a nothingness, since no one thing is itself good. But this nothingness is not a non-being, not something unreal. Everything that exists is unreal compared to it. This nothingness is at least as real as we are ourselves. For our very being itself is nothing else than this need for the good. The absolute good lies wholly in this need. But we are unable to go and lay hold of it therein. All we are able to do is to love gratuitously [. . .]. The love that conceals from us the absence of good among creatures does not reach up to God. That is why we have to know "how much the essence of the necessary differs from that of the good." Now, everything that exists, without any exception, is subjected to necessity—even the manifestations of the supernatural *qua* manifestations. Everything here below is necessity, defiled by force, and consequently unworthy of love. (N 491–2)

What is effected by this "emptying" knowledge is an Augustinian education of desire relative to its objects, but one qualified, in Weil, by a thoroughly modern negation of God in the world that is dialectical rather than Platonic. Love is constrained to learn that what it desires does not exist, cannot exist in principle. It undergoes a disillusionment, a loss of object, a confrontation with void, a wrenching detachment; but precisely this crisis makes possible a progress of another kind, at another level. Although we cannot stop ourselves from loving, we can choose what it is we love: "Nothing that exists is absolutely worthy of love. We must therefore love that which does not exist" (N 220); "he whom we must love is absent" (N 219 = GG 109). Here Weil witnesses a faith that resembles a modern-day Jansenism more closely than a Christian Platonism, for there is no continuity of "degrees of being" here, but a modern dialectical break between the abyss of God, who is good itself—a nonexistent "nothingness"—and the abyss of the world, which fully exists, but under the rule of necessity, force, evil, is marked by radical lack, an absence of the divine. This resemblance to Jansenism is explored in Chapter 6.

The good that we desire does not exist. This means that for us pure good is only representable in negative terms as a nonentity, a "nothingness." The world is empty of good precisely because the world offers nothing that is free of the grip of necessity, with its inexorable conditions, its ubiquitous mixture of good and evil properties. Everything that has properties presents us with a combination of good and evil, whereas pure good has no property at all except the fact of being good (N 545). The good is the actual object of our desire, yet it is nowhere to be found. Weil asks, "Is it, then, emptiness; is it negative? Yes, as long as we do not direct the whole of our attention towards this" (N 545). The good is negative through the course of our apprenticeship, during which we must direct our attention toward the negative and the empty. An extended "dark night" is necessary before the good can present to us any other aspect than the negative.

But to undergo this movement into the dark night is to exercise a new responsibility on the basis of a nonillusory understanding of desire. It is a movement of abdication, a withholding of attachment, and a consent to the reality that opposes the will. Through the period of apprenticeship, the desire for plenitude (the good) discovers everywhere only the total inadequacy of earthly goods, thus reorienting desire in the direction of that which does not exist. So it happens that desire, seeking an increasingly perfect fullness, can only satisfy itself with an ever more perfect emptiness. It enters the void. Only at the end of this process, Weil writes, is it revealed that "this emptiness manifestly appears as the only reality that is truly real" (N 545).

How is it that Weil can claim that "Good is a nothingness, yet real" (N 491)? Loving that which does not exist would seem to imply that the object of one's love is not real. Moreover, Weil explicitly states that "for a man there is no other reality but that of earthly existence" (N 384), and we have seen that only the real has value, according to Weil. In what sense, then, can the good be real for a human being if it does not exist? How does this nonexistent good, this plenitude of nothingness, have value—even absolute value—as more real than anything that exists? Weil's response to this question is deeply dialectical: *the reality of the good is created in and through the reality of the desire for it.* The good "exists" for desire precisely *in* desire, as the absent object of desire. The purer and more intense the desire for good, the more the good is negatively embodied as real. "This nothingness is at least as real as we are ourselves. For our very being itself is nothing else than this need for the good. The absolute good lies wholly in this need" (N 491).

This argument concerning absolute good differs essentially from all cases of relative good. It differs essentially from the claim, for example, that if I am a farmer who longs for rain, and I pray with sufficient intensity, then my fervency will cause the rain to come. This expectation concerns causation in the order of material effects (that is, rain), which is strictly ordered by conditions according to the rule of necessity. Such a claim, from Weil's perspective, can only be deluded and fallacious. But the good belongs to an essentially different order than does necessity: it is pure value—value as such, *in itself* (N 307)—a value that is actually *created by the act of valuing.* The good is actually created by the desire for it. Love of good creates good by the sheer virtue of its valuing regard. Good is not a thing in the world. It cannot be a thing in the world. It is love.

Thus Weil's claim that the good is *real* does not imply that the good "exists" or will ever come into existence in any material sense. On the contrary, the good absolutely does *not* exist, for the good is absolutely other than existence, which is ruled by necessity. The index of the good's reality—a reality that transcends necessity, and hence the material order in which we live—is that it is *really* desired by a desire that is indubitably real. The good that is desired, therefore, has reality beyond the dichotomy of existence versus nonexistence. Nonexistent in itself, it has a real relationship with existence through us, and the real effects of this relationship are empirically observable. Our desire empirically confirms the reality of the good for us whenever we desire; that is to say, whenever we *want* something—and we want something all the time, at every moment of our lives.

> I wrench away the whole of my desire and my love from worldly things in order to direct them towards the good. But—it will be asked—does this good exist? What does it matter? the things of this world exist, but they are not the good. Whether the good exists or not, there is no other good than the good [. . .]. It makes no sense to say the good exists or the good does not exist; one can only say: the good [. . .]. The desire for good is itself a good. (FLN 315)

Because all desire for the good *is* the negative presence of good, and because the good as such is inherent in the desire for it, good is an end in itself. It does not require any other object or condition to make it real as the good. It is unconditionally replete in itself. Desire for good, when it is detached from particular ends, is itself the good that it wants. Desire for good in this sense actually incarnates the good. Weil asks, "Will it be said that I shall be left without an object of desire?" She answers, "No, because desiring in itself will be my good" (FLN 316).

There is a conscious reduction to tautology in Weil's argument: desire itself is the good, the good is desire (in other words, love). However tautological this formulation may be, it is in deep continuity with traditional Christian theologies of grace. The Augustinian doctrine of grace, which in myriad variations is foundational for Christian thought, maintains that the love that we direct toward God is necessarily itself from God and of God. It is God's love alone that we return to God by the grace of God in us, and this holds true whether nature is understood to "cooperate" with grace or not, because our nature is also from God and enabled to love by God. But Weil is theologically a *sola gratia* thinker (N 130) who leaves a strictly negative role to nature; it is not *we* but "God within us who loves God" (FLN 177). Supernatural love is a condition of our reception of God's love, and by this grace it is given to us to love gratuitously (N 279). The holy spirit is the immanence of God's love in us, and this spirit is the only love in us that is capable of a supernatural or transcendent goal.

For Weil, as for Augustine, "Desire is in itself the good. Even when it is wrongly directed it is still the potentiality of good" (FLN 318). Desire is in fact the *sole* good immanent in the human being, and as such it is the *imago Dei* in us; as we have already seen, longing for good is the sacred element in every human being. Love directed toward God is the real presence of God in the soul; it *is* God in the form of holy spirit. When we love with an orientation toward the good, but without an object (N 203), we are actually loving love itself (the notion of *amare amabam* in Augustine's *Confessions* 3.1, see FLN 261), and to love love is to do exactly as God does when God loves himself (N 193). God is essentially the trinitarian love that loves love. Love of God in its essence is an unconditional feeling (FLN 194). This is the sense in which God, perfect good, is the only possible *finality* for desire. All created things are intermediaries of love; they—we—have value as signs, mediations, and mediators of love. The value is not in the sign, but in the signified, and what is signified by love is the good. God as love mediates between creatures; creatures, insofar as they love purely, with perfect detachment, mediate God.

Detachment of Desire

The human being is born in contradiction: a limited creature motivated by unlimited desire, an unlimited desire that is a desire for unlimited good. Constituted by this paradox, creaturely desire cannot be assuaged except—equally paradoxically—by death, by the total dissolution of the limitations that constitute it as a creature. The deep ambiguity of death stems from this existential paradox: death is at once the greatest horror and the most quiescent peace; an object of dread and no less of deep longing and temptation. This paradox has been articulated by Freud as a contest between eros and the death drive (*Todestrieb*): his notion is that "besides the instinct to preserve living substance and to join it into ever larger units, there must exist another, contrary instinct seeking to dissolve those units and to bring them back to their primaeval, inorganic state."[7] Weil similarly remarks on the ambiguity of death that it is at once the ultimate destiny of the limited being and a humiliation, an annihilation of the limited being (N 10).

How is it possible to live this contradiction: to live in the absence of good, to live in acceptance of necessity, its opposite, which means acceptance of suffering and death? The way to acceptance is not to extinguish desire, for desiring per se is good. "Without desire we should not seek the truly absolute, the truly illimitable. We have got to have passed by way of desire" (N 100).[8] All desires are precious, since they contain energy that can be revalorized by the void (N 175). The way to acceptance is to detach desire from its changeable objects in order to liberate it from everything that is only conditionally good. We should steal the energy from particular desires by taking away their orientation in time (N 251). This means wrenching desire away from objects in which the presence of good is conditioned by necessity, and transferring the energy of desire to a good that is unconditional. It is a movement from natural goods to a supernatural good. This movement of detachment is the most Platonistic aspect of Weil's thought.[9]

Logically, in a world constituted by necessity, which is to say by inescapable conditions, anything that can be called "unconditional" is absent from the world except for the unconditional quality of desire itself (FLN 143). Therefore, it is appropriate that unconditional desire be directed to an unconditional good, a good that by virtue of its perfection is absent from the world, and this is what Weil refers to in speaking of God. Only by directing our longing to the pure good, or God, can we escape reaching for things that turn to death and futility in our grasp, following the New Testament precept: "Lay up for yourselves treasures in heaven, where neither moth nor rust consumes" (Matthew 6:20). Anything that is taken for an "end" other than pure ineffable and nonexistent good is an illusion of good, an idol. "No human being escapes the necessity of conceiving some good outside himself toward which his thought turns in a movement of desire, supplication, and hope. Consequently, the only choice is between worshipping the true God or an idol" (FLN 308).

To love what is purely absent with all one's vital energy is to live a life in the likeness of death. It is to detach one's desire and cease to "feed" on things and persons in the world, to cease hoping for (expecting, willing) good from the world—precisely as though one were already among the dead. One has renounced "feeding on man" and resolved to feed on God (FLN 286).

> Really to die, in the moral sense, means consenting to submit to everything whatsoever that chance may bring. Because chance can deprive me of everything that I call "I". To consent to being a creature and nothing else. It is like consenting to lose one's whole existence. We are nothing but creatures. But to consent to be nothing but that is like consenting to be nothing. Without our knowing it, this being that God has given us is non-being. If we desire non-being, we have it, and all we have to do is to be aware of the fact. (FLN 217–8)

This is to accept death virtually as having already occurred. Even objects and persons existent in the present are to be regarded as "perhaps destroyed" and "perhaps dead"; and yet, Weil writes, we should not let such a thought of loss dissipate the sense of reality, but render it more intense (N 218–9). We should employ the loss itself as an intermediary for attaining reality (N 28).

To undergo this abnegation, this reduction of vital desire through suffering and death, is to be touched by the first dawning of truth, the beginning of receptivity to truth, for only in the grip of death is our desire capable of overcoming the primary lie that governs human life. It is precisely attachment to life that blocks our awareness of the omniqualifying truth of death. "In this world of ours life, the *élan vital* so dear to Bergson, is but a lie; only death is true. For life constrains one to believe what one requires to believe in order to live" (NR 249).

In what sense is "only death true"? In the sense that, due to the grip of necessity, the creature's existence can be directly and irreversibly reduced to death, whereas death is not conversely reducible to life. The nonreversible nature of this causal order means that the needs of life impose a subjection to a set of conditions, and this subjection to life's conditions, when it is a *servitude*, displaces the possibility of serving truth. One must choose between life and truth, Weil insists, because ultimately one cannot serve two masters: "When we have felt the chill of death—unless we make haste to forget it, or it leaves us numbed—we pass on beyond, and this universe itself becomes a draught of immortality [. . .]. Through dissolution having traversed death" (N 61).

To die virtually, not literally, is to be released from the life-enslaving illusions that attachment to life engenders. "It is death alone that teaches us we have no existence except as a thing among a lot of other things" (FLN 285). In accepting death and living in virtual death, one remains subject to necessity as before, but necessity is no longer confused with the good. The two are held at an infinite distance. That is to say, life is no longer regarded as the supreme object of desire; it is regarded as a subjection to necessity. Pure good displaces life as the object of infinite desire. To know this is to part with illusion and come over to the side of truth. Although necessity continues to impose conditions, the good is known to transcend those conditions infinitely. Precisely because it is absolutely good, the good is absolutely absent.

Waiting for God

The inescapable contradiction of desire—the fact that our imperious longing to possess the good can only be satisfied by ceasing to be, either literally or virtually—means that we can never simply rest in the immediacy of life as our native element. The suffering induced by the contradictions of existence is what projects us beyond our limits as creatures into a transcendent perspective on our own predicament. It is a fundamental alienation from the entirety of the temporal realm that leads one to God. Fueled by the paradox of desire, we desire something good, everything good, the good itself—but we would never experience such desire if there were no evil blocking our possession of it, creating our existential condition of radical lack. "God entrusts to evil the work of teaching us that we are not" (FLN 218). Indeed, "good would not exist without evil" (N 327); without evil, "we would never renounce this world" (N 261) and seek the pure transcendent good.

What is absolutely absent from the world, pure good, cannot be possessed but only desired. Or, rather, desire in this case *is* the sole mode of possession, when possession is viewed in a fully dialectical sense as the having of a lack. Desire is the only possible mode of possession of pure good because, precisely qua absolute, pure good is absolutely absent. In Weil's theology it is *desire* for the good that already constitutes possession of the good, or God:

> The only thing that doesn't ever become exhausted is my will to good. Pure and inexhaustible good resides only in this will itself. (N 490) / In the same way that "exists" and "does not exist" have no meaning in relation to the good, so privation and satisfaction have no meaning in relation to the desire for good. This desire is not fulfilled, since it is itself the good. It is not unfulfilled, since it is itself the good. (FLN 317)

To desire is to wait. Our longing for unconditional good, when it is detached from the world without being extinguished as infinite desire, is finally what is symbolized in Weil's trademark phrase *attente de Dieu*, ambiguously meaning "waiting for God" and "God's waiting." The French words *attente* and *attendre* have all the connotations of "to wait" in English: to expect, to count on, to hope for. But it is also cognate with the English "attention," "to attend," which connote to listen to, to be present at, waiting upon, to pay attention to. Each of these connotations is enfolded in Weil's use of "waiting" with reference to God.

The strong temporal determination implied in "waiting" is the reason for Weil's use of the term. It draws forth the ontological contradiction between temporality and eternity: time's violence rends the soul, and through the rent eternity enters (N 28). We wait for God, God waits for us, across the crucifying divide of creation:

> God waits like a beggar who stands motionless and silent before someone who will perhaps give him a piece of bread. Time is that waiting. Time is God's waiting as a beggar for our love [...]. God and humanity are like two lovers who have missed their rendezvous. Each is there before the time, but each at a different place, and they wait and wait and wait [...]. The crucifixion of Christ is the image of this fixity of God. (FLN 141 = SWR 424–5)

The "waiting" thus described must not be understood in a common or literal sense. Waiting for God is not like waiting for a bus. There is never a time—or there are only exceedingly rare moments of grace—when what is awaited "arrives" so that the status of waiting is suspended. Waiting for God is a mode of existing detached from objects in the world, with all of one's desire directed toward a transcendent "nothingness" as a way of preventing it from being attached to a serial string of objects in the world. In waiting, the energy of desire is lifted away from objects, liberated from fixation in particulars, and affirmed as a good in itself apart from all specific intentionality. One's desire should be directed transparently through the good in objects toward the good that transcends all objects, the good that is no object, no thing, or "nothing." That nothing is God.

This is where prayer and contemplation occupy a central role. Prayer is a way of asking for the good that one does not possess and cannot obtain by any effort. "The cry is the first resource granted to a human being. What we could never get by work, we cry for" (FLN 99). The condition precedent to receiving supernatural bread consists in having reached and felt the limit; on contact with the limit, to continue longing and waiting for good is the only way "not to lie to oneself, and to hold on though bereft of hope" (N 153). It is folly to wait for a good that we have no logical or experiential reason to believe will come in any decisive sense (WG 209), for it is to love *emptily*, without sense or reason, in the void. But it is a lesser folly than continuing to seek good where—due to the paradox of desire—good cannot be found.

> In the period of preparation the soul loves in emptiness. It does not know whether anything real answers its love. It may believe that it knows, but to believe is not to know. Such a belief does not help. The soul knows for certain only that it is hungry. The important thing is that it announces its hunger by crying [...]. The danger is not lest the soul should doubt whether there is any bread, but lest, by a lie, it should persuade itself that it is not hungry. (WG 210)

The presence of desire in the form of unabating hunger is a certainty, and it is this certainty upon which faith is grounded, for in itself it constitutes an assurance that ultimate good is real. It itself *creates* the certainty that ultimate good is real: "Faith creates the truth to which adheres [...]. The domain of faith is the domain of truths created by certainty" (FLN 291, WG 209). Because faith is its own foundation, its certainty is unconditional, depending on nothing whatever in the world.

> There is only one proof of the goodness of God—it is that we love him. The love that we have for him is the sole benefit worthy of our gratitude, and consequently this love contains within itself the proof of its legitimacy. When it has no other incentive than itself, nothing can shake it; for even at the point of "Why hast thou forsaken me" love does not falter, but takes on the form of absence instead of that of contact. It thus attains the extreme limit of purity. (N 267)

Weil writes that all real desire for pure good, once a certain degree of intensity has been reached, causes the good in question to descend (NR 263). In saying this she is speaking of a decisive experience of grace, like her own "possession by Christ" (see Introduction), but this is not a question of divine intervention as commonly conceived. The descent of the good is not an occult and miraculous action effected by an occasionalist act of God, but the eruption of an immanent revelation in the soul. Again, tautology is the active ingredient of this "descent"—the infinitely simple tautology that *love is the good, the good is love*. To love the good that is absent is already to possess that good, which is simply love itself. "If love finds no object, the lover must love his love itself, perceived as something external" (FLN 260). Contemplation of the realization that love *is* the good, when the soul is undergoing the acute tension of deprivation of good, may at any moment convert into an overwhelming revelation, since "even the most ordinary truth, when it invades the whole soul, is like a revelation" (N 233).

In a moment of dialectical reversal, the tension of hunger breaks through the limit and is unveiled as an infinitely fulfilling grace; the "nothingness" of void is revealed as a plenitude, and this void means more than all plenitudes put together (N 491). When love continues to love in the void, without an object, in the image of Christ abandoned on the cross, it is a purified and perfected love, a love that loves through us, a love that *is* us, that is and has been our deepest identity all along. This love overwhelms the void of ourselves with the reality of itself. "If we want only the absolute good, [...] a revelation of it comes to us—the revelation that this nothingness is really the fullest possible fulness, the mainspring and principle of all reality. Then we can truthfully say that we have faith in God" (N 492). To believe that the desire for good is always fulfilled—that *is* faith, and whoever has this faith is not an atheist (FLN 137).

The good is something we can never get by effort but neither can we desire it purely, unconditionally, without getting it (FLN 142). This tautological fulfillment that characterizes the relation of desire to good is not due to psychological suggestion, Weil insists, because we cannot obtain by suggestion things that are inherently incompatible: for example, we cannot convert the absence of good into the presence of good; only grace can do that (N 435, 434). But once all our desire is directed to the good, what other good do we have to expect? This is what it is to possess the good. It is absurd to imagine any other happiness (FLN 157), for the fulfillment of unconditional love is tautological. When desire is reality, it is possession (FLN 317, 158).

Everything that I desire, and consequently look on as a good, exists, or has existed, or will one day exist somewhere, therefore how can I fail to have my desires gratified? (N 294).

In the case of the good uniquely, the tautological relation of pure desire to fulfillment is due to the fact that desiring itself *is* the good: desire is love, and love is an end in itself, a sufficiency unto itself, since it is already the fullest possible good to *love* the good. As long as we are alive we feel desire, and this very desire is the fullest possible good if only we prevent ourselves from focusing it in a particular direction (N 493). Weil's theology is grounded in the insight that this pure desire for good *is* God as we are able to know him, without names and labels. It is only with respect to false goods that desire and possession are different things; with respect to true good there is no difference. Therefore God exists because I desire him; that is as certain as my existence (FLN 157).

The final step of detachment allows a detachment from oneself, that is, from the centrality and importance of oneself as the seeker in the quest for God. What is all-important is the good, not *my* moment of finding and sharing in the good:

> There really is perfect and infinite joy in God. My participation can add nothing to it, my non-participation take nothing from the reality of this perfect and infinite joy. Of what importance is it then, whether I am to share in it or not? Of no importance whatever. (N 335 = WG 84)

To know that God is the good, or more simply, to know that the absolute good is the good, and to have faith that the desire for good is self-multiplying—"nothing else is needed" except to keep steadfast in these two simple things (FLN 309).

The Earthly Criterion

In the end, we do not become absolutely detached, for that would be to cease to love altogether, to extinguish desire. Rather, what we do is *universalize* the object of our attachment: "We must attach ourselves to the All" (N 21). To restrict our love to the pure object without fantasy and illusion is the same thing as to extend it to the whole universe. Faith thus entails an apprenticeship in loving God through the things of the world:

> We begin at first abstractly to know that we must love God in all things. Only later the beloved presence of God, through all the incidents great or small that make up the stuff of each day, enters at each second into the centre of our soul. The passage to this state is an operation analogous to that by which a child learns to read, by which an apprentice learns his trade, but analogous above all to that by which a very young child learns the perception of sensible things. (IC 200)

Faith is a gift of reading: a reading of the natural world in a supernatural light. Although God is absent "here below," God's creative presence is of an equal density in all phenomena and all possible interrelations of phenomena (N 360). This makes earthly things the *criterion* of spiritual things (FLN 147). Through faith, or that belief which is "productive of reality" (PSO 138), we must come to understand that "supreme reality" consists in this absence of an object which is the object of love, and we must learn to read that supreme reality in all objects taken together as a whole and in each object separately (N 220). In order really to love God, we must love God by means of all that is not God.

In "waiting," the energy of desire is liberated from attachment, making it available as free, undisposed energy offered to the good. The motive of this detachment is not to remove our love from the world, but far rather to perfect it *for* the world. Desire is wrenched away from creatures and directed to God not because God needs love and creatures do not; on the contrary, desire is detached and directed to God in order that it be returned by God to creatures—including ourselves—in a perfect manner, for "the love of God is only an intermediary between the natural and the supernatural love of creatures" (FLN 144). Detachment purifies and transforms our relation to ourselves: "It is because God loves us that we should love ourselves. How could one love oneself without this motive?" (N 278). The ultimate value of waiting for God is not diversion of attention away from the world or creaturely need, but its redirection in the form of love for all creatures as equally and "indifferently" as God loves them: "After having traversed death in order to reach God," Weil writes, "the saint should in a sense incarnate himself in his own body in order to spread in this world, in this earthly life, the reflection of supernatural light" (SNL 112). When the soul is mystically caught up unto God, the world made up of sensations vanishes; but the world is "saved, transfigured by a redemption," when the soul that has espoused God now redescends and feels the sensations anew (N 383). When we make this movement of descent and incarnation in imitation of Christ, we participate in the redemption of the world.

This dialectic of redescent casts into question McLellan's claim that, due to her apparent Platonic framework, Weil "emphasises transcendence at the expense of empirical reality" (*Utopian Pessimist*, 211), and Vetö's similar claim that "even in decisive moments she yields to the profound temptation to condemn the finite" (RM 73, 38, 155, 159). Transcendence of the finite is only the first movement of Weil's theological dialectic: it is the movement that accomplishes detachment. The second, more decisive movement mandates a return to the world of temporality and life in the body, a "redescent" in imitation of God's descent, and this is a movement of pure compassion and transparence to divine love (Chapter 5). The identification of a perfect human being with God, Weil asserts, may be considered from either the point of view of ascent or that of descent, but "it is descent that matters" (N 243).

Since God has infinite love for finite things as such (N 482), a pure love for creatures is not a love of the world for the sake of God, but love of the world for its own sake that has passed through God as through a purifying fire. "It is a love that detaches itself completely from creatures in order to ascend to God, and then redescends from God linked with the creative love of God" (N 616). Pure love on the part of a human being is a love that "recreates" the world by consenting to the will of God to create. This is to give one's consent to necessity as the opposite of the good, which, qua opposite, reveals the good dialectically through absence and evil. To give this consent is equivalent to loving creation, Creator, and cross in a seamlessly interlinked movement of the soul. Thus the point of "waiting for God" is not to surrender oneself to God and to abandon the world, leaving the limitations of creatureliness behind. The objective is to redescend to live among creatures as a transparent mediator of creative–redemptive love. For, when a human being finds "this small inert thing of flesh, lying stripped of clothing by the roadside," it is *not* the time to turn one's thoughts toward God (WG 151).

Redescent into the world is a participation in God's descent in the acts of creation, incarnation, and crucifixion (Chapters 3–5). For the incarnation is not the finishing stroke in a plan of salvation *from* the world, focused on the promise of an afterlife in heaven, but is far rather an inaugural movement of inspiration of spirit *into* the world: "Christian inspiration has never been able to relate itself to the things of this world. So the Incarnation comes to seem like a crowning event, a completion, instead of a commencement" (FLN 264). If Christian inspiration is to relate itself to the things of the world, Weil writes, two forms of "attachment to divinity" have to be overcome: "To put off the false divinity is but a preliminary image. We have to put off the true divinity after having acquired it, as far as this is possible for human nature" (N 324). In other words, we have to be detached not only from idols, which draw the supernatural down to a natural level, but from the supernatural itself (N 249).

The "false divinity" is our image of God reigning in power and glory rather than in void and abdication, and this is put off by accepting the kenotic movement of divine descent and crucifixion. The "true divinity" is put off in recognizing that the crucified God does not appear to us glorified on the cross, but incarnate in the anonymous sufferings of fellow creatures, above all the most extremely afflicted. This is what Weil means when she writes: "In a sense, the fact that a certain beggar is hungry is far more important than if Christ himself were hungry" (N 324). This assertion is a blasphemy to one who has not put off the true divinity. Yet to recognize divinity first of all in an anonymous beggar is to refuse to glorify the incarnate God as reigning above humanity, but to recognize divinity as immanent within the nakedness and suffering of anonymous humanity, and indeed within the suffering of all creatures inclusively. We have to strip away the name of Christ to arrive at his immanent reality in the nameless, unknown, unglamorous, needy, often appalling other, who is simply the mirror of our own misery in another. To honor in actual deed the longing for good that is the deepest center of *every* creature—including the appalling other—is to put off all attachment to divinity and to honor the anonymous crucified.

We are called to imitate Christ, Weil submits, incarnating him in this immanent sensory world, because it is our vocation to be mediators between God and reality (N 383). True imitation of Christ marks the final detachment: detachment from divinity itself. "Not to be attached to the supernatural. The Word stripped itself completely of its divinity" (N 248). So a double humiliation is called for: first, to find God in the void by giving up will, life, all attachments in this world, seeking out the "nothingness" of pure good, or God; and second, to reverse this movement, giving up God in a redescent to the world, in order to direct attention and energy into the world, which is patently more beloved by God than his own divinity. This double humiliation is the reflection of a double love, which Weil symbolizes as, on the one hand, God's unfathomable love for the abject Christ abandoned in the world, and on the other, as Christ's equally unfathomable love for the absent God in the depths of abandonment:

> To love means loving created beings and things as the divine Word loved them at the moment when it emptied itself in order to become a slave; and it means loving God as Christ did at the moment when he cried on the cross "My God, why has thou forsaken me?" Love this world as the divine Word loved it when for the sake of this world it parted from God. Have these two loves at the same time. This double love, of which each part is impossible and their combination impossible to the second degree, is the love of Christ that passeth knowledge. This love

consists of a certain attitude towards the things of this world.
(FLN 260)

The deepest paradox of desire is that it is wrenched away from
creatures in order that it be given back to creatures, purified by the
discipline of loving in the void, a purification that purges love of
every vestige of attachment. Weil cherished Plato's thought that the
true lover of wisdom is ineluctably called to return to the cave, and is
called to do so by the generosity of love itself. All the mystery and
beauty of love is manifested in the decision to descend, putting off
true divinity—and in this way, embodying true divinity. To descend
is to imitate the God who emptied himself on the cross (Phil. 2:6–8);
it is to pour oneself out in the image of divine kenosis. This is why,
as Weil phrases it, "returning into the Cave takes us further than
St. John of the Cross" (N 324).

(Not) to Speak of Holy Things

Because God alone is absolute good, "God alone is worthy of interest,
and absolutely nothing else" (FLN 126). And yet to understand
Weil's earthly criterion is to realize that finally everything in the
world actually is "about" God, and all things exist only in order to
mediate God as *metaxu*.[10] Everything created is related incarnation-
ally to God as creator, and to accept that God is the providential
source of all existence is in effect to understand that all things in
existence "speak" of God somehow. What regard should we have for
the things of the world, constituted as they are by a mixture of good
and evil? Or, as Weil poses the problem: "What are we to think about
the multitude of interesting things that say nothing about God?
Must we conclude that they are the devil's shows?" She answers her
own question: "No, no no. We must conclude that they do speak
about God" (FLN 126). Weil thought that in light of engulfing
secularism (*laïcisme*) in modernity—the massive domains of human
life that are of immense human interest yet seemingly "say nothing
about God"—it is urgently necessary to establish the relation of
everything apparently "godless" to God: that is, to establish the

relevance of God to secular pursuits, and the value of secular pursuits as paths for seeking or "waiting" for God.

The contradiction between good and necessity, between God and world, means that God and the supernatural are hidden and formless in the universe (N 230). Absolute good is other than the limited good we find in the world, which is the opposite and correlative of evil, though absolute good is the pattern and source of all relative good (SE 214). Absolute good can never inhere within the structures of necessity, it can only exert its influence in the world invisibly, secretly, from "beyond" the world. Because of this secrecy, Weil maintains, it is good that God and the supernatural should remain hidden and nameless in the soul as well; otherwise one risks grasping at something imaginary, under a name only, with false or empty words. Catholics and Protestants alike talk too much about holy things; saintliness has to be hidden—even from consciousness to a certain extent. "Those who fed, clothed, etc. Christ did not know that he was the Christ" (N 230). In the same vein, to undertake a certain action with the thought that one is doing it *for* God is a bad thing if this makes the action easier than it would be when accomplished simply for the objective involved (N 625). "One of the most exquisite pleasures of human love—to serve the loved one without his knowing it—is only possible, as regards the love of God, through atheism" (FLN 84). When we perform an action, we should pray for the good while letting all thought of "God" remain anonymous in us, hidden from our awareness, lest we act on the basis of idolatry.

Stéphane Mallarmé, one of the few modern poets whom Weil admired for his purity, wrote that everything that is sacred and wishes to remain so must envelop itself in mystery.[11] Weil similarly affirms that true faith implies extreme discretion, even with regard to itself. "It is a secret between God and us in which we ourselves have scarcely any part" (WG 199). Grace must be permitted to operate in secret; we must not seek to draw its workings into the light for fear of degrading it or subverting it with something inferior, something impure. Many people degrade charity in themselves, Weil writes, because they want to make it occupy too large and too visible a place in their souls, whereas "our Father lives only in secret" (WG 199), therefore love should be accompanied by modesty.

But simply keeping discreet silence is not the answer, for Weil any more than for Augustine (*Confessions* 1.4). When it comes to holy things, neither silence nor homage will do; there is continual need for judgment and discretion as to how to speak of the sacred: "It is bad both to offend against sacred things, even in a joking way (while thinking one is joking), and to pay them homage at a certain level. Nor must they be altogether passed over in silence" (N 141). There can be no rule to determine when it is appropriate to speak about God, yet Weil's rule of thumb is that one should do so only when one "has to": when compelled in some sense, as though to do so is unavoidable. "Not to speak about God (not in the inner language of the soul either); not to pronounce this word, *except when one is not able to do otherwise* ('able' is obviously used here in a particular sense)" (N 234).

The quandary of language about God is that God can never be manifested by the word, because God is that by which the word is manifested (FLN 151). So it is that God has a foundational relationship with all words that attempt to speak the Word, for it is the Word that speaks in all words, not vice versa. And yet, Weil concedes, ultimately all things do manifest the love of God and the *Logos* of God, including speech about the multitude of interesting secular things that seem to say nothing about God. Supernatural love is at work, hidden in the way it illuminates and reveals the world:

> If I light an electric torch at night out of doors I don't judge its power by looking at the bulb, but by seeing how many objects it lights up. The brightness of a source of light is appreciated by the illumination it projects upon non-luminous objects. The value of a religious or, more generally, a spiritual way of life is appreciated by the illumination thrown upon the things of this world. (FLN 147) / The object of my search is not the supernatural, but this world. The supernatural is the light. We must not presume to make an object of it or else we degrade it. (N 173)

Thus, although Weil affirms time and again that only spiritual things are of value, she insists concomitantly that only physical things have a verifiable existence for human beings, since full reality for a human being lies within this world (N 374). The value of spiritual things can *only* be verified as an illumination projected onto material things. For human beings, spiritual value—that is, the good that is to be loved—has to be recognized and honored in physical things because human beings themselves are physical beings, vulnerable to harm and responsive to the effects of care. Excessive spiritualization of love, beyond detaching it from particular objects, threatens to render love objectless and empty—disincarnate—and therefore unreal. "If, on the pretext that only spiritual things are of value, we refuse to take the light thrown on earthly things as a criterion, we are in danger of having a non-existent treasure" (FLN 147).

One's regard for earthly things, then, becomes the touchstone of genuine faith, which is the love begotten between the hidden God and the hidden part of the soul that loves supernaturally. One loves God anonymously when one loves the world purely, and this is why it is possible to be an "atheist" at one level and a person of faith at another. Not to believe in God, but to love the universe faithfully, is to demonstrate the same faith as that which shines resplendent in religious symbols (N 469). Love for God satisfies the criterion of reality only when it is reflected in one's relation to the real things of the world.

One does not testify so well for God by speaking about Him as by expressing, either in actions or words, the new aspect assumed by the creation after the soul has experienced the Creator [. . .]. It is not the way a man talks about God, but the way he talks about things of the world that best shows whether his soul has passed through the fire of the love of God. In this matter no deception is possible. There are false imitations of the love of God, but not of the transformation it effects in the soul, because one has no idea of this transformation except by passing through it oneself. (FLN 144–5)

Weil draws an analogy: just as a painter does not depict the spot where he is standing, yet by looking at his picture we can deduce his position in relation to the things depicted, similarly, according to the conception of human life expressed in the acts and words of a human being, an observer with spiritual discernment can tell whether that person beholds life from a viewpoint "in this world" or from a supernatural, transcendent perspective (FLN 146).

So it is that saintliness is most readily discerned and verified not directly by speech about God but by one's relation to the things of the world. This is what Weil means in writing, "It is not the way a man talks about God, but the way he talks about things of the world that best shows whether his soul has passed through the fire of the love of God" (FLN 145). In fact, the soul's attitude toward God is not a thing that can be verified at all, not even by the soul itself, because God is elsewhere, "in heaven," in secret. The veracity and purity of love is to be judged by its fruits when it is directed to creatures (FLN 117), for the fruits of the tree are what bear the mark of an experience of God, not the tree itself (FLN 145). "What is a proof is the appearance of supernatural virtues in that part of [the soul's] behaviour that is turned towards men. The faith of a judge is not seen in his behaviour at church, but in his behaviour on the bench" (FLN 146).

If God alone is worthy of interest and "absolutely nothing else" (FLN 126), why should there be a primary concern for creatures? Because, Weil responds, care for creatures is the verifiable expression of love of God. What is good in a good act is that, in it, *love* acts. Although a good act is always at risk of having an admixture of evil in its effect, the love expressed in the act, if it is pure, is nonetheless a pure sign of love, a pure signification of good. "Good and evil works (e.g., feeding the hungry, swindling the poor) have been placed within our power to act as a language, and are essentially only signs of love or hatred. These signs are contagious like language, and within the same limits" (N 448, 357).

Since radical want is the human condition, the reality of *need*—deriving from necessity—is what creates the occasion for manifesting love as real, as gift and sacrifice, and not as a mere figment of idle or wishful imagination. Because every human being is in subjection to necessity, ever vulnerable to misery and need, actually or potentially, the "one possibility of indirect expression of respect for the human being is offered by men's needs, the needs of the soul and of the body, in this world" (SE 221). The fact that a human being possesses an eternal destiny imposes the obligation of respect, and this obligation is met only if the respect is expressed in a real and effective, not a fictitious or imaginary way. This can be done only "through the medium of man's earthly needs" (NR 6). Thus it is not how we speak of God in words but how we imitate divine generosity and compassion in our actions that is the touchstone of faith.

CHAPTER 3

GOD AND THE WORLD

Already before the Passion, already by the Creation, God empties himself of his divinity, abases himself, takes the form of a slave. (FLN 70)

Most of the unorthodox or anti-orthodox elements in Weil's religious thought stem from her unusual conception of the creation of the world as a *withdrawal* of God. Her lack of formal theological education left her unusually free to conceive the creation of the world in a strikingly heterodox manner as an act of abdication rather than an act of power on the part of God. This unorthodox conception of creation functions as the decisive center of her religious thinking as a whole, for it is primarily through God's voluntary abdication in creation that God is revealed as a "self-emptying" passion: a passion that is fulfilled or "finished" (John 19:30) not only through the death on the cross, but in the entire movement of abdication that comprises creation, incarnation, and crucifixion as moments of a single providential decision. On the one hand, Weil embraced the central Roman Catholic teaching that God is a trinity (Father, Son, and Holy Spirit); that God is love, and before all things God knows and loves himself; and that the immanent "friendship" that characterizes God *in se* is an infinite nearness or identity. On the other hand, Weil was by no means an orthodox trinitarian. As we shall see, Weil's God divides himself by "an infinite distance" yet remains one across the void of this distance, united by nothing but an unconditional, unintelligible love, which is an expression of God's "madness" (*la folie propre à Dieu*) (N 262, FLN 127, IC 182–3).

Creation as Withdrawal

Before creation—a "before" we can speak of only paradoxically—God is the sole reality: the godhead is in absolute unity with itself. The world cannot in any sense be created "outside" such a self-united God, for there is no godless point wherein to create, no "outside" or place of division, and for that matter no *nihil* out of which to create. In order to create, Weil reasons, it is necessary for God to undo this perfect unity and bring into existence something that is other than God. Only the imposition of what Weil terms "an infinite distance"—reminiscent of Kierkegaard's "infinite qualitative distinction"—can achieve this. The act of creation establishes the world at an infinite distance from the Creator, which is to say, as an infinite otherness. "God has created, that is, not that He has produced something outside Himself, but that He has withdrawn Himself, permitting a part of being to be other than God" (IC 193).

God, absolute and unlimited in himself, must renounce unbounded freedom if a world determined and ordered by finite limits is to exist. Out of his omnipotence, God abdicates power with the result that his freedom is limited. God lets his hands be tied, so to speak, and he himself does the tying. "God is more hidden in creation than in incarnation. [...] Everything is possible for him, but everything happens as if everything were not possible for him" (N 290). Creation, which is God's withdrawal and abdication for the sake of the world, is an act of renunciation of divinity: "In creating God renounces being all. He abandons a bit of being to what is other than Himself. Creation is renunciation by love" (IC 183).

This abdication introduces a contradiction within divinity. As Weil puts it, "It is contradictory that God, who is infinite, who is all, to whom nothing is lacking, should do something that is outside himself, that is not himself, while at the same time proceeding from himself" (N 385–6). The divine abdication must be understood as a movement of God "against" God, an assault on God by God in that it means the destruction of the divine unity: the rending of God from God (SNL 176). Yet from another point of view the movement must be understood as "for" God in that it enacts God's providential will, which is a self-rending will. In willing the creation as an object of love, God freely consents to renunciation of power and the evil that is its consequence: "This universe [...] is the distance put by Love between God and God. We are a point in this distance. Space, time, and the mechanism that governs matter are the distance. Everything that we call evil is only this mechanism" (WG 127).

Something is thus created that is not only *not* God, it is God's *undoing*; it comes to exist as contrary to God, which means that God suffers a real diminution: "God and all his creatures are less than God alone. God accepted this diminution. He emptied a part of his being from himself" (WG 145; N 217, 212). Weil's term for this something that is contrary to God—which issues from and enacts God's will to create—is *necessity*. Weil views the act of creation as "God chaining himself down by necessity" (N 191). Necessity is the limitation and suspension of the pure freedom of God, although that limitation is the actual consequence of the enactment of God's freedom. Necessity can come to exist only by a decision of God to withdraw himself and to institute a principle in opposition to the pure and limitless good that he is.

Several scholars have commented on the striking parallels between Weil's conception of creation and that of the Jewish kabbalistic thinker Isaac Luria (d. 1572).[1] As there is no clear evidence that Weil was aware of Luria's highly original theory of creation, we can only speculate that she may have absorbed the idea through indirect channels of exposure (perhaps via Böhme or Schelling). Although in the last years of her life Weil began to read several major Christian mystics, her antipathy to Judaism seems to have kept her away from Jewish mystical traditions.[2] In any case, whether she was aware of Luria's theory of creation or not, the conceptual problem that it purposed to solve is essentially identical to the problem Weil confronted in her theological thinking, leading her along a parallel course of reasoning.

For both Weil and Luria, who share a commitment to the idea of *creatio ex nihilo*, the problem is the *nihil* out of which God created: where did this "nothing" come from if the plenitude of God is infinite and omnipresent? In the course of commenting on Luria, Gershom Scholem summarizes the series of questions that the doctrine of creation *ex nihilo* provokes: "How can there be a world if God is everywhere? If God is 'all in all,' how can there be things that are not God? How can God create the world out of nothing if there is no nothing?"[3]

By way of solution, Luria conceptualizes creation as an act of *tsimtsum*, a Hebrew word denoting "contraction," "withdrawal," "retreat"; that is, God created the world by first withdrawing or stepping back into himself to form a primordial space empty of God. This precreative movement of *tsimtsum*, the self-contraction or withdrawal of the unlimited godhead *Ein Sof*, means that God's first act was a negation or limitation of infinite divine substance: "God was compelled to make room for the world by, as it were, abandoning a region within Himself, a kind of mystical primordial space from which He withdrew in order to return to it in the act of creation and revelation" (Scholem, *Major Trends*, 261). Moreover, every new manifestation by God is preceded by a corresponding movement of self-concentration and retraction in which God "pulls himself back" before sending forth the rays of his light in the creative movement of Genesis; "but for this perpetual tension, this ever repeated effort with which God holds Himself back, nothing in the world would exist." For Luria, the withdrawal of God is not a mythical idea but a conceptualization of an actual, pre-original *event* that must necessarily have occurred. Luria's conception of *tsimtsum* is intended to provide an explanation for the actual existence of something other than God, according to Scholem, thus it constitutes—remarkably enough— "the only serious attempt ever made to give substance to the idea of Creation out of Nothing" (261–2).

In strong contrast with Luria, Thomas Aquinas's reflections on the doctrine of creation *ex nihilo* argue that in the act of creation (as opposed to change) there is first of all "no thing," and then the whole substance of a thing is produced; he makes clear that the "nothing" of *ex nihilo* is not itself a thing, not a material cause, but is simply "not something," and the thing that is created is "not made from anything."[4] Created being is not first "nonexistent" and then existent; rather, it comes into existence *de novo* and that is all. But it is hard to see how Thomas's understanding of creation is not in some sense—a sense left unargued and unaccounted for—a *creatio ex Deo*, given that "before" the act of creation God is the sole subsistent being.

In subsequent tradition, Christian theology of creation has been heavily patterned on Thomas's thinking, sustaining his idea that the world as created being subsists in the power of the being of God, *ipsum esse*, and that God continues to govern creation with absolute power. Weil's concept of creation, quite purposefully and intentionally, reverses this understanding with an alternate deeply dialectical view: "Because he is the creator," she insists, "God is not all-powerful. Creation is abdication. But he is all-powerful in this sense, that his abdication is voluntary. He knows its effects, and wills them" (FLN 120). God, in giving rise to existence as a realm other than himself, at an infinite distance from himself, has forfeited omnipotence. "God's attributes do not overflow one another. They all have the same limit, the abdication that is God's creative act" (FLN 125). Thus God has abdicated the power of being God alone, a perfect unbroken unity, unfallen and absolutely free of evil. This means that the act of creation, for Weil, is a radical act of self-transfiguration of God by God: creation is already the crucifixion or passion of God.

The withdrawal of God, his abdication to necessity, results in the rending of God—a rending that is for Weil the theological origin of evil. God the Father and God the Son are torn infinitely asunder: "Between the terms united by the relation of divine love there is more than nearness; there is infinite nearness or identity. But through the Creation, the Incarnation, and the Passion, there is also infinite distance. The interposed density of all space and time sets infinite distance between God and God (SNL 176, N 428–9). As a consequence of the Father's withdrawal in creation, and the Son's corresponding acts of descent into flesh and abandonment in crucifixion, an "infinite distance" is interposed between the Father and the Son. Even the incarnation is simply a figure of the creation, recapitulating how God denied himself (*Dieu s'est nié*) and "abdicated by giving us existence" (WG 145, FLN 297). The incarnation does not bring God closer to us but increases the distance: God has placed the cross between himself and us: "The Cross is harder to bridge than the distance between heaven and earth. It is this distance" (N 298). The rending of God by infinite distance actually inaugurates the distinction between good and evil, for "evil is nothing else but the distance between God and the creature" (N 588). This distance is a negation of good, hence the dialectical opposite of good—evil—by definition; for God, who is the good, has withdrawn himself to make it possible.

Just as *tsimtsum* in Luria's thought distinguishes and concentrates the intradivine sternness within *Ein Sof* until it becomes recognizable as *din*, divine judgment or justice—an act of negation and limitation in which the root of all evil is already latent (Scholem, *Major Trends*, 261–3)—so Weil's God elects to withdraw himself to give place to *necessity*, which is the root of all evil owing to the infinite distance that separates the necessary from the good, the creature from God. "Necessity is the screen placed between God and us so that we can *be*" (N 402). The world is governed by necessity because God, in order to create, had to give the world over to a concatenation of determinations and limits whose boundaries judge one another in a Heraclitean sense: "Like the oscillations of the waves, the whole succession of events here below, made up, as they are, of variations in balance mutually compensated—births and destructions, waxings and wanings—render one keenly alive to the invisible presence of a plexus of limits without substance and yet harder than any diamond" (NR 288). Every limit that particularizes the order of the world establishes a *yes* and a *no*, a *good* and an *evil*, opposites that subsist in necessary mutual correlation. A real world governed by such limits cannot but entail the existence of evil: "God alone is pure good. Creation being both God and other than God is essentially good and evil" (N 414).

But Weil's statements concerning the evil of the created world must be balanced within the more comprehensive understanding that

"the possibility of evil is a good" (N 112). As will become clearer
in the chapters that follow, the world is neither good nor evil
intrinsically, but is both at once dialectically. The infinite distance of
the world from God is evil, but inasmuch as it actualizes the will of
God to create, giving himself to a godless other, it is good. The evil
within creation is a dialectical vehicle of good. From this perspective,
the world is ambiguously good or evil according to the aspect of its
relationship to redemptive grace: "evil" is the point of view of grace
withheld, "good" is the point of view of grace abounding. Although
in a relative sense evil is always evil, in an ultimate sense, evil as such
is entirely good.

The Absent God

The conceptual beauty of Luria's *tsimtsum* theory is that it establishes
an absolute distinction (an "infinite distance" in Weil's language) of
creatures from God, thus prohibiting any immediate pantheistic
grounding of finite beings in the being or substance of God. Every
being acquires a reality of its own, Scholem observes, which "guards
it against the danger of dissolution into the non-individual being of
the divine 'all in all.'" The creature is real as that which is created out
of nothing, not out of God, and is therefore substantially other to
God—truly distinct and independent from God, or "outside" of
God, occupying the space left by the divine self-retraction. By the
same token, *tsimtsum* is the deepest symbol of divine exile that could
be thought of, since God is in effect exiled into himself (*Major
Trends*, 261–2).

In a profoundly parallel respect, the negative ground of creation in
Weil's thought establishes a pure distinction between God and
creature. This takes the form of an inverse dialectical relation
between God and world. Weil's many contradictory statements about
God cannot make sense until this negative dialectic is recognized and
taken into account. In willing the existence of an actual "other," God
must necessarily withdraw, taking an infinite distance from that
other: "God has only been able to create by hiding himself. Otherwise
there would only be he" (N 230). The withdrawal of God engenders

the space of creation that is a "nothing"—the actual presence of the absence of God—for the presence of void is necessary in order that the world have need of God, and that presupposes evil (N 148). "It is impossible for God to be present in creation except in the form of absence" (N 419); only God's presence in the Eucharist is an exception (N 593). God has withdrawn, the good is absent, and precisely that absence or void is present to the creature as the purest negative revelation of God: "Pure goodness is not anywhere to be found in [this world . . .]. The existence of evil here below, far from disproving the reality of God, is the very thing that reveals him in his truth" (WG 145).

As the creature can only exist by the grace of God's absence, God respects the requirement of the negative relation and does not tamper with his creature in its otherness. God abandons creatureliness to necessity, a necessity embodied in the absence of God, the absence of good: "The distance between the necessary and the good is the selfsame distance separating the creature from the creator. God, with respect to creation, in so far as perfectly present and in so far as perfectly absent" (N 379). Where the world exists in space and time, God is necessarily absent. This absence of God is the condition of the world's existence, and remains ever present to the world as its negative foundation. That the world is created *ex nihilo* means that, by virtue of its origin, the world is *a-theistic*, without God, bereft of God. The world is negative from the point of view of God, and God is negative from the point of view of the world.

> Everything is upside down in our world of sin. What is negative appears as positive, and what is authentically and fully positive appears to us as negative. This constitutes a criterion. What appears to us as positive never is, cannot possibly be, positive. Only what appears to us as negative is authentically positive. (N 433)

Weil alternates language of positive and/or negative, of presence and/or absence to a paradoxical effect in speaking of this fundamental dialectical relation between God and world.

For example, the presence of the absence of God in the material substance of the world can be expressed in terms of either *presence* or *absence* dialectically, or both at once paradoxically. "God, in so far as he exists, is the universe composed of phenomena. God, in so far as he is other than the universe, is other than existence" (N 328); the universe both manifests and hides God (N 149). As in the case of any true paradox, neither opposite negates the other; each remains paradoxically true in relation to its opposite, and the comprehensive truth is expressed in their dialectical coincidence and correlation. Thus Weil's conception of creation as a withdrawal of God provides the theoretical grounds for what can be called her "religious atheism," or even her atheistic mysticism. In the dialectical terms of Weil's thinking, experience of the world negatively reveals the reality of the absent God. Precisely insofar as the things of the world mark the absence of good and the reign of necessity, they signify and make palpable the negative ground of creation: the withdrawal and abdication of God. The very existence of the world is the abiding proof and sacramental presence of God's abdication.

This makes possible for Weil an experience of intense negative mysticism and negative sacramentalism. For, although contact with human creatures is given to us through the sense of presence, "contact with God is given to us through the sense of absence"; compared with this divine absence, presence becomes "more absent than absence" (N 239–40). As classically defined by Augustine, a sacrament is the visible sign of an invisible grace. But while sacramental tradition understands the relation between visible form and invisible grace as a positive continuity between degrees of good, Weil's thinking renders the visible–invisible relationship inverse or dialectical. The visible form of the world renders sensible the *absence* of God as the form of his hidden presence; absence per se reveals the visible and palpable form of his grace. It is in this vein that Weil can write in a tone of mystical rapture of God's "everlasting absence," and can insist that consciousness of the absence of God is our most powerful experience of grace in the world:

The occasional contacts resulting from inspiration between [God's] creatures and Him are less miraculous than is his everlasting absence, and constitute a less marvelous proof of his love. God's absence is the most marvelous testimony of perfect love, and that is why pure necessity, the necessity that is manifestly so different from good, is so beautiful [...]. Everything that makes this absence manifest is beautiful. (N 403)

Divine absence is the very substance of God's love for the creature. That God consents to this infinite distance from himself, to letting necessity reign so that the creature may *be*, is a gift of radical otherness, of "godlessness"—even of evil—to the creature. If "evil is nothing else but the distance between God and the creature" (N 588), then evil is the primary condition of creation: no world can exist without a fall into evil. For God, to love something truly other, something infinitely distant from himself, is to let it exist abandoned to necessity, and this act of abandonment is the actual embodiment of his love for the creature. It is only by willing absence of good, thus a voluntary "fall" into evil, that God can reveal his goodness to a created world: "The apparent absence of God in this world is the actual reality of God [...]. This world, in so far as it is completely empty of God, is God himself. Necessity, in so far as it is absolutely other than Good, is Good itself" (N 424).

"Original Sin"

The withdrawal of God not only opens a space for the possibility of evil, but actually constitutes that space as qualified by evil, for by definition evil is a condition of separation from God, who is the good. In creating the world, "God renounces—in a sense—being everything. This is the origin of evil" (N 193). Evil is born when God, in the act of creation, renounces being the only reality in order that a world exist ruled by necessity and the conditional limits of existence. Thus evil is the unavoidable concomitant of God's decision to create; it inheres necessarily in the constitution of existence per se. Existence projects evil as its inescapable shadow and nemesis, for the consuming shadow of nonexistence inheres in every relative good of existence. From this perspective all of creation is shot through with evil, an evil that takes the form of violence or suffering or both.

Can it be said, then, that God *wills* evil when he creates? The answer given by Weil's theology is dialectical: yes and no. We must always be mindful that God's willing of evil is not an act of power but a consent to withdraw and become powerless in relation to necessity: "Everything that occurs, without any distinction, is permitted, that is to say consented to, by God. But this consent is an abdication. So it is not the exercise of a kingly power [. . .]. God's will is to abdicate in favour of necessity" (FLN 296). For love of an other, the created order of the world, God wills the *nihil*, the nonbeing, the evil that necessarily attends a created existence. Inasmuch as God positively wills the existence of the world and everything that happens in it, he concomitantly wills evil, for "nothing happens here below unless He wills it" (FLN 136). And yet this willing of evil is "innocent" in a higher sense, for the alpha and omega of the world's evil aspect is a creative and a redemptive good. We are called to love evil not from the natural standpoint of a creature but from a supernatural perspective: "We must love evil as such" (N 431) because the goodness of God abdicates to it and in that sense fully wills it. Because we are called above all else to love the divine will, we must love the will of God not apart from evil or dissociated from evil but *through* evil as such. Recognition of the true God allows the horror of evil to subsist, and even renders it more intense; while one has a horror of this evil, at the same time one loves it as emanating from the will of God (N 505, 431). "We have to love God through evil as such: to love God through the evil we hate, while hating this evil: to love God as the author of the evil that we are actually hating" (N 340 = GG 75). As God is the author of evil, to love God's will is to love that authorship, and that means to love evil in an ultimate sense as providential. For, although the good is never a product of evil, evil is in a sense produced by good: "God allows evil to exist. Love consents to be an object of hatred" (FLN 300).

All evil in nature, including human nature, is associated with the creative will of God. Sin, in Weil's unorthodox theology, is that portion of natural evil that has its source in the willing of a created will. Such evil is "voluntary" in that it is actively willed by the creaturely will pursuing its own objects, quite apart from knowledge of or regard for the will of God for it. This will is the locus of the creature's otherness and separation from God. In creating the creaturely will, God has created this otherness, this contrariness to himself of voluntary evil, or sin (FLN 211). "Creation and original sin are only two aspects, which are different for us, of a single act of abdication by God" (FLN 140). The possibility of sin is attached not to freedom, but to existence—a separate existence (N 192). To will as a human creature is to will as a separate and distinct existent, alienated from the will of God—a separateness of will that as such cannot be distinguished from sin.

Original sin is a sin committed *before* any sin; it is outside time, transcendental (N 192). Weil is therefore consistent in her deep heterodoxy when she situates the fall of Adam outside the beginning of time, before existence has come into being. The original sin of Adam did not erupt in breaking a taboo or commandment; this traditional account, Weil maintains, is only a "translation of the real sin into human language"; rather, to her thinking, "time proceeded out of the sin and did not precede it" (FLN 127).

> Adam before the Fall is inconceivable; one can only conceive a causal, non-temporal anteriority between his creation, his sin and his punishment. The whole of humanity has sinned in a non-temporal sense by possessing its own will. It has been created with a will of its own and the vocation to renounce it [. . .]. The order from God was an ordeal proving that Adam had a will of his own. He was in a state of sin in view of the fact that he had a will of his own. It is clear that there never was a period of time in which he was in a state of innocence. (N 268)

A sin that is conceived as coeval with the creation of the will is necessarily a sin for which God himself is responsible. "If we are born in sin, it is evident that birth constitutes a sin" (FLN 303). Just as God, in willing abdication, wills the evil inherent in creation, he likewise wills the "original sin" of the human will; but again, God wills it "innocently" inasmuch as sin is a dialectical means toward an ultimate revelation of good, a good that cannot actually be manifested qua good otherwise than indirectly, through the contradictory actualites of evil and sin.

According to Weil's nontemporal understanding of original sin, there is no pristine age of innocence before the fall. Creation as such is identified with fall, that is, creation brings into existence an "ungodly" will, which qua ungodly is nonetheless willed by God: "God undoes the harmony of which He is constituted in creating man—a creature that prefers itself to God" (N 560). When God creates the human will, God not only permits or consents to, but actually *enacts* the fall, and in that sense God's own innocence "falls" with that fall. While humanity falls upon being created with a will, God "falls" preveniently as the original provenance of that fallen will.

Challenging traditional Christian assumptions on this point, Weil questions, "Why should one be reluctant to think that God willed Adam's sin?" (N 235), for it is in view of redemption that the advent of sin is willed by God.[5] Only consciousness of the evil of evil, the sin of sin, can reveal to humanity the absolute desirability of good. The serpent in the garden promises Eve, "You will be like God, knowing good and evil" (Gen. 3:5), and Weil reads the serpent's promise positively, as did Hegel, averring that only in view of redemption does this likeness to God become strictly true, and the fall into sin is a condition of becoming "like God," of becoming perfect as the heavenly Father is perfect (Matt. 5:48).

God has created man with the capacity of becoming like unto Himself, but in a state of sin consented to by man. The Fall expresses this essential character of consent attached to sin. Sin lies within man, not outside him; it comes from man; but man has been created such. Man has been created such, and yet God is innocent. This innocence is not harder to conceive after this fashion than is, for those who represent to themselves the story as unfolding itself in time, God's innocence at the moment when Adam disobeys. For everything that takes place is the will of God. (N 309)

So God consents preveniently to humanity's constitutive predisposition to sin, and does so in order that grace abound, for "where sin increased, there grace abounded all the more" (Rom. 5:20). But this is not to make light of the radical negativity of sin—which is a voluntary evil. It is *real* sin that makes possible *real* grace. Real sin is accompanied by guilt and resentment against oneself, against one's existence, and ultimately against one's creator. This is the ground of what Nietzsche came to understand as *ressentiment* and what Dostoevsky portrayed in the self-rending agonies of Ivan Karamazov. Viewed theologically, the deep problem of sin is that to pardon oneself or one's neighbor is not a sufficient remedy for voluntary evil: a human pardon does not get to the ontological root of the resentment because ultimately sin is not a merely human guilt. To forgive humanly cannot touch the primordial origin and provenance of the wound of sin. The guilt is ours *in God*, and equally it is God's *in us*. This is why, according to Weil, "one can only excuse men for evil by accusing God of it" (FLN 94). "We lay the blame for our failures and shortcomings upon things and creatures other than us. In the end, we are accusing God. If we forgive God for our sins, he forgives us for them. All our debts are to God, and God is also our only debtor" (FLN 210). Having created us, he owes us everything (FLN 177).[6]

Only a forgiveness directed toward God, the ultimate source of human existence and fallibility, can redress and heal the primordial wound of the fallen will. There is no ultimate release from our resentment over sin unless we can forgive God for our existence: "The most difficult remission of debts consists in forgiving God for our sins. The sense of guilt is accompanied by a sort of rancour and hatred against the Good, against God, and it is the effect of this mechanism that makes crime harmful to the soul" (FLN 140). Without recourse to ultimate forgiveness, resentment eats the soul, a rancor bitterly feeding on itself, a self-consuming negativity that is given powerful expression in the words of Satan in Milton's *Paradise Lost*: "myself am Hell."

Since the guilt of the human creature and the guilt of the Creator are the fruits of reciprocal "crimes," they require a reciprocal forgiveness, a mutual redemption: "God's great crime against us is to have created us, is the fact of our existence. And our existence is our great crime against God. When we forgive God for our existence, he forgives us for existing" (FLN 263). To forgive God for his abdication in creating us is at the same time to consent to exist as he created us, outside his kingdom (NR 277). To pardon God for our sins is to embrace God's will that we exist, for our sin is our existence apart from God. "God pardons us for existing so soon as we are willing to consent to exist only in so far as God wills our existence" (FLN 263). In forgiving God, then, we are simultaneously consenting to a "repetition" of creation qua fall; we consent to creation by saying *yes* to God's abdication of power. This enactment cuts to the root of sin:

> One can only excuse men for evil by accusing God of it. If one accuses God one forgives, because God is the Good. Amid the multitude of those who seem to owe us something, God is our only real debtor [...]. Sin is an offense offered to God from resentment at the debts he owes and does not pay us. By forgiving God we cut the root of sin in ourselves. At the bottom of every sin there is anger against God. If we forgive God for his crime against us, which is to have made us finite creatures, He will forgive our crime against him, which is that we are finite creatures. (FLN 94–5)

Human forgiveness in Weil's thought is an *imitatio Dei:* when we blame God for our afflictions, for all the evil we give and receive, we are imitating the action of God in Christ when God accuses himself of this very guilt through the mouth of his Son: "Just as God, through the mouth of Christ, accused himself of the Passion, so we should accuse God for every human affliction. And just as God replies with silence, so we should reply with silence" (FLN 94, 83). To reply with silence means to consent, not to refuse or rebel. It is to love

God's will even though caught in the teeth of evil because God's will is ultimately the good, the sole source of the beauty and wisdom that pervades all things. As all that we love is received from this will, so all that we hate must be returned to it, offered back to it in the form of sacrificial consent.

All crime is a transference of evil from the one who acts to the one who suffers the action. The one who suffers evil wants to be relieved of it in turn by putting it elsewhere (FLN 154). Such transference does not diminish evil but multiplies it. Thus every evil enacted in the world circulates and multiplies, passed from one to another, until it alights on a perfectly pure being who suffers it in completeness and thereby destroys it (FLN 153). To be absolutely just, one must be able to suffer injustice without it doing one any harm, and God alone, pure love, is able to do that (N 627). We must offer our hatred to God; we must leave it to God to avenge the offenses we receive, so that the hatred in us is burnt up by contact with pure good (FLN 331). For it is only through contact with God, the Just One, that evil falls into its own proper nothingness.

> Where, then, are we to put the evil? We have to transfer it from the impure part to the pure part of ourselves—if we have such a thing in us, even though it be only a speck—thus transmuting it into pure suffering. The crime that is latent in us we must inflict on ourselves. In this way, however, it would not take us long to sully our own speck of inward purity if we did not renew it by contact with an unchanging purity placed outside us, beyond all possible reach. Patience consists in not transforming suffering into crime, and that in itself is enough to transform crime into suffering. (N 624–5) / The false God changes suffering into violence. The true God changes violence into suffering. (N 507 = GG 72).

The alienation from goodness that we experience in the evil and fallenness of the world is an alienation that God has already suffered in himself, accused himself of, and forgiven himself for. We can only reenact the cry of God within himself, unto himself: "'Father, why. . .?' God accuses himself of Christ's passion. 'He that delivered me unto thee hath the greater sin. . .'" (FLN 94; see John 19:11). In Weil's radical interpretation of this gospel passage, the one who "delivers" Christ is not Judas, or the Jews, or the Romans, or human sin, but God himself, and *God* therefore has the greater sin. God has delivered himself into evil; God is guilty of the blood of the innocent; and God is also the innocent who has consented to this crime against himself.

The satisfaction that we seek by throwing the offense of evil away from ourselves in sin consists, for God, in submitting to it (FLN 154). Human beings have the choice of being either willing or unwilling participants in this sacrifice, the crucifixion of God, which has been enacted already once and for all. Our vocation is to transcend evil by recognizing evil for what it is, consenting to it as emanating from the will of God (N 505), and suffering it as a participation in the cross. This is why, Weil asserts, "One should ask for circumstances such that all the evil that one does falls solely and directly upon oneself. That is the Cross" (N 418, 414). Thus we may give or refuse consent, but the will to fallenness is God's, and that will is done on earth as it is in heaven. Even in the light of divine grace, there is no escape from or consolation for the suffering caused by evil: "It is impossible to contemplate without terror the extent of the evil which man is capable of causing and undergoing. How are we to believe that it is possible to find a compensation, a possible consolation for this evil, when because of it God suffered crucifixion?" (N 564, 227).

The Self-Emptying God

To grasp Weil's understanding of creation in its full implications is to grasp that finally all suffering is God's suffering. God, for love, has consented to and undergone all possible suffering preveniently in an infinite degree. The God who loves with a purity beyond comprehension likewise suffers with a purity beyond intimation. To believe that God "so loved the world that he gave his only Son" (John 3:16, FLN 113) is to believe that God himself suffers ultimately (FLN 82). This is why, Weil writes, "None goes to God the creator and almighty without passing through God EMPTIED OF HIS DIVINITY (*VIDÉ DE SA DIVINITÉ*). [. . .] We have to *empty God of his divinity* in order to love him" (N 283–4 = OC 6.2.393–4, emphasis in original).[7]

Here Weil's scriptural ground is the early Christian hymn embedded in Paul's letter to the Philippians, which she quotes in her notebooks in the original Greek (N 208). The hymn recapitulates the kenosis of Christ, "who, though he was in the form of God, did not count equality with God a thing to be grasped, but emptied himself, taking the form of a servant [or slave], being born in the likeness of men. And being found in human form he humbled himself and became obedient unto death, even death on a cross" (Phil. 2:6–8). But her theological construal of the hymn is a free one: her conception of creation as abdication links Father and Son in mutual kenosis. Not only the Son but also the Father "did not count equality with God a thing to be grasped," for the Father, provenance of all creation, humbled himself and became obedient. Thus, in advance of the passion of Christ on the cross, "creation itself is already a Passion" (N 560): the passion of the Father. It is not only Jesus Christ but the Creator who empties himself and becomes a servant: "God possesses power of life and death, but he voids himself of both and is made a slave" (FLN 258, 70). This crucial theological point is summed up in Weil's affirmation that even God's power is also obedience (FLN 338), a statement that refers not to Christ's obedience, but to God the Father's obedience in abdication to necessity: "God has abandoned God. God has emptied himself. This means that both the Creation and the Incarnation are included within the Passion" (FLN 120 = OC 6.4.152).

Clearly such a claim radically inverts the traditional Christian conception of God as omnipotent ruler of heaven and earth, and Weil was well aware that her kenotic conception of the Creator runs against the grain of established doctrine. This was precisely her intention, and at this crucial point she was resolutely non-Catholic. She held that the Roman Catholic conception of God, centered on God's absolutely sovereign omnipotence, was a corruption foreign to authentic Christianity, introduced into it by the influence of imperial Rome's adulation of power. When the Christian religion was officially adopted by the Roman Empire, "God was turned into a counterpart of the Emperor" (NR 271). Ever since, the Roman spirit of imperialism and domination has retained its hold over the Church; hence she believed that much of Catholic mysticism (for example, Marguerite Porete, Meister Eckhart, John of the Cross) was aimed at purifying faith of this corrupt personification—"the infinite equivalent of a Roman slaveholder"—in order to reveal the invariable universal justice of an impersonal God of providence worthy of love: "In the mystic traditions of the Catholic Church, one of the main objects of the purifications through which the soul has to pass is the total abolition of the Roman conception of God. So long as a trace of it remains, union through love is impossible" (NR 277–9).

What is to be gained theologically by viewing the Creator as "powerless" vis-à-vis necessity—a necessity that is equivalent to the order of the world, indeed, is the world itself? What value is there in thinking of God, the omnipotent primordial reality, as impotent in relation to creation? From Weil's viewpoint, the gain is *love*. For the key duality in Weil's thought is the universal dichotomy between power (force, gravity) and love: it distinguishes nature from grace; necessity from the good. If it were true that God ruled the world with sovereign power, then God could be thought of as a sort of supernatural tyrant—much in the way that Dostoevsky's character Ivan Karamazov judges God to be tyrannical—because God does not respond to the horrors of evil and the sufferings of the innocent on earth. Having read *The Brothers Karamazov* in French translation, Weil at several points expounds her theodicy as a critique of Ivan Karamazov's stance (N 283, 287, 288, 293, 432–3). Ivan harbors bitter resentment against God in the face of innocent suffering because he views God as a transcendent power: a sovereign will removed from the world and unaffected by its pain. His God is inexplicably unwilling to intervene where he is conceived to have infinite power to do so: "to rebel against God because of man's affliction, after the manner of [...] Ivan Karamazov, is to represent God to oneself as a sovereign" (N 283).

But in Weil's analysis, it is our own longing for power, for infinite being and control, that tempts us to imagine God as possessing this unlimited power to intervene arbitrarily in time, to manipulate particular events, to alter circumstances much as a monarch or dictator would do, though infinitely more effectively. We picture God this way, as reigning in almighty power, Weil points out, because "it is very much easier to place oneself in imagination in the position of God the Creator than it is in that of Christ crucified" (N 411). Such an image of God reigning in power contradicts the God who has emptied himself of divinity and abdicated to necessity in order to establish the existence of an absolute other. God does not exercise his all-powerfulness, for if he did, neither we nor anything else would exist (N 191). Limitation is the evidence that God loves us (N 613).

But the human creature, suffering the limits of existence, is inclined to refuse this powerlessness of God because of its own craving for power and being. It is prone to imagine God in the image of its own will; it longs for a divinity extrapolated from earthly images of power and sovereignty. "To represent God to oneself as all-powerful is to represent oneself to oneself in a state of false divinity. Man is only able to be one with God by uniting himself to God STRIPPED (*DÉPOUILLÉ*) OF HIS DIVINITY (EMPTIED of his divinity)" (N 284, emphasis in original). Yet it is God-in-his-powerlessness who will judge us, who will be the arbiter between God-in-his-power and us (N 542).

At this point, for Weil, trinitarianism is essential for understanding God as love. When God is conceived as One rather than Three, the "fall" into evil of the Father who abdicates to necessity is not redeemed by the sacrificial suffering of the Son; rather, God the Creator reigns in the image of a transcendent power without the descending and self-emptying movement of divine love incarnate in Christ. God conceived as One, purely one, is an *object* (N 264); whereas God who is Three is pure relation, pure *mediation* (IC 176, FLN 87), the self-abdicating movement of love outside itself while remaining itself. The Father does what is necessary to create; the Son, through voluntary suffering, redeems the necessary as the good. In these reciprocal acts of Father and Son, the dialectic of necessity and the good is maximized to the extreme and reconciled in a transcendent harmony. Accordingly she can write, "the Trinity implies the incarnation—and *consequently* the Creation" (FLN 130).

Because our status as created beings is as nothing, we can only imitate God in his powerlessness, not in his power. We become separated from God by desiring to share in his divinity "through power and not through love, through being and not through non-being" (N 539). Hence our spiritual rebirth, our ability to love unconditionally in the void, depends on our acceptance of and consent to "*God all-powerless*" (*Dieu impuissant*) (N 284 = OC 6.2.395). It is not the God of power but the God who made himself a slave who educates us concerning the chasm between creator and creature, between necessity and good. Certain of Weil's affirmations sound startlingly like Luther expounding his *theologia crucis*, although Weil knew little of Luther: "So that we may feel the distance between us and God, God has to be a crucified slave. For we can only feel this distance looking downward" (N 411).

We should clarify that when Weil uses the expression "stripped" or "emptied" of divinity she does not mean that the Creator or Christ ceases to be *divine*, but that God abdicates the *power* and *prestige* of divinity, which are not the locus of his essential divinity. God's essential divinity consists in not power but love. God the Father voluntarily empties himself of omnipotence in the act of creation; on the cross, Christ the Son is stripped of power and social prestige. Both acts of abdication reveal true divinity under the form of love, and this kenotic enactment is the whole meaning of incarnation and crucifixion for Weil. God who is essentially love not power—who is love *sacrificing* power—cannot intervene because love bids that an infinite distance be allowed to exist *in extremis*.

> God here below cannot be anything else but absolutely powerless. For all limited power is a union of power and powerlessness, but in accordance with a unity belonging to this world; whereas in God the union of these opposites is found in

its very highest degree. (N 542) / God has to [cross] the infinite
thickness of time and space. Love is here, if anything, greater. It
is as great as the distance that has to be crossed. (N 428)

Weil's view of creation means that God has abdicated power to act
within the world, from the beginning of the world, for the love of the
world. This love consists of desiring simply that a thing should be
and not wanting to tamper with it: "God loves us in this way;
otherwise we should immediately cease to exist" (N 541–2). "He
stays far away from us, because if He approached He would cause us
to disappear" (FLN 142).

Given that evil is defined by Weil as distance from God, to
eliminate evil would be to eliminate creation and creature. This
means that with respect to innerworldly power—or capacity to act
within the world—the creature is actually more powerful than the
creator (FLN 129, 312). Having an essentially negative (dialectical)
relation to existence, God can bring about effects in the world only
indirectly by inspiring human desire to action. Grace is God's means
of "begging" for action from a human being and "waiting" for our
consent and obedience, given that he cannot directly alter the
machinations of necessity.

> One must approve God's creative abdication and be glad to be
> oneself a creature, a secondary cause, with the right to perform
> actions in this world. A victim of misfortune is lying in the
> road, half dead of hunger. God pities him but cannot send him
> bread. But I am here and luckily I am not God; I can give him a
> piece of bread. It is my one point of superiority over God. "I was
> hungry and you fed me." God can beg for bread for the afflicted,
> but he cannot give it to them. (FLN 312)

This impotence vis-à-vis necessity is the Father's cross to bear, a cross
that he shares with the Son, suffering equally, though differently,
every moment of the world's existence. That there is a God in heaven,
that God is pure love, does not change anything on earth: it does not
remove evil or eliminate the necessity to suffer; on the contrary, Weil

asserts, Christ was killed out of rage because he was powerless: "because he was only God" (N 221).

From Weil's perspective, Ivan Karamazov is not wrong to feel overwhelmed and broken by the world's evil, for Christ himself was humanly broken by it. Ivan is not simply failing to see the good in the world that would supposedly overbalance this evil, as optimistic theodicies attempt to argue. The world is truly as evil as Ivan finds it, and there is no greater good anywhere in the world to balance it. The world cannot contain such good, since the world exists by virtue of necessity, which imposes conditions and limits that engender evil. But Ivan is mistaken, Weil insists, in pitting the world's evil against the goodness of providence. For the good that alone is capable of balancing evil in the world is a good that lies "outside" the world. It is a *nonexistent* but nonetheless real, knowable, experienceable good, and it is a good that is actually known *through* the world's evil—even by the God who is crucified. The world's existence manifests the reality of good negatively—dialectically—through the palpability of its absence, and therein the world is a negative sign pointing to good, incarnating it in the form of absence, void, and longing in the void.

In the novel, Ivan claims that he accepts God's wisdom and the inscrutability of his purpose, but refuses to accept the world: "it is not God that I do not accept, but the world he has created." But this stance is disingenuous, an example of what Weil calls illegitimate contradiction. Can the two be separated this way, given that the providence that creates the world is the principal act of God's wisdom and purpose? Indeed, providence is nothing other than God's will, and the will of God and the order of world are so indistinguishable in providence that to reject one is to reject the other. Ivan himself recognizes that his unwillingness to accept the world because of innocent suffering is related to the problem of ultimate forgiveness. One who deigns to forgive the sins and evils of the world must have an absolute *right* to forgive them. When Ivan demands, "Is there in the whole world a being who could or would have the right to forgive?," his brother Alyosha answers precisely as does Weil's theology: "There is such a being, and he can forgive everyone and everything and *for everything*, because he gave his innocent blood for all and for everything. You've forgotten him, but it is on him that the edifice is founded" (Dostoevsky, *Brothers Karamazov*, 125, 287, 288).

To forgive is to exercise a dreadful responsibility, an ultimate decision to override justice with love. Ivan is torn between his resentment toward God on the one hand, and his powerful reverence for the way of freedom and love offered by Christ on the other. He must either hate God, the world's providence, as a cruel tyrant, or else accept Christ as having a real, actual, effectual "right" to forgive and accept what God has done. Ivan's professed "acceptance" of God is really an accusation, an attribution of responsibility: there *is* a God, and it is God who permits innocent suffering in the world. God is absolutely guilty of this crime. Where Ivan struggles is in relation to Christ: will he grant Christ the right to forgive God?

Scandalized by God's renunciation of power for love, Ivan rebels against the kenotic will of God. Only a renunciation of his own, in imitation of God's renunciation, would enable Ivan to accept the world and become, in effect, a co-creator. As it is, Weil calls his rebellion an "abscess on the world" (a Stoic metaphor she borrows from Marcus Aurelius) since "not to accept some event taking place in the world is to desire that the world should not exist" (N 297). Ivan's urgent desire to escape this dilemma is nonetheless a sign of the good in him, for in general "the desire to escape from duality is the sign of love in us" (IC 110). Love for good is evident in Ivan's spiritual agony, including the resentment and betrayal embodied in his poem of the Grand Inquisitor.[8]

It is God's love that lets the world and creatures exist in a condition separated from good. "The dereliction in which God leaves us is his own way of caressing us. Time, which is our one misery, is the very touch of his hand. It is the abdication by which he lets us exist" (FLN 142). Though this love is incomprehensible to the creature, who is entrapped in time, it is love that prevents God from willing to eliminate evil, for "love is on the side of non-action, of powerlessness" (N 541). Because God *will* not prevent evil, in a real sense he *cannot* prevent it; he cannot because his power is limited by his will: "The limits of will and power are the same in God. He wills only what He can, and if He is unable to do more it is because He does not will to be able to do more" (FLN 124). The love of God consents absolutely to the powerlessness of God. "God, out of love, limits his power [...]. God is at the same time absolute power and absolute powerlessness" (N 541–2). As it is love that renders God powerless vis-à-vis the creature, so it is by means of love alone, not power, that God crosses the infinite distance to the creature, transfiguring the abyss of evil by the light of love, without eliminating or altering the conditions of necessity.

This means that God's abdication to necessity—and in that sense his willing of evil—is the opposite of tyranny or indifference, being a decision of suffering love. "God's power tends toward annihilation, but his love produces salvation. This opposition between the power and the love of God represents supreme suffering in God" (N 542). The renunciation that empties God of his divinity is the Father's own sacrificial agony; it constitutes the crucifixion not only of the Son in the world but of the Father "outside" the world, and so it constitutes the sacrifice of his omnipotence, his very divinity, on the cross of created time and space.

Crucifixion as Redemption

For God, to create is concomitantly to will the advent of evil, since it is evil that "causes the distinction," and makes it impossible for God to be all (N 126). This is an evil for which God is ultimately responsible and in which we, as creatures, participate. Here a deep question must arise, which Weil herself poses, concerning the good of creation: "Why is creation a good, seeing that it is inseparably bound up with evil? In what sense is it a good that I should exist, and not God alone?" (N 191). Why the world, given that evil in the form of an inflexible necessity attends it? For the world as such is the reign of necessity, as Weil reiterates time and again: "There is an infinite distance between the nature of the necessary and that of the good. Our world is the kingdom of necessity" (IC 142).

God, in creating, has willed a "fall" from himself—undoing the perfect good of himself, inaugurating an alien reality, a conjunction of good and evil that is dialectically evil in relation to God. What can explain this paradox, that God would give existence to the world in full knowledge of the concomitant descent into evil? For a resolution, Weil resorts to a theological response that can make sense only in the light of grace, since it transcends human understanding: "Insoluble contradictions have a supernatural solution. The solution of this one is the Passion. But it is truly a solution only for those souls who are entirely possessed by the light of grace. For the others, the contradiction endures" (IC 142). We can only grasp the "solution" to the paradox when we consent to the existence of the world, including its evil, as being necessary for God.

God is perfect good, but it is intrinsic to the perfection of this good that it reveals itself by passing into its pure opposite, evil. In this sense, God is essentially a God of absolute passion: God is the one who rends himself with infinite distance, and—paradoxically—withdraws, waits, watches, and in all these indirect ways loves with infinite compassion, powerless to use his power (the Father); yet at the same time God descends, becomes incarnate, suffers, dies, and is resurrected (the Son); God is this absolute unity-in-separation (Holy Spirit), which constitutes the supreme supernatural harmony that is the trinitarian godhead.

> In God, at the point where the two opposites, Power and Love, are separated, a supreme anguish exists [. . .]. In order that there may be a perfect, an ideal model for the reuniting of the opposites, it is necessary that the unity of the two supreme opposites should be disrupted. The Holy Spirit withdrew for a moment from Christ. It is in this way that the Passion constitutes at the same time Redemption. (N 539)

In his deepest essence, then, God has suffered subjection to existence and evil. God *is* essentially God's enactment of abdication, self-emptying, incarnation, and passion. "God not incarnate is not really God; he has been incarnate and sacrificed from the beginning; 'the Lamb slain from the beginning of the world'" (N 222). This God, sacrificed from the beginning, is the crucified God, and we know this, in a sense, simply because the world *exists*. But we know it more perfectly and explicitly as revealed in the cross of Christ.

We must remember that for Weil theological language is never strictly true, and this includes language of the Trinity. Supernatural truths as set forth in verbal figures of expression are ever subject to the risk of falsification by a too direct and univocal understanding. This danger can be minimized by the use of paradox, which holds the truth above the reach of language and direct affirmation. Transcendent inspiration alone can "grasp" the reality toward which the language of religious paradox gestures. It is only in a highly figurative sense, then, that Weil means what she asserts of the relation between God's decision to create and God's passion: "God is trapped by evil when he contemplates what he has created. He is caught and subjected to the Passion" (FLN 329). We are not mistaken to think that, for God, creation absolutely implies the passion, but the necessary link between creation and passion in God is strictly nontemporal; only in temporal analysis are the two distinguishable, in the will of God they constitute a pure unity. Hence, the reverse causality holds equally true: in order to be subjected to the passion, God realized that he had to be trapped by evil, so he created the world. Passion and creation are one and the same movement, co-implicated in the divine will.

This means, furthermore, that the creation, incarnation, and crucifixion, which are aspects of one and the same passion of God, are not essentially enacted for the benefit of humanity. Rather, they are self-realizing, self-enacting movements of God in which humanity has the privilege of participating.

> Our misery gives us the infinitely precious privilege of sharing in this distance placed between the Son and his Father. This distance is only separation, however, for those who love. For those who love, separation, although painful, is a good, because it is love. Even the distress of the abandoned Christ is a good. There cannot be a greater good for us on earth than to share in it. God can never be perfectly present to us here below on

account of our flesh. But he can be almost perfectly absent from us in extreme affliction. For us, on earth, this is the only possibility of perfection. That is why the Cross is our only hope. (SNL 177)

Weil insists that, because "God is prior to humanity in all respects" (IC 198), the incarnation should be presented not as destined for humanity, but on the contrary, as that to which the destiny of humanity is related. We must view ourselves in relation to the passion, not the passion in relation to ourselves. The passion expresses and enacts God's relation to God; it is not something God has done for *us*, except insofar as we "are" him through the decreation of our will.

> The Son separated from the Father by the totality of time and space, by the fact of having been made a creature; this time which is the substance of my life—and of everybody's—this time so heavy with suffering, is a segment of the line that stretches, through the Creation, the Incarnation, and the Passion, between the Father and the Son. (FLN 83, see WG 127)

Taking this stance frees Weil's theology from traditional anthropocentrism, setting in its place a *cosmocentrism*, which is concentrically united with a *theocentrism*. The world, though radically other than God, is actually an event in the life of the godhead. The passion of God is the real center of everything inclusively that happens in the world; it is the real meaning of the existence of the world as a whole:

> The effects of misfortune upon innocent souls are really unintelligible unless we remember that we have been created as brothers of the crucified Christ. The absolute domination throughout the whole universe of a mechanical, mathematical, absolutely deaf and blind necessity is unintelligible, unless one believes that the whole universe, in the totality of space and of time, has been created as the Cross of Christ. (IC 198)

In this vein, Weil affirms that every particle of matter partakes of the nature of the Eucharist (N 322), which is to say, the body of Christ; every particle of matter in the world is God crucified.

Christ is the incarnate God who, by expiating the evil of the world, expiates the guilt of the disincarnate God for having created the world. "God has expiated creation [by crucifixion], and we who are associated in it expiate it also" (N 80). This is achieved through Christ's redemptive suffering, a divine suffering that gathers in and purifies evil of its evilness, while in another sense leaving it unchanged: "Evil itself may be pure. It can only be pure in the form of suffering" (N 234). Redemptive suffering, the essence of Christ, is what transfigures the very evilness of evil into good; this is achieved not through action, but through voluntary passion, for "no action destroys evil, but only the apparently useless and perfectly patient suffering of it" (FLN 218).

Redemptive suffering reveals evil in all its evilness as the real presence of the absence of the Father, from whom all pure good, of whatever order, derives (FLN 122). That is to say, whereas the Father, in this world, is embodied as an *absence*, the Son, in this world, is embodied as *real presence*, a presence corresponding inversely and dialectically to the Father's absence, suffering that absence perfectly in the form of abandonment. So it is through the Son's abandonment that God is present in extreme evil, for "God [the Father]'s absence is the divine form of presence that corresponds to evil—an absence that is felt" (N 343). The Father, who has withdrawn in order that the world exist, can suffer the world only indirectly across an infinite distance; he cannot redeem the world directly, since by entering or even touching it he can only destroy it. It is God the Son, the incarnation of the Father, who suffers the world directly and infinitely in order to redeem it, thereby enacting the will of the Father: "God who is in heaven cannot destroy evil; he can only send it back in the form of a curse. It is only God in this world, having become a victim, who can destroy evil by suffering it" (FLN 154), for indeed to suffer evil is the only way to destroy it (FLN 218). The pure one arrests the malediction of evil by becoming accursed, for to become a curse it is necessary to be pure (FLN 69). The Son, through the movement of incarnation, consents to the Father's will, enters the world, and voluntarily suffers its evil perfectly, totally, and redemptively as the Father cannot.

As God alone is the ultimate source of evil, God alone can destroy evil ultimately and thus redemptively (FLN 358). The totality of evil that the Father has engendered in creating, the Son takes upon himself in his consent to suffer the world infinitely. The Son consents to be delivered into evil for the Father, emptying himself of his divinity to manifest the Father's goodness, to redeem his innocence. When the Son enacts the Father's will in crucifixion, this entails a mutual and concurrent suffering of evil by both in pure unity of will: the Father suffers evil passively, possessing a power that cannot be used for love, while the Son suffers it actively, as a pure suffering love bereft of power. "The abandonment, at the culminating point of the Crucifixion—what unfathomable love this shows on either side" (N 403).

Inasmuch as all evil traces back to God's abdication in creation, it is inflicted on the world by a decision made "outside" the world. Evil is the inescapable consequence of the original constitutive abandonment of the world by God: "The Creation is an abandonment. In creating what is other than Himself, God necessarily abandoned it" (FLN 103). The world suffers God's abandonment without a power of choice in the matter, and in this specific sense all of creation, including the most horrible intentional criminality, is finally "innocent" of evil. Viewed as a totality, the world simply suffers what God has done, without any power to choose otherwise: "The Creation as a totality is without a blemish. All the evil in it is only suffering" (FLN 207). Christ, however, is God's means of allowing the world to suffer the decision with a choice: he voluntarily takes all the world's evil upon himself as a malediction.

Crucifixion is divine atonement: by becoming a malediction, Christ redeems God from the evil effected in the creation–fall, transfiguring it into voluntary suffering, and in so doing redeems humanity from its complicity in the "fall" into voluntary evil. Weil embraces the idea that "God suffered in place of man," but this does

not mean that Christ's affliction in any way diminishes the affliction
suffered by human beings; rather, it means that human suffering,
which would otherwise be utterly useless, is transfigured into
divinely redemptive suffering when it is consented to in imitation of
Christ. "Through the affliction of Christ (in the preceding centuries
as much as in the following) the affliction of any afflicted man
acquires the meaning and the value of expiation, if only he desires it.
The affliction then acquires an infinite value, which can only come
from God" (FLN 152, 345).

So individual human beings, through voluntary suffering, are able
to share in the destruction of evil, and in a sense every effort to relieve
affliction and diminish the spread of evil is a voluntary suffering of it.
But this is possible only through the prevenient action of Christ, not
through a virtue of one's own, for "all expiation implies that it is God
who is expiating" (FLN 152). The cross is something infinitely
greater than martyrdom (N 415) because it is the self-damnation of
the Son that achieves the redemption of the Father, who cannot enter
the world except as necessity (absence and evil) or as grace (powerless
suffering love).

In view of the crucifixion, the unavoidable suffering of a human
being, which has no real remedy, acquires a supernatural use when it
is consented to with the pure intention that God's will be done: "An
innocent being who suffers sheds the light of salvation upon evil. He
is the visible image of the innocent God" (N 234). For Weil, the
redemptive power of God is centered on and revealed in the
crucifixion rather than the resurrection: "The death on the Cross is
something more divine than the Resurrection, it is the point where
Christ's divinity is concentrated" (IC 142–3). The truly "blessed"
(*heureux*) exemplified in the gospel beatitudes are those who have no
need of the resurrection in order to believe (NR 269), those for whom
Christ's perfection as manifested on the cross is the full glory of God.
Like Luther and Kierkegaard before her, Weil excoriates the
"theology of glory" that obscures and displaces the greater glory of
the crucifixion: "After the Resurrection the infamous character of his
ordeal was effaced by glory, and today across twenty centuries of
adoration, the degradation that is the very essence of the Passion is

hardly felt by us [...]. Today the glorious Christ veils from us the Christ who was made a malediction" (IC 142–3).

From the perspective of a theology of glory, the resurrection of Christ "reopens" the door of life that crucifixion "closes," whereas quite the reverse is true for a theology of the cross. The cross itself is the open door. In a striking passage, Weil faults an undue emphasis on the resurrection in Christian teaching for *closing the door of separation* that was opened by the crucifixion: "The crucifixion of Christ has almost opened the door, has almost separated on one side the Father and the Son, on the other the Creator and creation. The door half-opened. The resurrection closed it again" (IC 195). Separation—that is, the movement of infinite distance, abandonment, crucifixion—is the movement that "opens" the door of truth, not the resurrection as it is commonly understood, which blocks the door shut with false glory.

For Weil, it is the voiding of prestige, not the physical suffering, that is the essence of Christ's passion, and this voiding of prestige is what is inverted by liturgical and dogmatic glorification of Christ. Christ, who had little prestige in life, was totally stripped of it after the Last Supper, when even his disciples abandoned and denied him, including Peter—that Peter, Weil comments, "who today is wrapped in a mantle of prestige deriving from the Church and twenty centuries of Christian history" (IC 137). Although it was extremely difficult to remain faithful to Christ during his life, Weil maintains, there is an even greater difficulty today because this prestige itself acts as a screen: it is possible to be faithful even unto death without being sure that it is truly Christ to whom one is faithful.

For God, who is pure good, to become flesh and dwell in the world is to become subject to every possible suffering, and indeed, "the extremest form of suffering" (N 414–5). As Christ is the existence in this world of the greatest possible good, a goodness that surpasses human understanding, so to accept the crucifixion is to consent to the greatest possible evil, for in crucifixion the greatest harm is inflicted on the greatest good, and "if one loves that, one loves the order of the world" (FLN 144). Conversely, also, to love the order of the world is to love the cross of Christ as the manifest will of God, for the "cross" of which Weil speaks is not only the cross on which Jesus died; it is the more comprehensive cross of creation and incarnation, the cross that God bears, in himself, already before the creation of the world— the cross that incites him to renunciation of divinity. For the creation of the world is already a crucifixion of divinity (FLN 70), and all human suffering, whether willing or unwilling, participates in this crucifixion, but only affliction that is consented to *because* it is the cross of Christ participates in the redemptive power of that cross, which is the perfection of suffering love in God.

Supernatural Harmony

Suffering turns us ever again to ask the question *why?* Why affliction? Why necessity? Why the world? The answer Weil offers is that God created the world as that infinite distance across which the absoluteness of absolute love could be perfected in full actuality. Evil is the infinite distance separating God the Father from God the Son; love is the passion that at the same time crosses the distance, spanning the void. Both effects are made real by the real existence of the world, and God cannot be God in actual perfection without it.

> Those who ask why God permits affliction might as well ask why God created. And that, indeed, is a question one may well ask. Why did God create? It seems so obvious that God is greater than God and the creation together. At least, it seems obvious so long as one thinks of God as Being. But that is not how one ought to think of him. So soon as one thinks of God as Love one senses that marvel of love by which the Father and the Son are united both in the eternal unity of the one God and also across the separating distance of space and time and the Cross [. . .]. God is joy, and creation is affliction; but it is an affliction radiant with the light of joy. (SNL 193–4 = SWR 463)

Weil calls this a "Pythagorean harmony" in which the maximum distance and the maximum unity between the contraries is realized

(IC 169). The cross symbolizes at the same time the union between and separation of the opposites, and the unity that characterizes this union and this separation (N 578). It constitutes a supernatural harmony: the harmony of Father and Son across the extremest void of distance and the bitterest suffering. This moment is the incomprehensible perfection of love: the love that passes all understanding (IC 169). Supernatural harmony is audible as a cry of love dissolving into the absolute silence of God:

> God allowed God to send up a cry to him and did not answer. It is when from the innermost depths of our being we need a sound that does mean something—when we cry out for an answer and it is not granted us—it is then that we touch the silence of God. (N 627) / The cry of Christ and the silence of the Father together make the supreme harmony, that harmony of which all music is but an imitation, that to which our harmonies, those at once the most heartbreaking and the most sweet, bear an infinitely far away and dim resemblance. The whole universe, including our own existences as tiny fragments of it, is only the vibration of that harmony. (IC 199)

This divine unity-in-separation constitutes a more encompassing universal harmony than any in nature or any representable in the forms of human language or music. All music is finally a mimesis of the plenitude of God's silence (N 232).

Father and Son are united by a reciprocal love that makes each the true God for the other: "Through love, the Father causes the Son to be, because the Son is the Good. Through love, the Son desires not to be, because only the Father is the Good. For the Father, God is the Son. For the Son, God is the Father. Both are right, and this makes a single truth" (FLN 102). This single complex truth articulates the essence of God: God at once separated from himself and conjoined with himself; other to himself and one with himself. Self-love and love between absolutely separated persons are one and the same thing in God, since "God alone is both himself and another" (N 192). God is one and two simultaneously by virtue of being three essentially;

that is, two united by a mediating third—the Holy Spirit—who abides in the beginning with the Father and Son, making God always one and always three. The separation effected by creation between Father and Son is real and infinite, but in the Holy Spirit it remains a union (IC 68–9): not an absolute diremption but a supernatural coincidence of opposites. Weil has the model of the trinitarian God primarily in mind when she affirms that "unity is not a thing in itself, but an act that cannot be divided" (N 618).

What unites God to himself, then, has nothing to do with the power of being, its attachments and conditions; what unites him ultimately is only love. The love between God and God is a love that rests on nothing, depends on nothing: suspended in the void of separation and suffering, grounded in mutual self-emptying, it reverberates in silence. God is pure love, nothing but love, spanning the void of distance. "God is so essentially love that the unity, which in a sense is his actual definition, is the pure effect of love" (WG 127). God is essentially three because the love uniting God with God is itself the divinity of God.

> The love between God and God, which in itself *is* God, is this bond of double virtue: the bond that unites two beings so closely that they are no longer distinguishable and really form a single unity and the bond that stretches across distance and triumphs over infinite separation. The unity of God, wherein all plurality disappears, and the abandonment, wherein Christ believes he is left while never ceasing to love his Father perfectly, these are two forms expressing the divine virtue of the same Love, the Love that is God himself. (WG 127)

God is good because he is love, and loves himself because he is good; or as Weil puts it, "God desires to be, not because he is himself but because he is the good" (FLN 102). Indeed, the goodness of God, which causes God to love himself infinitely, *is* God: "The intrinsic being of God resides in the fact that he is good—he is not a being to whom good is attached as an attribute, but is absolutely pure good in itself" (N 383); Weil identifies this idea as at once Augustinian and

Platonic (SNL 104). But in Weil's kenotic logic, it is because God is absolute goodness that he must abdicate power and empty himself to manifest absolute love. Weil characterizes this sacrificial generosity as a "divine madness" (*folie de Dieu*): an excess of divine love (*excès de l'amour divin*) that effects a total and unreserved self-expense for love. God stakes *himself* when he creates, for "the creation is a very much greater act of madness still than the incarnation" (N 262, IC 183).

Why would God lay down his divinity, his power and plenitude of being, his unity with himself? Because, Weil answers, divine love, being truly unconditional, goes to the furthest possible length; it knows no bounds or conditions, which in itself makes it a madness: "Love is supernatural when it is unconditioned. An unconditional love is a madness" (FLN 127). Unconditional love is God's creative madness, a madness that creates, and by creating gives itself in infinite sacrifice. Unconditional love is the madness that subjects God to crucifixion, for God, who is not compelled to do anything by necessity, elects to be crucified as an expression of superabundant goodness.

This can be expressed in alternate terms: that God creates in order to give himself not only to everything good (himself), but to necessity and evil, to everything void of good, to everything other than himself and infinitely distant from himself. He creates the realm of necessity and the void of evil in order to give himself to it, and he gives himself to it precisely by creating it, by letting it *be* apart from good, making it possible for necessity and evil to be illumined by the good. "God, who is nothing else but Love, has not created anything else but love. Relentless necessity, misery, distress, the crushing burden of poverty and of exhausting labour, cruelty, torture, violent death, constraint, terror, disease—all this is but the divine love" (N 401). Faith consists in believing that reality is love and nothing else (FLN 260).

The crucifixion is a model of love that passes understanding (IC 169): a love that tests itself beyond natural measures of reasonableness, a love that goes to the furthest extreme. "The supreme reason for which the Son of God was made man was not to save men, it was to bear witness for the truth. To bear witness that the love between the Father and the Son is stronger than the distance between the Creator and the creature" (FLN 240). If *Christ crucified* is a stumbling block and a folly, according to Paul (1 Cor. 1:23), contradicting every reasonable idea of God, then *God crucified* is surely a supreme madness. Yet, Weil writes, we are called to consent to and imitate this madness—not, along with Tertullian, because it is *absurd*, but because it is *good*. And we know it to be good not because it is intelligible, but because it is *beautiful*, and its beauty gives us joy.

The beauty of this good, the joy we take in it, is unintelligible (N 221). Faith alone can embrace it, consent to it, and feel joy in spite of suffering. This is a joy that redeems the sorrow of the world; it can only be encountered in immediate experience, and cannot be communicated outwardly except through the paradoxical conjunction of contradictory meanings. It is a complex supernatural joy—a joy available in the midst of the deepest anguish. It is a joy in the knowledge that, even in the greatest possible abyss of separation, love is stronger than separation. Love redeems every stringency of the void.

The most extreme separation of all is not the distance between the Creator and the world, but the infinite distance that alienates God from himself (N 560; IC 169, 197). Weil symbolizes this infinite rent in God by imaging God as divided, with the entire universe interposed between the Father and the Son. The universe, which occupies the distance between God and God, exists as an echo chamber for the theophanic—or theophonic—reverberation of an ultimate harmony: the silence of God (N 627). "This tearing apart, over which supreme love places the bond of supreme union, echoes perpetually across the universe in the midst of the silence, like two notes, separate yet melting into one, like pure and heart-rending harmony. This is the Word of God. The whole creation is nothing but its vibration" (WG 124).

The supernatural harmony that reverberates through the universe is heard as a silence, but an *essential* silence that is not a mere absence of sound (FLN 83, WG 213, 72). It is the positive silence of divine "speech" that is deeper than being, deeper than nothingness: it underpins, transgresses, and transcends the distinction between being and nothingness. Hearing this Word in silence, faith receives in time what God has decided from the beginning outside time. If the love that bridges is in proportion to the distance (N 616), then distance is the soul of love, and infinite distance is the soul of infinite love.

Chapter 4

Necessity and Obedience

Christ was crucified; his Father let him be crucified; two aspects
of the same powerlessness [...]. But everything that I suffer,
God suffers it too, for that is the effect produced by necessity,
the free play of which he refrains from violating. (N 191)

God "turns himself into necessity" to create the world (N 191).
Necessity is the principle or mode by which God, in abdication,
orders the world and sustains it in existence. God's will to create is
effected through necessity, and as a result necessity is what
constitutes the intelligibility of reality for us: "Reality for the human
mind is contact with necessity. There is a contradiction here, for
necessity is intelligible, not tangible" (IC 178). There can be no order
at all in our experience, not even our immediate perception, without
the notion of necessity, which is the principle of determinacy and
limitation (N 452). Thought encounters reality by being fettered by
obstacles that seem to be the opposite of thought, and yet are
themselves only thoughts, such as space and time (N 134), which
delineate matter and the order of the world for us. From our point of
view within the world, God's will is legible in the intelligible form of
the providential ordering of the world. The things of the world obey
necessity as the manifest form of the will of God, for "necessity is the
obedience of matter to God" (IC 186); conversely, also, all things

obey the will of God inasmuch as God wills things to exist according to the determinations of necessity. Everything that occurs without exception is consented to by God, but this consent is an abdication: "God's will is to abdicate in favour of necessity" (FLN 296).

Abdication to Necessity

Time, space, and "all the density of second causes" thus lie between God and the world (N 316). Indeed, Weil writes, there is no better proof that creation is an abdication than the fact that God himself cannot prevent what has happened from having happened (FLN 140). God as creator is not in time except negatively in the form of absence and abdication; he is "waiting" outside time while we wait for him in time. Matter, by suffering time, in a sense creates time, as time is defined by changes in matter and could not otherwise be measured. Matter, a non-good (N 496), is infinitely alien to God as ultimate good, and as such it is a mysterious creation: "Matter: something that is not spirit, something that is not God. What an extraordinary phenomenon! It is thanks to matter that creatures like ourselves have being" (N 405). If we were exposed to God directly without the "protection" of matter, of space and time, we would evaporate like water in the sun; necessity is the screen placed between God and us so that we can exist at all (N 402, 191).

The deep mystery of matter is its *evil*—defined precisely as distance from God (N 342)—for the advent of matter can only be the contradiction and undoing of divine unity and perfection. Matter is the actual stuff that makes distance from God real and actual, not merely potential; its advent *ex nihilo* is the inauguration of a realm of finitude and limitation, hence of evil and suffering. Necessity is the web of determinations that govern matter, ourselves included, along a course of suffering and ordeal in time: "God does not send sufferings and woes as ordeals; he lets Necessity distribute them in accordance with its own proper mechanism. Otherwise he would not be withdrawn from creation, as he has to be in order that we may *be*" (N 403).

Weil views the cosmos as a realm of perpetual becoming animated by an energy whose differential movements, like oscillations of waves on the sea, continually rupture equilibrium, but "this becoming, composed of ruptures of equilibrium, is in reality an equilibrium because the ruptures of equilibrium compensate each other" (IC 185; NR 288). Every phenomenon is a modification of the distribution of energy, and consequently is determined by the laws of energy (NR 293, 270). However limitless certain phenomena in nature may appear, ultimately there is a limit to each and every thing that is not God, a limit that serves as its nemesis and that imposes equilibrium in time. Everything that exists is finite, determinate, and as such obeys limits; this means that force is overmastered by something that limits it, for limit, imposed by necessity, is transcendent in relation to what is limited (matter, force, energy) (N 484). So it is that "Eternal Wisdom imprisons this universe in a network, a web of determinations" (NR 285) and it is necessity that governs the network of limits obeyed by material forces in the world: "Forces in this world are supremely determined by necessity; necessity is made up of relations that are thoughts; consequently, the force that is supreme in the world is under the supreme domination of thought" (NR 291). Human beings, as thinking beings, are therefore on the same side as that which dominates and overmasters force, and here lies the key to salvation.

Necessity is bound up with chance, the arbitrary, but not with injustice (N 410). This is because, precisely through chance, through the reign of the arbitrary, the mutual "injustices" of things cancel one another. This is the idea that Weil finds expressed in the famous fragment of Anaximander concerning the retribution that things pay to each other for their injustice "according to necessity." Anaximander is paraphrased by Simplicius: "The source of coming-to-be for existing things is that into which destruction, too, happens, 'according to necessity; for they pay penalty and retribution to each other for their injustice according to the assessment of Time.'"[1] Because all things are equally and uniformly subject to the vicissitudes of chance, there is no preferential bias in the order of the world. The chance factor that governs the play of necessity ensures that nothing is favored, nothing preferred. All events manifest an equal reality and value:

> God wants everything that takes place *to a like degree*, not certain things as means and certain other things as ends. Similarly, he wants *to a like degree* the whole and the parts, each portion, each slice that can be cut out of continuous reality. This can only be represented to the human intelligence in the following terms: he wants necessity to exist. The will of God cannot be for us a subject of hypothesis. To know it we have only to observe what takes place: what takes place is his will [. . .]. Necessity is the veil of God. (N 266)

Motivated as we human beings are toward particular ends, and predisposed to judge things good or evil with reference to particular desires, we are for the most part incapable of seeing the world from this perfectly indifferent perspective. Consciously or not, our imagination infuses elements of the world with differential values, which continually shift and change along with our purposes and desires, obscuring the world's essential justice and distorting the *imago Dei* that the order of the world presents to us: "The universe is the image of God, but not the universe as seen from a point of view [. . .]. The universe as seen by God is for man a nameless and formless constant" (N 146).

One of Weil's fundamental ideas is that necessity rules the world through *obedience* not force. When things of the world obey necessity, they obey a principle that is not force, but itself limits force: "The brute force of matter, which appears to us sovereign, is nothing else in reality but perfect obedience" (NR 285). Force cannot rule the world, according to Weil, for the reason that every force is limited by another force; and so it is *limit* not force that has the upper hand. Necessity is inflexible, unyielding in its determinations, but is essentially effected through obedience; the "proof" is that every force finally succumbs to its limit, and this universal obedience to limit is what renders the world beautiful—a contemplable cosmos rather than an inapprehensible chaos—contemplation being the criterion of the beautiful (N 81).

> The brute force of matter, which appears to us sovereign, is nothing else in reality but perfect obedience [. . .]. That is the truth that bites at our hearts every time we are penetrated by the beauty of the world. (NR 285) / Things are beautiful in their vicissitudes, although they allow one to perceive a pitiless necessity. Pitiless, yes; but which is not force, which is sovereign ruler over all force. (NR 288) / Obedience is the very essence of the brute force inherent in Necessity itself. Everything that hurts me, everything that weighs upon me is obedient to God. Everything that smiles upon me also. The tree that covers itself with blossom also. (N 600)

Weil believed that the principal thought that enraptured the ancient world as a whole, and Plato above all, was that what makes the blind forces of matter obedient is not another stronger force; it is a providential persuasion eliciting consent by love (NR 288). Love is a consent that neither exercises nor submits to constraint by force, but instead persuades and is persuaded by love (IC 65).

> Brute force is not sovereign in this world. It is by nature blind and indeterminate. What is sovereign in this world is determinateness, limit. (NR 285) / In this way, necessity becomes related to man, not as master to slave, or as an equal, but as a picture that is looked at. It is in this looking that the supernatural faculty of consent comes to birth. It is not to force as such (because it compels) that consent is given, but to force as necessity. (FLN 89)

This liberating insight makes possible the joy and freedom of the ancient Stoic philosophers, as Weil understands them (LP 178–9), and her own notion of providence is thoroughly Stoic in character: the order of the world is itself revelatory of the divine. "The order of the world is providential. It teaches us only about God" (N 480). But as we will observe in more detail (Chapter 6), this Stoic regard in Weil is thoroughly imbued with the modern mechanistic understanding of nature found in such thinkers as Descartes, Pascal, Spinoza, and Malebranche. It is not a premodern Stoicism we are confronted with in Weil, but an utterly modern one. Moreover, the God that this world teaches us about is the *crucified* God of Christian faith, so we are not dealing with a Platonic framework but a modern Christian framework. Through resourceful and irenic interpretation, Weil infused her readings of Plato into this modern Christian framework, but the fundamental framework itself is decidedly not Platonic or Neoplatonic (this is argued more fully in Chapter 6). The necessity of the order of the world as Weil understands it originates *ex nihilo* in God's decision to be crucified.

Providence

Providence, for Weil, is simply everything that happens. Reality as such is providential, which is to say, the perfect manifestation of the will of God (N 266). Everything that is real and actual is in conformity with divine will precisely by being in accord with necessity: "On the plane of events, the notion of conformity to the will of God is identical with the notion of reality" (NR 270). When God "turns himself into necessity," there are two sides to that necessity, the side exercised and the side endured (N 190). The two key aspects of providence correspond to these sides: on the one hand, providence = *necessity*; on the other hand, providence = *obedience*. Necessity and obedience are inverse sides or views of same phenomenon. *Necessity* is the name for determinate limits when they are viewed as imposed from outside (what Spinoza terms *natura naturata*); *obedience* is the name for the very same limits viewed as consented to by everything limited (*natura naturans*), whether that consent is thought of as active or passive, voluntary or involuntary.

Necessity is the work of providence from the viewpoint of limits imposed by the Father in abdication, while obedience is the same work of providence from the viewpoint of limits consented to by the Son in incarnation and crucifixion. Finally, necessity and obedience are one and the same, since God wills existence as necessarily limited and, equally, as obeying necessary limits: "God causes the existence of necessity to be spread throughout space and time by the fact that He thinks it. God's thought is God, and [...] is also the order of the world" (IC 185).

This is an order from which God, the pure good, is withdrawn, for God displaces himself with necessity. In his absence, in lieu of himself, his thought (*logos*), his Word or providential will, is operative in the world in the form of obedience to necessity; for the Word is already incarnate in the order of the world before the Incarnation properly so called (N 264). God has withdrawn in order that the world exist and his will be done through the hand of necessity. Thus Weil can write that God, insofar as he exists, is the universe composed of phenomena, while God, insofar as he is other than the universe, is other than existence (N 328). In Weil's heterodox trinitarian thinking, the former is the incarnate Son, the Word who does the will of the Father; the latter is the hidden or absent God who abdicates for the sake of the world. When God creates by turning himself into necessity, he likewise turns himself into obedience, such that "even God's power is also obedience" (FLN 338). Indeed, God's obedience *is* necessity; necessity as we encounter it in the conditional world is none other than the obedience within God. That principle in God, which is analogous to obedience in us, is "the free play that, in this world, he leaves to necessity" (N 615).

This dual-faceted account of providence as necessity and obedience is explicitly opposed in Weil's thinking to what she calls the "ridiculous conception of Providence" pervasive in popular religious imagination (NR 282–3): that is, the commonly held belief in occasionalist interventions on the part of God to achieve certain particular ends, accompanied by superstitious credence in miracles, visions, voices, occult powers, all of which are to Weil "a sort of impiety" (N 272, 297). In contradistinction to this conception, which Weil considers incompatible with genuine faith, we should always recognize that the sum of God's particular intentions is the universe itself. All the secondary causes that weave the tissue of nature and history are what already manifest God's particular intentions. God as creator does not enact one intention in contradiction or contravention to another. "Divine Providence is not a disturbing influence, an anomaly in the ordering of the world; it is itself the order of the world; or rather it is the regulating principle of this universe" (NR 285). Necessity is an image that the intelligence can grasp representing God's indifference and impartiality (N 297). Providence is impersonal (NR 263). The will of God is not the intervening cause of any single occurrence, but rather the very being of everything that exists (N 313). No event whatever can be viewed as a particular favor on the part of God, with the sole exception of grace.

> God sends affliction to the wicked and to the good without distinction, as he does rain and sunshine [. . .]. He only enters into contact with the individual human being as such by means of purely spiritual grace that responds to the gaze turned toward him [. . .]. No event whatsoever is a favour on the part of God; grace alone. (N 272)

Weil considers the popular notion of providence to be a veil that obscures the clear notion of *condition of existence*, with necessity as the strict determining principle (N 452). "God wants each atom, each event, together with all the innumerable combinations that they form between them, all the perspectives that they offer, without any exception whatever" (N 302). So necessity governs the conditions within space and time that constitute the landscape of existence, and causal relationships between conditions are allowed to play freely according to a set of boundaries, a web of determinations. Because the play is free, nonteleological, without directedness toward an end (here Weil follows Spinoza), the play is arbitrary, and in this sense necessity has to do with chance, with the arbitrary (N 410). But, paradoxically, precisely because the play is nonteleological, and in that sense arbitrary, it is ultimately indiscriminate, equal, and just.

An intrinsic justice is meted out through the law-like arbitrariness of necessity: nothing that happens is favored by providence over anything else that happens. Every occurrence is equally willed by

God. Moreover, faith in providence consists in being certain that the universe in its totality is in conformity with the will of God (NR 271). Weil writes of the indifference we sense in the world around us: "Space and solitude—the indifference of things. Certain events are no more charged with significance than others; even Christ's crucifixion is no more charged with significance than is a pine needle that falls to the ground; God wants all things that are to an equal degree. Time and space make us feel this quality" (N 400). All phenomena equally manifest perfect obedience to the will of God, for their obedience to necessity is finally the effect of God's obedience to his own will. Weil's fundamental idea in thinking the world as a cross, as crucifixion, is that we should be able to see God crucified in every pine needle that falls to the ground.

Everything that exists, simply by virtue of existing, exhibits God's abdication and obedience to necessity. Paradoxically expressed, this means that God is powerless against his own will: he cannot let the world exist without abdicating to necessity, therefore his will cannot undo or countermand the governance of necessity. God is not of two minds about letting the world exist: "God does not mix up established orders; he acts supernaturally within the sphere of the supernatural, and naturally (that is to say, in a sense, not at all) within the sphere of nature. Creation represents this respect for established orders. He does not unmake creation" (N 243). As the creator, God's sole effective action in the world is inaction; he upholds the world by refusing to enter into the world. He expresses his love by withdrawing and communicating his absence in the form of abdication and powerlessness.

God is involved in the world, sharing in its sufferings, primarily in the capacity of powerlessness, which is to say, as an infinitely participating bystander. Christ crucified is the unique image of God *in* the world that corresponds to God the Creator *outside* the world, exiled and unable to intervene. God is not the immediate governor of events in the world, necessity is, in all its imperious and impartial arbitrariness:

God is weak because he is impartial [. . .]. He sends sunshine and rain to the good and the wicked alike. There is a correspondence between this indifference of the Father and the weakness of Christ. Absence of God. The kingdom of heaven is like a grain of mustard seed [...]. God does not change anything. Christ was killed out of rage because he was only God. (N 221)

God "does not change anything" in the sense that God's infinite love for the world cannot remit or reduce suffering under the yoke of necessity. It follows that Christ on the cross is the image of redemption *through* suffering not *from* suffering. For the "tremendous greatness" of Christianity, Weil proposes, is that it does not seek a supernatural remedy against suffering but a supernatural use for it (N 386–7). Hence all suffering that does not detach us, all nonaccepted suffering, is wasted suffering (N 216).

Beauty

Necessity as manifested in the obedience of everything to determinate limits is the source of all suffering and at the same time the source of all beauty. When we experience beauty we grasp the "rightness" or "fittingness" of the limits of things in their determinate relationships: the fact that things are just so and not otherwise gives us unutterable joy (NR 270). Those same limits imposed by necessity, when they are experienced as painful, cruel, inflexible, unforgiving, inalterable—in short, as in opposition to our wishes, our *will*—are likewise the root of suffering. Love of necessity only becomes possible when attention to beauty waylays the will and beauty shines in the heart of suffering itself, illuminating it as an intrinsic dimension of the world's beauty. It is the beauty of the world that permits us to love necessity (IC 190), for "beauty alone makes it possible for us to be satisfied with that which is" (N 596).

To be satisfied with *what is* is to arrive at a finality without an end; indeed, the sacred value of beauty lies precisely in its being a finality that has no end (N 550). This is the unique property of beauty, the only finality here below (WG 165). But the finality of beauty is mysterious in that it has no purpose, no goal beyond itself, for it is a finality without an objective. It arrests desire, gives it a place to concentrate itself, flow back upon itself, while remaining empty of any determinate object or intention. "We want to get behind beauty, but it is only a surface. It is like a mirror that sends us back our own desire for goodness" (WG 166). Beauty does not furnish desire with an end. Rather, for a time it suspends the pursuit of ends. The beautiful puts a stop on the fabricating imagination (N 200). Only in this sense does beauty give us what we want, satisfying our desire: it dissolves our will to future-oriented particular ends by submerging it in a joyfully fulfilling state of momentary endlessness in the present. "Beauty seizes upon the finality in us and empties it of all ulterior end; seizes upon desire and empties it of all ulterior object, by presenting it with an object actually present and thus preventing it from launching out toward the future" (N 553).

The joy with which we respond to the sense of finality in beauty establishes a distance that our end-seeking will cannot cross in order to grasp or feed on the object; the will can only stand back, withhold its projects, and receive this grace, for "beauty is the face of the eternal 'yes'" (FLN 194). To gaze on beauty and say *yes* to it is to depotentiate the will—and this is what Weil means when she writes that there is as much sacrifice and renunciation at the bottom of joy as there is at the bottom of pain (FLN 235). In the spell of beauty, desire displaces will, and distance displaces the imperious urge of the "I" to possess and consume: "We should like to feed upon {beauty} but it is merely something to look at; it appears only from a certain distance" (WG 166). Distance is the soul of beauty. Because it makes possible an acceptance of distance, the "eternal yes" that beauty inspires teaches us obedience to necessity. It teaches us to consent to *what is* rather than willing our own objects and ends, and this consent itself—a consent to the distance of things from our will—constitutes obedience to necessity. "The knowledge of the distances that are observed by things teaches us obedience, eradicates the arbitrary element in us, which is the cause of all error" (N 615). Beauty is reality without attachment (N 319).

Necessity, the ruling hand of providence, is the very source or provenance of the world's beauty. All beauty is a shining forth of necessity—a mysterious shining forth that makes necessity appear as lovable, affirmable, embraceable, contemplable. Beauty is the appearance of necessity when it manifests itself as desirable. As such, it is beauty that allows us to give our pure attention to necessity, to contemplate necessity without the desire to flee or evade it. "It is the beauty of the world that permits us to contemplate and to love necessity. Without beauty this would not be possible" (IC 190). Because beauty alone makes contemplation of necessity possible, it follows for Weil that contemplation, not pleasure, is the aesthetic criterion (N 260).

In the depths of aesthetic response is a consciousness of necessity in which joy and sorrow are inseparably intermingled: a joy that things exist as God wills them, and a sorrow that things do *not* exist, that is, exist for a radically impermanent moment in accordance with the limits imposed by necessity. One tastes this double-sidedness of necessity in contemplating beauty: that things *really* exist, that things do *not* exist. The vulnerability of precious things is beautiful because vulnerability is a sign of *existence* in all its tenuousness and fragility (N 366). Natural beauty is the visible face of the obedience of all things to providence in the guise of necessity. When we read this obedience immediately in the face of nature, "beauty touches us all the more keenly where necessity appears in a most manifest manner, for example in the folds that gravity has impressed upon the mountains, on the waves of the sea, or on the course of the stars" (IC 191).

Weil considered it impossible to define beauty because contemplation of the beautiful disallows reflexive observation of the experience (N 240). Whatever one would describe as the experience of beauty would not be the rapture itself but an imaginary reconstitution, therefore an unreal and useless idea of it. In one note she writes: "Whenever one reflects upon the beautiful one is brought up against a blank wall. Everything that has been written upon the subject is miserably and obviously inadequate, because it is a study that must take God as its starting point" (FLN 341). What would it mean to take God as the starting point for beauty? It would mean experiencing the sensible appearances of things in their fleeting existence as the palpable realization of God's wisdom, the divine Word, that is, the decision to create and become sacrificially incarnate in the world both as absence (abdication) and as presence (incarnation and crucifixion).

For Weil, aesthetic response is inherently sacred, the key to supernatural truths (N 627), because it is the experience of the sacrificial presence of the divine. All art of the first order is essentially religious because it "testifies to the fact of the Incarnation" (N 440). It is a matter of sensible contact with divine incarnation, and this incarnational understanding of beauty is equally Greek and Catholic in her mind (N 440, 335). She alludes to "the *actual presence* of God in all that is beautiful; the sacrament of admiration" (N 455, FLN 83), for love came down into this world in the form of beauty (FLN 341). The aesthete's point of view on beauty is sacrilegious not only in matters concerning religion but even in those concerning art (NR 93). For art only imitates the beauty of the world, a beauty that instills detachment of desire and reverence for *what is:* "The suitability of things, beings, and events consists only in this, that they exist and that we should not wish that they did not exist or that they had been different" (WG 176).

The power of beauty is that it purifies the one who experiences it of attachment at the same time that it stimulates desire for the good. Beauty teaches the beholder what it is to love rightly, purely, without attachment, disengaging the will from its ceaseless pursuit of ends.

> Beauty is the supreme mystery of this world. It is a gleam that attracts the attention and yet does nothing to sustain it. Beauty always promises, but never gives anything; it stimulates hunger but has no nourishment for the part of the soul that looks in this world for sustenance. It feeds only the part of the soul that gazes. While exciting desire, it makes clear that there is nothing in it to be desired, because the one thing we want is that it should not change. If one does not seek means to evade the exquisite anguish it inflicts, then desire is gradually transformed into love; and one begins to acquire the faculty of pure and disinterested attention. (SE 29 = SWR 333)

Beauty feeds the part of the soul that gazes, which is to say, the pure part that receives and consents to the real, to *what is*. Whereas the will desires to *feed* on the world, purified desire or supernatural love utters its "eternal yes" to the world across a distance, a space of resignation, through gaze alone. Feasting on the world through gazing alone is what Weil calls eternal beatitude, a state where to look is to eat, for "man's great affliction [...] is that looking and eating are two different operations" (N 637). Looking is what saves us (WG 192).

An infinite desire can only be satisfied, paradoxically, when it finds satisfaction in that which cannot be an end, because no end in the world can put an end to desire. Beauty can do so, however, by virtue of being a finality without being an end. Beauty is the image of God in this world—not the specific form of the beauty, but the quality of *beauteousness* per se. As God is the only pure end-in-itself, so beauty is the still mirror of this divine finality: in it the good is made immediately visible and available as spiritual food for our ontological hunger. And although she affirms that "the pure taste of apple is as much a contact with the beauty of the universe as the contemplation of a picture by Cezanne" (SL 189), neither our stomach nor our will is fed by this beauteousness per se, but only the part of our sensibility that consents to let things be across a distance, unpossessed. So beauty persuades us to abdicate our will.

Ultimately the real is identified with the beautiful, for the beauty of the universe is the sign that it is real (FLN 99), and indeed the world's beauty is indistinguishable from the world's reality (FLN 341). Since everything that *is* is providential, the world is the beauty of God incarnate, and therefore "the beauty of the world is God's own beauty" (IC 150). Love is always connected with a body, and God has no other body that is offered to our senses except the universe itself (N 322). According to a commutative logic, if the real is beautiful because it is real, and the real is providential because God wills everything that is, it follows that the providential is the beautiful. This clearly implies, moreover, that necessity itself is beautiful, for necessity is wholly providential, being the very principle of providence embedded in reality. And if necessity is beautiful, evil is beautiful, as Weil repeatedly affirms: "The universe is beautiful, even including evil" (FLN 329).

Weil's understanding of beauty is based on *contradiction* and *scandal* rather than univocal harmony or appropriateness. The beauty of God as incarnate in the world is scandalous because all the evil of the world radically inheres in it:

> Beauty is the manifest appearance of reality. Reality represents essentially contradiction. For reality is the obstacle, and the obstacle for a thinking being is contradiction [. . .]. The essence of beauty lies in contradiction, scandal, and not at all in appropriateness; but it must be a scandal that forces itself upon one and fills the heart with joy. (N 387–8) / To render horrible things as such lovable, simply because they exist, is to make an apprenticeship of the love of God. (N 451) / To want only to direct our steps above—in the direction in which it is impossible to go. To want the impossible. Embrace absurdity with the mind. Love evil. (N 493)

The scandal that must be grasped in tandem with beauty is suffering; for if the beautiful is the contact of the good with the faculty of sense (FLN 98), then suffering is surely the contact of evil with the faculty of sense. Both are forms of contact with the real, the necessary, the providential.

Suffering

Suffering, Weil asserts, can be regarded as a koan: "God is the master who supplies this koan, plants it in the soul as something irreducible, a foreign body, impossible to digest, and constrains one to think of it" (N 484). In being constrained to undergo irreducible suffering, one is brought to the realization that the koan points to an emptiness, a void at its center: "Suffering has no significance. There lies the very essence of its reality. We must love it in its reality, which is absence of significance. Otherwise we do not love God" (N 484). The koan of suffering teaches the reality of void, for suffering is defined by efforts in the void (N 227); it wrenches away illusion, social armor, ulterior hopes and dreams, and it constrains one to exist in the naked present and enforces renunciation of the fruits. Again, as when in the thrall of beauty, one is arrested by *what is*. "I must not love my suffering because it is useful, but because it *is*" (N 266). The feeling of our wretchedness is the feeling of reality: "For our wretchedness is not something we concoct. It is something truly real" (N 411). Rather than being arrested by joy, in this case the sufferer is arrested by brute necessity: the irreducibility and ineluctability of *what is* solely because as a matter of fact it *is*, and for no more logical or less scandalous reason.

> The *irreducible* nature of suffering, which makes it impossible for us not to have a horror of it at the moment when we are undergoing it, is ultimately designed to arrest the will, just as an absurdity arrests the intelligence, or absence, non-existence, arrests love. So that man, having come to the end of his human faculties, may stretch out his arms, stop, look up and wait. (N 415)

For what does the sufferer wait? For that unique finality, the good, which is absent. Suffering is the absence of the good perfected, become palpable with every breath, every heartbeat. Suffering is absolute waiting, absolute longing for that which "I" am not and can never be. Thus suffering, insofar as it is redemptive—not merely degrading or expiatory (N 222)—wrenches desire for the good out of its natural mooring in the will and transports it beyond the "I"-centeredness of the creature. As long as the sufferer continues to love and wait for the good, extreme suffering severs the attachments of the will, purifying the intentionality of love in the void, thereby rendering it universal. "This irreducible 'I', which is the irreducible foundation of my suffering, must be made universal" (N 293). This is the purgation through which conditional love is rendered unconditional, and therein like unto God's.

Though suffering has no significance, it does have a use value. The principal use of anguish is to teach me that I am nothing (N 261), liberating me from "I"-centeredness, releasing me into the nothingness of the void. For the creature cannot travel toward the good except via nothingness, since the limit of both good and evil is nothingness: "the soul's only choice is between travelling towards nothingness through more and more good or through more and more evil" (FLN 310). Nothingness, because it is the creature's origin, is also the creature's inevitable destiny, but that nothingness may be differentially met as either heaven or hell, love or damnation, absolute good or absolute godlessness: "If death is annihilation, there are two annihilations, annihilation in nothingness and annihilation in God" (N 463). Indeed, Weil conceives "heaven" and "hell" as essentially the same thing, the *same* nothingness; the difference between them depends entirely on the refusal or the acceptance of nothingness as a destiny by the soul. "Hell is a flame that burns the soul. Paradise also. It is the same flame. But depending on the orientation of the soul, this single and unique flame constitutes either infinite evil or infinite good" (N 468).

The urgency of suffering is what forces this decision between consent and refusal, hence the decision between heaven and hell, damnation and salvation, eternal death (through the will's attachment to life) and eternal life (through the will's consent to death). Because suffering teaches void and nothingness, it teaches the ultimate meaning of the *yes* or *no* that we utter in response to nothingness. The moment of decision is particularly acute at the "laceration point" when abject despair is imminent. At this critical moment, the sufferer faces the risk of final damnation; the eclipse of beauty and joy in suffering poses an ultimate danger to the soul, for on reaching a certain degree of pain, we lose the world (N 22).

Always at the first onset of affliction there is a privation of beauty, and invasion of the soul by ugliness. And then, unless we keep our love oriented, in defiance of all common sense, in the same direction, although it has ceased to have an object, we lose all contact with the good, perhaps finally. (FLN 139) / In the case of our own suffering, [...] there is one irreducible moment when it has not yet been transfigured, when it is quasi-infernal, and when nevertheless we must love. This is the laceration point. We always remain exposed to this laceration when considering others. (N 256)

Christ's cry of abandonment on the cross, "Why have you forsaken me?" is this laceration point in God (N 256, N 403). It is the moment of decision when love must either cross an infinite distance into "heaven," or cease to love and perish in "hell." Both movements occur in the same void, the void of crucifixion. But one realizes God as love and the other realizes a final damnation.

Pain is the root of knowledge (FLN 69) because suffering alone causes us to feel that human life is impossible, that death alone is possible, that nothingness is true and irreducible. This realization is the beginning of truth, of spiritual understanding; it initiates a purification from illusion and constitutes the first genuine contact with reality. "When one understands the nature of affliction, one loves it" (N 311). The bitterness of extreme affliction does not prevent one from feeling beauty, and therefore neither does it prevent love of God; it is, on the contrary, a condition for feeling it (N 258). Indeed, beauty and pure joy, the "complicity of the body and the natural part of the soul in the faculty of supernatural consent," are indispensable even for those whose vocation is the cross (FLN 90). As darkness is the dialectical measure of light, so extreme suffering is the dialectical measure of the reality of ultimate good, or God. Suffering constitutes the purest possible measure of divine love as it is embodied in abdication, absence, and abandonment.

> It is in affliction itself that the splendor of God's mercy shines, from its very depths, in the heart of its inconsolable bitterness. If still persevering in our love, we fall to the point where we cannot keep back the cry, "My God, why hast thou forsaken me?" if we remain at this point without ceasing to love, we end by touching something that is not affliction, not joy, something that is the central essence, necessary and pure, something not of the senses, common to joy and sorrow: the very love of God [. . .]. The knowledge of this presence of God does not afford consolation; it takes nothing from the fearful bitterness of affliction; nor does it heal the mutilation of the soul. But we know quite certainly that God's love for us is the very substance of this bitterness and this mutilation. (WG 89)

Suffering is the scandal of evil, just as beauty is the scandal of the good (N 387–8). For is it not scandalous to affirm, as Weil does, that since everything obeys God, therefore everything is perfect beauty— embracing in the sweep of that affirmation all the suffering that evil causes, including the actions of "the worst criminals" (IC 194)? The scandal of Weil's theology is that it is the *love of God* that is the originary cause of all evil, the mad ulterior reason of all suffering. The human being, as a thinking sentient creature, has no choice at all in the end but to suffer crucifixion with God:

> One should not speak to those in affliction about the kingdom of God, it is too remote from them, but only about the Cross. *God suffered. Therefore suffering is a divine thing. In itself.* Not because of compensations, consolations, recompenses. But the very suffering which inspires horror, which we endure against our will, which we seek to escape, which we beg to be spared. (FLN 82; my emphasis)

The conditions imposed by the rigorous mechanism of necessity mean that God leaves us in this world exposed to evil (FLN 143) exactly as God leaves *himself* exposed to evil. This evil, transfigured by redemptive suffering, is the cross—the supreme contact with God in his essence as love. Untransfigured by redemption, it is simply hell.

Necessity: Root of Beauty and Suffering

Beauty and suffering teach us the *reality* of reality, and reality gives birth to joy. Pure joy is always joy in the feeling of reality (N 360)— so much so that perfect joy excludes the very feeling of joy (N 179). Affliction reveals reality in such a way that we consent to it only through a lacerating and painful reduction, purgation, and purification by death, but this death is also present in the extreme joy inspired by contemplation of beauty: "By dint of suffering, one wears down the 'I', and one abolishes it altogether when suffering goes as far as death. One also wears down the 'I' through joy accompanied by an extreme attention" (N 291). Pleasures and pains can be equally useful for wearing down the "I" (N 462). Although beauty reveals reality in such a way that we say *yes* to it immediately, in joyful consent, this joy is secretly pregnant with the bitterness and sorrow of affliction, for "in all beauty are contained an irreducible contradiction, an irreducible bitterness, and an irreducible absence" (N 415). Hence Weil considers the two paths—affliction and pure joy—as essentially equivalent (IC 198–9). But the first way, the way of the cross, the way chosen by Christ, is more rigorous, more perfect, for this principal reason: the cross teaches a purer beauty precisely because it teaches a purer affliction. "Such is the grace of God that sometimes he makes us feel a beauty in our affliction itself. It is then the revelation of a beauty purer than we knew before" (FLN 139).

Weil regards this marriage of pure joy and bitter affliction as the hallmark of first-class art. No work of art can be truly beautiful— which is to say, sacred—without this core of bitterness (N 258). Certain artworks convey a "mysterious bond between suffering and the revelation of the beauty of the world" (IC 102). Here, as examples, she cites the Book of Job and the first verses of Aeschylus's tragedy *Prometheus*, though she might have listed most of her favorite texts, above all the *Iliad*, Sophocles's tragedies, and modern works such as Shakespeare's *King Lear* ("a tragedy of *gravity*," N 138) and Racine's *Phèdre* (N 155). Greek and courtly poetry provide further examples, for in Greek poetry "sorrow was expressed with such purity that there shone from the depths of an unalloyed bitterness a perfect serenity," while some of the troubadours' verses expressed joy in a manner so pure that "there shone through it a piercing grief, the inconsolable grief of the finite creature" (SE 50). Tragic art of this magnitude embodies the essential contradiction of creaturely existence—that life is impossible, that existence per se is the crucifixion of infinite love by inescapable necessity.

The question provoked by affliction and beauty alike is—*why?* (SNL 197 = SWR 466–7). The naked vulnerability of affliction asks *why?* even as the heartbreaking over-fullness of beauty provokes precisely the same question. This *why?* is a question that arises with perception of the irreducibility of the real as something impenetrable, mysterious, an obstacle to thought that simply cannot be grasped. "In beauty—for example the sea, the sky—there is something *irreducible; exactly as there is* in physical suffering: the same irreducibility; impenetrable for the intelligence" (N 308). One is confronted with stark reality, the real existence of something other than oneself; one is thrust beyond the perspectival limits of one's will, impelled to pose a question vastly greater and more consequential than oneself, a question whose answer lies outside the orbit of one's petty conditional hopes and expectations.

Why? is a question provoked by both affliction and beauty. It expresses a search not for a cause but for an *end*. When we ask *why?* we are seeking a finality, an ultimacy, a purpose that transcends all purposes, an end that has the power to stop our question, to suspend our search for good. For Weil, God's silence is the only answer that has this power: "The word of God is silence. God's secret word of love can be nothing else but silence [. . .]. In this world, necessity is the vibration of God's silence" (SNL 197 = SWR 467). The silence of God is the Word of God, but only when we ourselves become quiet and attend in patience do we become able to hear it.

Silence is the answer to our question *why?* when it is posed at this level of questioning. No other answer is possible:

> If the word "*why*" expressed the search for a cause, the reply would appear easily. But it expresses the search for an end. This whole universe is empty of finality. The soul that, because it is torn by affliction, cries out continually for this finality, touches the void. If it does not renounce loving, it happens one day to hear, not a reply to the question that it cries, for there is none, but the very silence as something infinitely more full of significance than any response. (IC 198–9)

Silence dissolves our question *why?* into the absence of a *because.* The question itself disappears into *what is*, and *what is* is simply necessity. Necessity is the vibration of God's silence (SNL 197 = SWR 467). Necessity does not furnish the end that would answer our question *why?*; to the contrary, it provides only the endless frustration of our desire for an end. Necessity is the essence of the reality of the things of this world: this essence lies in not being ends. Their very reality consists in the fact that they are not manifestations of good (N 496). Necessity is what we cannot bear, yet *must* bear as long as we continue to exist in the contradiction that is life. "Necessity makes all our love objectless. It is our one and only enemy. And for this reason it is necessity itself that we must love" (FLN 324).

The paradox of desire is that in desiring an end, we desire that which cannot exist, while at the same time refusing that which *is*: necessity. To live with this paradox a conversion must take place: we must find a way to love *what is* as the actual manifestation of the ultimate end we desire, the good that is absent. In other words, we must love *what is* as the real presence of the absent good. This is what it is to love the will of God. There are only two objects for us to love, and both require a love that is paradoxical: "First, that which is worthy of love but which, in our sense of the word existence, does not exist. That is God. And second, that which exists, but in which there is nothing it is possible to love. That is necessity. We must love both" (FLN 324).

We must love the good and the necessary precisely in their contradiction; we must reconcile them in our love. This is to consent to necessity as a painful finality, a finality in the image of the end we desire, the good, though necessity is infinitely distant from that good. This is to accept that we ourselves are part of the infinite distance that separates God from God (FLN 83), necessity from good, and precisely as such we are participants in the event of crucifixion: "We are what is farthest removed from God, at the extreme distance whence it is yet not absolutely impossible to return to him. In our being God is torn asunder. We are God's crucifixion. My existence crucifies God" (N 564).

The term for this acceptance and consent on our part to the crucifying contradiction in which we exist is *obedience*. Obedience transforms necessity, that which cannot be loved, into finality, that which *is* nonetheless loved.

> If we look upon ourselves as an end in the world, the world is a chaos and without finality. If we eliminate ourselves, then the

finality of the world is manifest; but there isn't any end. God is
the sole and unique end. But he is not really an end at all, since
he is not dependent on any means. Everything that has God for
an end is finality without end. Everything that has an end of its
own is deprived of finality. That is why we have to transform
finality into necessity. And it is what we manage to do through
the notion of obedience. (N 613)

In other words, through obedience we love the absent God indirectly
by loving his will in the form of necessity; this is to love the world
precisely as God does, with God's own love.

Obedience of Matter: Gravity

Weil portrays necessity as the mediator between matter and God.
Although matter exists only inasmuch as it is willed by God, we are
right to think of necessity as nearer to God's will than matter because
it is the mediating principle (IC 186). One way to represent this
nearness of necessity to God, she writes, is to relate it to the second
person of the Trinity: necessity is the ordering action of God's
Wisdom or Word. As the Word is the order of the world, so the chaos
that we imagine to have existed "before" creation is a mythic
expression of what the cosmos would have been without ("before")
the mediation of necessity (IC 186). Matter obeys God by obeying
necessity, and so it is that "necessity is the obedience of matter to
God" (IC 186).

   As we have seen, it is not force that ultimately rules the world, but
necessity. Every force is subject to necessity as its limiting principle.
Although force is not supreme, it is nonetheless real and active in the
world, making the world what it is: a realm of contesting forces,
grounded in what Weil calls the master force of forces: *gravity*.
"Gravity is the outstanding example of force—and is there, strictly
speaking, any other kind?" (N 71). Weil employs the term "gravity"
as a metaphor for that force operating in the world that pulls
everything down to a lower level and apart into dissipation and
entropy, away from God, away from the "nothingness" of the good,

toward the nothingness that is an empty vacuity—for we must remember that the limit of both good and evil is nothingness (FLN 310). "There exists a 'theofugal' force," Weil writes, "otherwise all would be God" (N 229). Gravity, as she uses the term, is this theofugal force, and force per se "is naturally below, towards the lower; gravity" (N 123). It is because of the pull of gravity that "everything suggesting an upward movement suggests an increase in value" (N 71).

In the dialectic of Weil's thinking, gravity is the force that actively resists and opposes grace, and which, precisely by opposing it, makes the realization of grace possible, for without gravity, grace would have nothing to realize itself in relation to: "good would not exist without evil" (N 327). Just as without matter everything would be God, so without gravity everything would automatically tend toward God, and never tend away. Gravity, the natural force that is active everywhere within the limits of necessity, is willed by God; the non-good of this force exists in the world, like the non-good of matter (N 496), only because God wills it. Nonetheless, in the realm of human affairs, force is the essence of evil: "Force is injustice. Force is the evil principle. It reigns everywhere [...]. Only that which is non-subject to force is pure" (N 457).

Here, once again, Weil's theology affirms that by abdicating power in the act of creation, giving the world over to necessity and delivering humankind into "original sin," God actually wills the advent of evil. But in so willing God remains pure good, innocent, for the ultimate meaning and final cause of evil is good. This idea is captured in Weil's paradoxical statement that "God created because he was good, but the creature let itself be created because it was evil" (FLN 123). The creature is evil for the simple reason that it is emancipated from God, created "outside his kingdom" (NR 277), and this evil is a condition of decreation (N 261), since without evil we would never be free to renounce this world, renounce feeding on other human beings (FLN 286), and direct our love and hunger wholly to the good (N 261). "If there were no such thing as gravity, good would be a matter of course; evil would be unexpected, surprising, and would please on that account. As a result of gravity, it is the reverse" (N 154). It is pain on contact with evil that first instills an infinite desire for good in the creature. Pain, fear, lack, powerlessness, suffering, affliction: these brutally acquaint the creature with the abyssal difference between evil and good. As evil is the root of mystery, Weil writes, pain is the root of knowledge (FLN 69).

The omnipresence of force in human affairs is denoted by Weil as *moral gravity* (N 129, 285). Moral gravity is the natural tendency of human beings to incline toward evil, injustice, baseness *(bassesse)*. This force encompasses all of human existence insofar as it is governed by natural inclination, and "in all that smacks of the social order, force is to be found" (N 466). The pull of moral gravity is present wherever the "original sin" of human will is operative within the universal reign of necessity, which governs everything under the sun, random natural forces and human impulses alike. Weil asserts that "everything whose origin is natural, is alien to the good" (FLN 120); this is precisely because force in one form or another is the fundamental basis of all natural relations: "So long as man submits to having his soul taken up with his own thoughts, his personal thoughts, he remains entirely subjected, even in his most secret thoughts, to the compulsion exercised by needs and to the mechanical play of forces. If he thinks otherwise, he is mistaken" (NR 291).

Thus for Weil moral evil is a species of natural evil. The possibility of sin is attached not to freedom, but to existence—a separate existence (N 192), as we have seen. In creating the creaturely will entirely subjected to the compulsion exercised by needs and the mechanical play of forces, God has created voluntary evil, or original sin (FLN 211). Creation and original sin are two aspects of a single act of abdication by God (FLN 140). Nevertheless, it is crucial to realize that both gravity and grace are forms of obedience to God, for everything that takes place is willed by God, and "there cannot be anything in us that does not obey God" (N 263). Even when we refuse to obey God, or are prevented from doing so by weakness, we are still obeying him because "nothing happens here below unless He wills it"; even when I refuse to obey him, I still obey him (FLN 136). But for a human being capable of thought, to obey God according to the force of moral gravity is to obey as matter, whereas to obey God according to grace is to obey as spirit (WG 129). "If we obey him as matter, the spirit is absent. God in us is dead" (N 263).

Here Weil's thought is in part Spinozistic, distinguishing orders of obedience according to whether they occur under the aspect of extension (*extensio*) or under the aspect of thought (*cogitatio*).[2] For Weil, as for Spinoza, true understanding of the world—and through it, valid ethical activity—can be achieved only by way of a comprehensive critique of the associations and constructs posited by the imagination, forming what Weil calls "ersatz reality" or illusion. Illusions created by the imagination dominate the mind, especially the collective social mentality, for imagination always constitutes the fabric of social life and the dynamic of history (SE 150). Imagination is essentially a liar (N 160). This state of affairs persists until the intelligence is actively employed to replace these imaginary relations with knowledge of true and necessary relations between things. Working within this loosely Spinozistic conception, Weil characterizes the two kinds of obedience:

> We can obey the force of gravity or we can obey the relationship between things. In the first case, we do what we are urged to by the imagination that fills up voids. We can affix thereto, and often with a show of truth, a variety of labels, including righteousness and God. If we suspend the filling up activity of the imagination and fix our attention on the relationship between things, a necessity becomes apparent that we cannot help obeying. Until then we have not the notion of necessity, nor have we the sense of obedience. (N 155)

As for Spinoza, true freedom is a matter of acting in accord with the necessary relationships between things. For Weil and Spinoza alike, to grasp the essential relationship between God and necessity is the sole means of liberation of the individual toward effective action.[3] There can be no question of a liberation *from* things as they are but only a liberation of one's thinking in relationship to things: "Everything that is in this world is conditional. The only thing in us that is unconditional is acceptance" (FLN 112).

This liberation of perspective is the fruit of true knowledge. To know necessity as divinely determined is to perceive one's proper role in relation to things.[4] In the language of Spinoza, one's role is to become *active* rather than acted upon by extrinsic causes; in the language of Weil, it is to become *obedient* as spirit rather than matter. The two terms describe something very similar: that to live in maximal accord with necessity is the only possible ground of human freedom. Weil writes, "The pair of contraries constituted by necessity in matter and liberty in us, has its meeting in obedience, for to be free, for us, is to desire to obey God. All other liberty is false" (IC 186).

Obedience is the only true freedom in a world so bound by necessity that even God is bound by necessity, for even God's power is also obedience (FLN 338). Obedience, whether in us or in God, is the unity of necessity and freedom (FLN 90). Any human action that is not voluntarily obedient to God (as God himself is voluntarily obedient), any action that is not *free* in this sense, is simply the passive result of moral gravity:

> When [...] a man turns away from God, he simply gives himself up to gravity. He thinks that he can decide and choose, but he is only a thing, a stone that falls. If we examine human society and souls closely and with real attention, we see that wherever the virtue of supernatural light is absent, everything is obedient to mechanical laws as blind and as exact as the laws of gravitation. To know this is profitable and necessary. Those whom we call criminals are only tiles blown off a roof by the wind and falling at random. Their only fault is the initial choice by which they became such tiles. (WG 128)

It follows from this notion of obedience as true freedom—which is at its base as much Augustinian as Spinozistic in inspiration—that refusal of necessity can only result in a total lack of freedom, a servitude to gravity. When necessity is not obeyed in full knowledge and consent, it is nonetheless obeyed, but in ignorance and illusion, in falsehood, without the light of truth.

It is in this vein that Weil interprets the words of Jesus on the cross, "Father, forgive them, for they know not what they do" (Luke 23:34). Love of one's enemies in the form of forgiveness and non-rejection is the logical result of seeing pure necessity—the force of gravity—at work in all human actions whose fruits are evil. Human injustice and crime, which is the cause of most affliction, is the work of blind necessity enacted by criminals who, in the grip of moral gravity, "do not know what they are doing" (WG 125). What they are doing is following the impulsions of moral gravity rather than recognizing and consenting to the truth of necessity: the truth of death, of powerlessness, of radical poverty, of nothingness. They are operating under the illusion of power, of freedom from necessity, but that very illusion is the mark of their servitude:

> The beings gifted with reason who do not love God [...] are wholly obedient but only in the manner of a falling stone. Their soul also is matter, psychic matter, humbled to a mechanism as rigorous as that of gravity. Even their belief in their own free arbitration, the illusions of their pride, their defiance, their revolts, are all simply phenomena as rigorously determined as the refraction of light. Considered thus, as inert matter, the worst criminals make up a part of the order of the world and therefore of the beauty of the world. Everything obeys God, therefore everything is perfect beauty. (IC 193–4)

The most potentially scandalous and offensive aspect of Weil's religious thought is her theology of evil, which treats evil not only as a work of providence willed by God in abdication of power, but as actually therein *beautiful*. Viewed in itself, every manifestation of evil is dreary and monotonous (N 140–1), for the void, not accepted, produces hatred, harshness, bitterness, malice (N 139). But this very ugliness, viewed dialectically as an effect of moral gravity, reveals a "terrible beauty"; this Weil affirms again and again: "The universe is beautiful, even including evil, which, as part of the order of the world, has a sort of terrible beauty. We feel it" (FLN 329). This quality of beauty derives from the perfect obedience of things to gravity, whether natural or moral gravity: "Mountains, pyramids, the folds in statues—such beautiful things, and they are all of them manifestations of gravity. Will not ugly, vulgar, shameful, or criminal things be beautiful, if we read in them the other form of gravity?" (N 152).

In Weil's analysis, all crime is a transference of evil (N 621, 624), a transmutation of suffering into evil. In response to our own suffering, we have the tendency to spread evil outside ourselves (N 128). That is why real crime is not felt as crime, but as deliverance. The evil in crime is essentially hidden from the agent; it only declares itself in the sensibility of the innocent victim. Therefore, "I must desire that this harm not degrade me out of love for him who inflicts it, in order that he may not really have done me harm" (N 621). Seeing crime in this way is the only possible path to ultimate forgiveness of evil in human action. There is only one way of never receiving anything but good: "It is to know, with our whole soul and not just abstractly, that men who are not animated by pure charity are merely wheels in the mechanism of the order of the world, like inert matter" (WG 157).

Just as one attributes no blame to a rock for falling and killing a human being, so one should view all human crime, however premeditated, intentional, and abhorrent it may be, as a manifestation of necessity, unfreedom, moral gravity, in exactly the way the falling of a rock is governed by physical laws of gravity. If under certain physical conditions the rock cannot but fall, so, say, military personnel under certain specific socio-psychological conditions cannot but obey commands to commit torture or indiscriminate killing with a sense of fulfilling a necessary and rightful duty. "When we are the victims of an illusion we do not feel it to be an illusion but reality [. . .]. Evil when we are in its power is not felt as evil but as a necessity, or even a duty" (N 108 = GG 71). Due to moral gravity, in the absence of grace, there is no genuine alternative when evil is mistaken for good. In the realm of nature, including that of psychology, good and evil are continually mutually producing each other (N 306). Only contact with perfectly pure good reveals every lesser good as inherently mixed up with evil, and this is the specific paradoxical sense in which Weil asserts, "one must be very pure to do evil" (N 87). Evil is something external to itself, which means that in the place where it is, it is not felt; it is felt where it is not: "Evil is only felt within a pure being, but in him it is not evil" (FLN 69).

We may ask, is the torturing or murdering agent not "free" to do otherwise? Weil's answer, in essence, is no. If he were truly free to do otherwise—that is, actually freed from the grip of moral gravity by supernatural love—then he would do otherwise without fail, even to the point of self-sacrifice, for to conceive the possibility of good in a genuine sense of conceiving—free of false *imagining*—is to carry it out (N 110–1). In the grip of gravity and its illusions, the torturer does not *know* the evil he is doing, for truly to know would be to do everything possible to prevent this infinite harm. He tortures convinced that his action is necessary, good, and justified. It is a lie, but it is the real power of this lie that in fact fuels his action. Although, on the one hand, this may seem pessimistic in the extreme, on the other hand, it means in effect that no one is willfully criminal:

> The unreality that takes good away from good—that is what constitutes evil. Evil is always the destruction of sensible objects in which good is really present. Evil is accomplished by those who are not cognizant of this real presence. In this sense, it is true that no one is willfully wicked. The relationships of force give Absence the power to destroy Presence. (N 563)

Though force appears to be exercised by the one who is in power, it is really only submitted to (N 499). Power depends in every respect on a combination of conditions, and the conditions that govern force are such that no one can possess and control them, but only seem to. One appears to be master, but the appearance is an illusion. In reality, human beings only submit to force and never actually exercise it, whatever may be the circumstances: "The ability to exercise force is an illusion; nobody possesses that ability; force is a mechanism. The devil presides over this illusion" (N 499). The illusion of possessing and exercising power is keenly desired precisely because the powerlessness and poverty of creatureliness is ineluctable. One reaches for power as an antidote to nothingness and death. Yet however great the power one seems to possess, existence remains conditional and *being* eludes the creaturely will to possess it. To accept lowliness and poverty in a quite literal sense, as did Francis of Assisi (Weil's beloved example), is to accept being nothing in appearance just as one is nothing in reality (IC 175).

Power is not an end but a means—it is *pure* means. As such it creates the appearance of greater being in the one who seems to possess it. Power aggrandizes the will, undergirding the capacity to say "I": "Men only love riches, power, and social consideration because they reinforce the faculty of thought in the first person" (IC 175). Although the "I" inevitably dies, reduced to nothing in time, possession of power supports the illusion that this powerlessness and nothingness may be evaded. In the virtually universal longing to maximize this illusion, Weil sees the truth of Thucydides's "terrible pronouncement," which she paraphrases: "Through a necessity of nature, every being whatsoever, as far as it is able, exercises all the power at its disposal" (N 83, see 198). Elaborating this tendency, she outlines the key principle of moral gravity: "In given circumstances, a being reacts in such a way as to preserve and expand itself to the maximum extent. There is no choice" (N 83). This is the "will to power" as Weil explicitly appropriates this Nietzschean term (N 270, SL 150): force, gravity, attachment to being, refusal of death and void, are the ground of this will.

It is the will that first discovers necessity as the way of the world. Necessity is the obstacle that makes the projects of the will possible, just as the resistance of water makes swimming possible. This means that perception of necessity is tied up with expectations of the will. "In the universe, man experiences necessity only so far as it is at once an obstacle and a condition of accomplishing his will. Henceforth the experience of necessity is never entirely free of illusions inevitably connected with the exercise of the will" (IC 181). To know necessity with the will is not the same as to know it in truth—essentially, purely, without attachment and without expectation of gain. The latter way is to know it in a sense mathematically, as the principle of limit abstracted from time (FLN 135). To think of necessity in a way that is pure, it must be "detached from the matter that supports it" and conceived as a fabric of interwoven conditions (IC 181).

If necessity is the root of all evil, this means that God is ultimately responsible for all evil since God is responsible for all effects of gravity, effects that make the world a realm of pure obedience: a realm of pure evil and pure beauty simultaneously. The world's evil and the world's beauty meet in suffering, which is nothing but obedience to necessity. Only the nonillusory knowledge of necessity, released from the natural ambitions of the will, makes a supernatural consent to this created order possible, a consent that liberates one's perspective from the grip of gravity and issues in the other kind of obedience.

Obedience of Spirit: Grace

If force is the essential principle of moral gravity, purification of all susceptibility to force, and the reign in its place of love and justice— which are finally identical in Weil's judgment—is the essential principle of grace. Desire for the good, where it abides in the human heart, is the sole locus of the *spiritual* presence of God in the world as pure good rather than as necessity, for "the gifts of grace alone escape the power of circumstances" (N 123). This presence of the good in us occupies an "infinitely small" portion of the soul, that is, the irreducible core that desires pure good. Never does it constitute the whole soul except in the case of Christ and a few saints, and this is the only place where good can actually be present in the world without any admixture of force. Only that which escapes from force's contact deserves to be called good, but "God alone escapes from this contact, and partly also those men who, by love, have transported and hidden a part of their souls in him" (IC 117).

Everything in the world is subject to necessity; only when universal subjection to necessity is transcended in thought can it be grasped or "read" alternately as pure obedience. Insofar as we are fleshly creatures whose existence depends on material conditions, we obey necessity as everything else does. But insofar as we are thinking beings, Weil contends, we can recognize necessity as a form of obedience and consent to it voluntarily in a spirit of sacrificial redemption. The creature who transcends necessity in thought has the privilege to obey the will of God not as matter (obedience to force) but as thought (voluntary obedience to necessity) (N 150). Spiritual obedience is an interior response to grace: a spontaneous reciprocating response to the love that sustains us and the world—indeed, that creates us and the world—in and through the ineluctable rigors of necessity.

Because this is *our* response, a response in the interior center of ourselves, God cannot save us without our consent. Yet Weil remains Augustinian with respect to the need for preconditioning grace: our ability to respond to necessity with consent and obedience is possible only given prevenient grace. The action of grace in the individual soul is the only special favor, the only miracle, the only supernatural counteractivity to gravity that God effects in the world. God only enters into contact with the individual human being by means of purely spiritual grace, which responds to the gaze turned toward him: "No event whatsoever is a favour on the part of God; grace alone" (N 272). Grace is supernatural love, the spirit of God acting in us (IC 195):

> At the moment when we are resolved to consent to necessity, we cannot foresee the fruits of this consent. This consent is truly in the first place pure absurdity. Also it is truly supernatural. It is the work of Grace alone. God works in us without us if only we allow ourselves to be worked upon. When we become conscious of this, the work is already done, we find ourselves pledged without ever having taken a pledge; we can no longer turn away from God except by an act of high treason. (IC 187)

As creator, God upholds necessity always; but by the gift of grace, a gift descending directly from God, the soul's fundamental relationship to necessity is transfigured. Necessity is recognized for what it is, the very embodiment of divine love, and when the soul responds to this love with love, consent is given, obedience is effected. This is the advent of "holiness" or "saintliness," a state of obedience responsive to the irresistible impulse to act on behalf of God. Obedience does not act *for* God, the way a servant fulfills the command of a master, but *by* God and on *behalf* of God (FLN 152), as supernatural love directly impels one's actions toward finite creatures (FLN 123): "The unique supernatural fact in this world is holiness itself and what lies near to it; it is the fact that the divine commandments should become for those who love God a motive, an active force, motor energy in the literal sense, like gas in an automobile" (NR 267).

The action of grace in the soul is secret, silent, infinitesimally small, free of all contact with force, yet real. Its reality is proved by its real effects, including physical effects (N 225), which are the authentic fruits of love and justice borne out in the actions of individuals who respond to it. Grace is the only direct power God can wield in the world (N 402): a spiritual power heteronomous to all worldly power, gravity and force. It is only a "powerless power" to elicit a response of love, an action on behalf of love, by persuasion alone. It is through grace that God calls on our freedom, begging it to respond. As God has created us outside his kingdom, our consent alone can bring about an inverse operation, with time, converting us into "something inert, something analogous to nothingness, where God is absolute master" (NR 277).

In abdicating to necessity, God elects to become *"God all-powerless"* (N 284), and hence has no other resource against gravity than grace. Grace is the communication of divine love that converts the soul to the motive of pure charity, in radical opposition to relations of force.

> God is only all-powerful here below for saving those who desire to be saved by Him. He has abandoned all the rest of his power to the Prince of this world and to inert matter. He has no power other than spiritual. And spirituality itself here below has only the minimum of power necessary for existing. Grain of mustard seed, pearl, leaven, salt. (FLN 100)

Weil makes clear that only a tiny part of the soul, the "supernatural part" (comparable to Eckhart's "divine spark"), can respond purely to grace in this way, but when it does it is on this small part that everything else in the soul depends for support and direction. This part of the soul is analogous to the center of gravity in a body: it is that point which, if sustained, abolishes weight; so the supernatural point of the soul, if it is sustained by God, transcends moral gravity (N 463). This tiny part of the soul is like the mustard seed in Jesus's parable symbolizing the kingdom of God: when the soul is faithful to it, it increases exponentially according to the laws of grace. "There is an exponential power contained in seed" (N 615, FLN 350), including this spiritual seed.

The mystery of grace is precisely that although it is gratuitous, it is not arbitrary (N 182). "A divine inspiration operates infallibly, irresistibly, if one does not turn the attention away from it, if one does not reject it. There is no need to make a choice in its favour; all that is necessary is not to refuse to recognize its existence" (N 303). Provided that it is received and consented to, grace incrementally increases the kingdom of God in the soul, the "only sphere in which God is an immediate cause" (N 225). This means that rather than obeying necessity in the form of moral gravity, one is liberated by an exponentially increasing freedom to obey the laws of spiritual phenomena. Although one's whole exterior being remains subject to necessity, this infinitely small part of the soul acts in freedom: "Supernatural freedom (there is no other kind) is something infinitely small in the soul" (N 464).

This is a freedom to act directly "by God," that is, on the basis of a spiritual motive and energy rather than a vegetative energy derived from nature or matter. The generative source of this energy is renunciation itself, as new disposable energy is released by the breaking of the bonds of attachment: "This renunciation is a source of energy; there cannot be any other" (N 221, see 558–9). As in the saying of John 12:24, "Except the seed die..." we must die in order to release tied-up energy, detaching it from existing forms to allow it to develop into new liberated forms, "an energy that is free and capable of understanding the true relationship of things" (N 178–9 = GG 35), but for that a "violent wrench" is necessary. As this liberation germinates like a seed, taking root and increasing, the natural part of the soul is reordered in response to the needs of the supernatural part, for faith is the submission of those parts of the soul that have no contact with God to the one that has (FLN 132–3).

Necessity is as operative in the "mechanism" of spiritual obedience as it is in the mechanism of natural obedience, for supernatural mechanisms are at least as dependable as are the laws of gravity (NR 264). While natural mechanisms are the conditions that produce events as such, supernatural mechanisms are the conditions necessary for producing pure good as such. Necessity thus mediates between the natural part of us and the supernatural consent (FLN 89). Just as physical law governs the natural motives of force according to material necessity, so spiritual law governs the supernatural motives of grace according to spiritual necessity.

> When a man consents to obey God, the spirit in him obeys, that is to say, it becomes subject to the laws of spiritual phenomena; and by a mechanism of which we know nothing the rest of his being adapts itself to the spirit sufficiently for those laws to operate. When a man does not consent to obey God, then there is no spirit in him. But the carnal soul and the flesh that compose his whole being are obedient; that is to say, they are subject to mechanical law. (FLN 263)

Force versus justice, gravity versus grace—these opposing principles distinguish the two kingdoms: the kingdom of God and the kingdom of this world. Justice, wherever it is real, is absolutely opposed to force, for "there is something in us that lies completely outside the range of relationships of force [...] and that is the supernatural principle of justice" (N 457). It is important to note that Weil locates justice not in the world per se but in the soul, for the only foothold of justice in the world is in the purest part of the soul. Justice occupies a place in this world only to the extent that a thirst for it resides in the human heart, where the kingdom of God establishes its claim. Outside the human heart, outside its infinite longing for good, force remains ever the ubiquitous principle, for our world is the kingdom of necessity and real justice is not of this world

(IC 142). Where force is absolutely sovereign, justice is absolutely unreal except in the hearts of human beings: "The structure of a human heart is just as much of a reality as any other in this universe, neither more nor less of a reality than the trajectory of a planet" (NR 243). But because of the mystery of the absence of good within the sphere of human society, a person of purity accomplishes nothing, or whatever he or she does accomplish turns to dross (N 484). Good, when it becomes incarnate in this world, takes the form of a slave (N 134), a suffering servant; this is the epitomic image of pure good in relation to worldly power. "In order to be just, one must be naked and dead" (N 411), and finally "the absolutely Just One can only be God incarnate" (N 627).

Weil echoes the proclamation of Matthew 22:14 that "many are called but few are chosen," construing it in her own fashion: "One is called; one either comes running up, or one doesn't" (NR 265). Everyone is called by grace in the sense that every human being's essential core is constituted by an infinite longing for good, a longing for justice that could, if converted to obedience, potentially nullify the evil of moral gravity. But due to the grip of illusion and the counteractive compulsion of moral gravity, few respond in such a way that the principle of justice actually supplants that of force as the motive of action in body and soul—the body being "the indispensable intermediary through which the soul brings real action to bear upon itself" (FLN 288). This, when it happens, entails a radical conversion, a total transformation of the natural creature by means of obedience similar to that practiced by the religious orders (N 125). "We are born and [. . .] live in sin, which is an inversion of the hierarchical order. The first operation has to be one of reversal. Conversion" (N 528).

Wherever justice supplants force in the soul, a new mechanism is set in place, a spiritual mechanism governed by the demands of a purely spiritual necessity; a necessity that gradually, through a temporal process, liberates one's action from the bondage of moral gravity. One is under a new compulsion:

All the parables about the seed are connected with this notion of an impersonal Providence. Grace descends from God upon all beings; what becomes of it depends on what they are; there where it really penetrates, the fruit it bears is the result of a process similar to a mechanical one, and which, like a mechanical one, takes place in a time continuum. The virtue of patience, or to translate the Greek word [*hupomone*] more accurately, of immobile expectancy, is relative to this necessity of duration. (NR 263; see SL 137)

Weil repeatedly reiterates that this spiritual mechanism, which establishes and increases the kingdom of God in the soul, is a mysterious process. It can be witnessed through its effects—a good tree bears good fruit—and it can be known experimentally through experience, but its operation remains hidden, secret, and like all operations of faith it is super-rational.

Grace is the privilege of a few who experience divine mercy in the inner life of their souls, while the great majority continues to obey gravity (FLN 151). This privileged experience of mercy is often strongest when the outer life is most afflicted, when the misery inflicted by necessity is at its greatest extreme. Because our misery is literally a participation in the distance between the Father and the Son, it is in the deepest depth of misery that we touch God; our misery itself makes us the receptacle of the Holy Spirit (FLN 83). This perception of misery itself as a mercy enables one to accept God, to love God right through affliction or *malheur*, when based on objective grounds God would appear most unspeakably unmerciful, as in the case of the God who tries Job, the God who abandons Jesus on the cross. It is then that witness to mercy is borne against all worldly evidence, against all sense—a witness verging on a kind of madness. At this point, the "evidence" of divine mercy is wholly a matter of spiritual rather than earthly fact:

Those who are privileged to contemplate God experience the fact of his divine mercy in the supernatural part of their inner life. It is God's divine mercy as Holy Spirit. Their only reason for believing that God as creator is merciful is that these contemplative states exist in fact and form part of their experience as creatures. There is also another reason—the beauty of the universe. No other trace of the divine mercy is to be found in creation. But these privileged beings are outwardly a witness of the fact in so far as they let fall sensible signs of what is within them. The existence of such signs constitutes, indeed, yet a third type of evidence of the divine mercy. (N 449)

Obedience is the supreme virtue (N 96); to be obedient is simply to love necessity and to act in a way that one is convinced to be spiritually necessary. Obedience is the name Weil gives to action motivated purely by the love of God, understanding this "of" in the genitive not the dative sense—for "it is God within us who loves God" (FLN 177). One obeys God truly by obeying love and truth, not the name or image of "God," which masks many inferior, imperfect, idolatrous notions (FLN 138, 145). What makes an action truly good is that it is motivated by love descending from God, not that its consequences are good, since all good in this world has some evil attached to it and it is impossible to avoid this evil; the objective interconnection between good and evil in this world is irreducible (N 414, 251).

Obedience to pure good, despite evil, is our way of participating in the incarnation of God (FLN 150). Through obedience we respond to God's will in the form of love rather than necessity, though this process is mysterious and depends on our being detached from the supernatural. A soul perpetually ruled by this feeling, from birth to death, is God become man (N 249), and it is because our obedience gives us the precious opportunity to incarnate God that sin is a waste of our freedom. For even if the possession of a treasure implies the possibility of losing it, "losing a pearl is not the same as having a pearl" (N 256). Resources that might have been lavished on other creatures out of charity—by God acting in us—are wasted on nothingness by our "I" acting for itself. Everything that proceeds from a source other than grace, everything originating in our will, is alien to the good (FLN 120).

One of the profound paradoxes of Weil's thought—underscored for emphasis in her notebook—is that *man has no power whatever, and yet he does have a responsibility*" (N 97). One is responsible for the use made of one's ability to consent to or refuse *what is*, though this is an ability that does not change *what is* in the least. What *is* already is, yet the faculty of consent is responsible ("response-able") for consenting to it. By nature we tend to respond to the world and others with a mixed *yes* and *no*, discriminating goods from evils, affirming goods that please us and rejecting evils that frustrate and defy our will. But our responsibility is to recognize that these goods and evils are inseparable inasmuch as they are delivered with equanimity through the same hand of necessity. Everything in nature is both good and evil together, as we have noted; in a relative sense, *mixed*, in an absolute sense, *dialectical*.

One of the values of fundamental reflection on God for Weil is precisely that it forces a total decision, a consent or refusal that is absolute: a decision that is dialectical, not mixed. Ultimately, one must consent to or refuse the comprehensive dialectic of necessity and the good as constitutive of all of reality. Only in consenting to everything, the totality of the universe, as *absolutely* good—including all evil and everything that thwarts one's "I"-centered will to exist, one's will to power—only then does one become grounded in the truth that makes one free. This consent effects the ultimate detachment: the wrenching of one's energy and perspective away from oneself as a limited, mortal creature. The "I" is a fiction, an illusion; the sooner it perishes, the sooner the reality of the whole universe is gained—and through the reality of the universe, the reality of God.

Amor Fati

Divine love never suffers anything without having consented to suffer it. When we accept divine love, we do the same. We imitate God when we consent to suffer in our turn what God has consented to suffer in the movements of creation, incarnation, and crucifixion. For a human being to imitate divine love perfectly, "it suffices for him to consent fully, at every instant, with love for the order God has created in the world, to all wounds without the least exception that the course of events may bring him" (IC 120). To do this is to utter an unconditional *yes* to the decision of God to create the world with all its tragic strife and finitude, beautiful and horrible at once, bound by the strict limits of necessity, thrust in the grip of gravity. Utterance of unconditional consent in the soul is the very substance of obedience, the very essence of holiness, sanctity, spiritual beauty. This is the highest virtue: it is the *amor fati* of ancient Stoics as Weil interprets them.[5]

> This unconditional "Yes" that is pronounced in the most secret point of the soul, which is but silence, is entirely withdrawn from all danger of contact with force. Nothing else in the soul can be withdrawn from it. This method is simple. There is no other. This is *amor fati*, it is the virtue of obedience, the Christian virtue excellent above all others. But this "Yes" has no virtue unless it is absolutely unconditional. (IC 120)

Weil views Stoicism and Christianity as "two twin conceptions" (NR 290), rooted in a shared religious reverence for the order of the world, as well as the core virtues of humility, obedience, and love (NR 290). In both traditions Weil saw a common core: the insight that love of the world, purified of attachment, *is* love of God. Weil refers to this as a "tautology," though strictly speaking it is a commutative equivalence: "We must love all facts, not for their consequences, but because in each fact God is there present. But that is tautological. To love all facts is nothing else than to read God in them" (N 267). To love all facts regardless of their consequences is to be detached from the suffering that facts cause, and this detachment is itself a work of love only possible through grace—a love descending directly from God and actively consenting in the soul.

Supernatural love loves "indifferently" in response to good and evil, even while perceiving the distinction between good and evil ever more intensely: "One must accept everything, all things, without any reservation, both inside and outside oneself, in the whole universe, with the same degree of love; but evil must be accepted as evil and good as good" (N 305). The feeling of evil is not an evil (FLN 69) because the *awareness* and *certitude* of evil—by shining a pure light exposing it—is itself destructive of evil, provided that it is apprehended explicitly as such (N 605).

> Only supernatural love is able to contemplate stark necessity. It ceases then to be an evil. (N 480) / Pain is not an evil. The misery of the creature is not an evil. Creation is not an evil. (N 251) / Suffering is an evil for those who think that suffering is an evil [...]. If I think that suffering is not an evil for me, then it is not one in fact. In this way I can accept suffering for myself and feel compassion for other people. (N 323)

Stark necessity ceases to be an evil not because it ceases to cause suffering but because the suffering is consented to as grounded in the order of the world: "Whilst one has a horror of this evil, at the same time one loves it as emanating from the will of God" (N 505). Love that transcends the distinction between good and evil does not deny the importance of the distinction, but far rather confirms it. Yet the distinction is now seen to be non-ultimate, relative and endurable, because evil is finite and infinitely redeemed.

All the seemingly unredeemed evil in the world is finite and relative (N 451, 621), susceptible to appropriation by and for an absolute good. Absolute good absolutely transcends the good that is the opposite and correlative of evil, and this good is only encountered by means of a supernatural love that passes beyond the sphere where good and evil are in opposition (SE 214), that is, beyond the natural universe. Thus for supernatural love, and *only* for supernatural love, creation is not an evil (N 251) and an unqualified faith in providence is possible. For faith in providence is the spiritual certainty that in this universe good outweighs evil (NR 271), that redemption is universally actual. So Weil can affirm that "pantheism is true only for saints who have reached the state of perfection" (FLN 111).

The endurability of evil for love is the key realization of *amor fati*. Love of necessity is simply love of what befalls one, what befalls every creature, simply because it is necessary as a consequence of God's will to abdicate and for no other reason. God, who created the world by emptying himself, is perfectly just inasmuch as necessity is for him necessary: it is the condition of the existence of the world and the creature, the condition of incarnation and redemption. Necessity is indeed deaf and blind to creaturely need, but it is necessarily so.

The bitterest reproach that men make of this necessity is its absolute indifference to moral values. Righteous men and criminals receive an equal share of the benefits of the sun and of the rain; the righteous and the criminals equally suffer sunstroke and drowning in floods. It is precisely this indifference that Christ invites us to look upon and to imitate as the very expression of the perfection of our heavenly Father. To imitate this indifference is simply to consent to it, that is, to accept the existence of all that exists, including all evil, excepting only that portion of evil that we have the possibility, and the obligation, of preventing. (IC 184)

Precisely in view of the "moral indifference" of necessity, Weil considers the deepest benefit of becoming a "friend of God"—one who responds to grace with obedience—to be this ability to act in the world as a surrogate of God: to act as God would act if he were a human being. Though God the Father is powerless to give bread to an afflicted stranger suffering from hunger because he is disincarnate (FLN 312), through obedience one is privileged to act as God's surrogate and give the stranger bread. Clearly, this is Weil's roundabout way of conceiving the *imitatio Christi*: "An act that is good is one which in a given situation would be accomplished by God incarnate" (N 509). To love God is not only to accept necessity but to act constructively to prevent suffering and manifest love wherever one has the opportunity to do so, whenever one experiences the need to do so as an immediate command of love.

Indeed, Weil affirms repeatedly that it is not one's own suffering but the suffering of others—above all the suffering of the innocent— that stands as a barrier to pure obedience, to the holy virtue of *amor fati*. One must be willing to say yes to the sight of perfect innocence on the cross, and this seems a horrible offense, a moral crime, a blasphemy. In accepting it, one becomes complicitous with God in his decision to create and thus shares in the guilt of the Creator. It is due to a mystery, the "madness" of unconditional love (FLN 127), that it consents to suffer what it cannot bear to see: "Christ on the Cross, the greatest harm inflicted on the greatest good: if one loves that, one loves the order of the world" (FLN 144).

God must be accused of all evil, yet God must be forgiven it too, since God is subjected to it in its totality. All evil is inflicted on God by God in the creation of the world, and all evil is transfigured redemptively by God who suffers it. This transfiguration is communicated to us when we give our consent. There is no justification or compensation for evil, yet supernatural love redeems it as a divine work.

> Evil is to love what mystery is to the intelligence. Just as mystery constrains the virtue of faith to be supernatural, so likewise does evil act in regard to the virtue of charity. And to try to find compensations, justifications for evil is as harmful for the cause of charity as it is to try to expound the content of the mysteries on the plane of the human intelligence. (N 341 = GG 75)

Insofar as we become able to love *what is* unconditionally, we are in fact loving with a love that descends from God. Nothing in nature is capable of such detachment, such liberation from the particularity of perspective. Such a love, when it occurs in us, has already said yes to the fall, to the advent of evil, to the torture of innocence, to every earthly darkness and tragedy, to the crucifixion of the greatest good. "Wherever there is complete, authentic and unconditional consent to necessity, there is fullness of love for God; and nowhere else. This consent constitutes participation in the Cross of Christ" (IC 184).

To give this consent to the will of God is to answer the divine "madness" of creation with the further madness of affirmation, and "this consent is a folly that responds to the triple folly of God (Creation, Incarnation, Passion) but, to begin with, to the first of the three" (FLN 89). Creation is the folly of follies, the supreme folly, and only supernatural love working in us is mad enough, super-rational enough, to consent to the madness of God in this act. When we experience *amor fati*, it is the holy spirit in us consenting to everything God has wrought (IC 195). The fact that we are able to consent at all is itself, for Weil, a proof of the reality of God: "The world is only beautiful for him who experiences *amor fati*, and consequently *amor fati* is, for whoever experiences it, an experimental proof of the reality of God" (N 242). Just as there is only one proof of God's goodness—that we love him (N 267)—so the one proof of God's reality is that our love for his will can be real.

We consent to God's madness simply by not standing in the way. We remove ourselves, our "I," so that the love of God for God may be communicated transparently through us. This work of the spirit of God in us is our own madness, offered back to God in reciprocity:

> No mover, no motive can be sufficient for such a consent. This consent is a madness, man's own particular madness, just as the Creation, the Incarnation, the Passion together constitute God's own madness. These two madnesses answer each other. It is no surprise that this world should be par excellence a place of affliction, for without perpetually suspended affliction [*malheur*] no folly on man's part could echo that of God, which is already wholly contained in the act of creation. (IC 182–3, translation altered)

This madness on our part—identical to *amor fati*—is the image in us of the creative will of God, which upholds equally and impartially all that exists (IC 190). Weil interprets the Lord's Prayer as a spiritual exercise of this image of God in us: it petitions for the end of the world (the end of evil, which would necessarily entail the end of the world) and simultaneously for the continued existence of the world in accordance with the will of God: "'Thy kingdom come' means let evil disappear [. . .]. 'Thy will be done'. God's will is to abdicate in favour of necessity. So this petition implies consent to the existence of the world" (FLN 296).

Where *amor fati* reconciles beauty and suffering in a transcendent joy in the real, there is true love of God. Transcendent joy as Weil describes it is a complex dialectical joy—a joy in the reality of the good that is absent and simultaneously a joy in the order of the world as the sacrificial manifestation of that good. *Amor fati* effects a *coincidentia oppositorum* of necessity and the good: that is, it constitutes an affirmation that necessity is necessity, that good is good, and that the contradiction between them ultimately is no contradiction but a supernatural harmony. When it is understood in the depths of the soul that necessity is only one of the faces of divine beauty, of which the other is the good, then all that makes necessity felt—sorrows, ills, obstacles—becomes a further reason for loving supernaturally (IC 101). For the beauty of the world is simply the order of the world that is loved (WG 170):

> The order of the world is to be loved because it is pure obedience to God. Whatever this universe accords us or inflicts on us, it does so exclusively out of obedience [. . .]. Everything, without any exception, joys and sorrows alike, ought to be welcomed with the same inward attitude of love and thankfulness. (NR 289)

Therefore love of God is pure when joy and suffering equally inspire gratitude, for "felicity is beyond the realm of consolation and pain, outside it" (N 237). We apprehend this felicity through a sense of another kind, outside all ordinary sensation of pleasure and pain. This felicity is a transcendent joy, a joy in God as perfectly good, despite evil, and a joy in the world as perfectly beautiful, despite evil. It is a joy in the supernatural realization that all necessity, including evil, is finally obedience to the good.

Many of Weil's affirmations suggest that *transcendent* joy can be experienced at its fullest only through extreme suffering, and extreme suffering can be redemptive only through transcendent joy. Although suffering is perhaps indispensable for achieving the final break-through (N 291), on the other hand, suffering can have no redemptive value without the illumination of joy. She asserts that in

order to find reality in suffering, the revelation of reality must come
to one through joy, for otherwise life is nothing but a more or less evil
dream (N 291). It is finally the *yes* of joy that gives finality to all the
senseless, insignificant givenness of suffering. For evil could not be
evil without revealing the good, which it discloses negatively in the
eclipse of joy:

> To say that this world isn't worth anything, that this life isn't
> worth anything, and to adduce evil as the proof, is absurd; for if
> it isn't worth anything, of what exactly does evil deprive us?
> Thus suffering in affliction and compassion for others are all the
> purer and more profound the better we are able to conceive the
> fullness of joy. (N 290)

It is a madness on our part to consent to God's madness, but finally
the madness of our consent is given in response to an ultimate joy, a
joy that passes understanding and is so transcendent, unconditioned, and selfless that it is able to say: "What does it matter that
there should never be joy in me, since there is perpetually perfect
joy in God?" (N 268). All else withers away in the face of the
certainty that God possesses himself eternally and perfectly (FLN
136). This joy in the reality of God qua good gives the unique
consolation that even if I fall into the lowest depths of evil, the
abject wretchedness that befalls me does no harm to the good
(FLN 311).

To experience such joy in God is to accept that one will never in
this life possess the good; one must rather renounce possession of the
good, even while continuing to "wait" for it. We wait for God
because waiting is our paradoxical way of holding the good in time.
"We have all those impossible desires within us as a mark of our
destination, and they are good for us when we no longer hope to
accomplish them" (WG 126). All that we vainly desire "here below"
is perfectly realized in God, and this presentiment of God's finality is
all the salvation we need, for salvation consists in knowing that God
is absolute good, and that absolute good is real and irreducible,
inalienable, and therefore already entirely ours in the only sense that

matters. All our attachments are nothing but an insufficiency in our feeling for reality (N 365). To realize this is to realize that we do not need to be attached to ourselves; my "I" does not need to be saved if there is God (FLN 199), and this understanding, achieved through faith, itself constitutes salvation.

CHAPTER 5

GRACE AND DECREATION

Supernatural good is not a sort of supplement to natural good
[...]. In all the crucial problems of human existence the only
choice is between supernatural good on the one hand and evil
on the other. (SE 23)

God abdicated, giving us existence in the world. It is by refusing
existence that we abdicate, becoming in that way similar to God
(FLN 297). We must imitate God's renunciation in creation and
crucifixion. To find God we have to exhaust duality—the opposition
of good and evil—by going to the very extreme of duality, and this is
what is done in crucifixion (N 436); in it, the greatest harm is
inflicted on the greatest good (FLN 144). God emptied himself of
divinity and filled us with a false divinity; we are called to reply by
emptying ourselves of this pretense or illusion (N 216–7, 212–3).
This act of decreation is the whole purpose of the act by which we
were created (FLN 140). "God renounces—in a sense—being
everything. This is the origin of evil. We have got to renounce being
something. Herein lies our only good" (N 193).

In the subjective existence in which we say "I," God is torn
asunder; our desire to exist crucifies God (N 564). Every thinking
finite being who is subjected to necessity, space, and time knows that
as a finite being he or she is "God crucified" (N 213). Such a thinking

being's vocation is to be "like God"—but like God *crucified*—for "God created us in his image, that is to say he gave us the power to abdicate in his favour, just as he abdicated for us" (FLN 297). As it is God's will to establish infinite distance through creation, and to expiate the evil of it through crucifixion, so it is our vocation to participate in that decision through our knowledge of good and evil and our consent to expiatory and redemptive suffering: "God has expiated creation [in crucifixion], and we who are associated in it expiate it also" (N 80).

Sin Says "I"

In creating us as a creature that says "I," God has created a finite being that is possessed by a self-orbiting ersatz reality and is therefore unable to love God. But through the action of grace the "I" gradually wears away and disappears until God loves himself by way of the creature, which "empties itself, becomes nothing" (N 331), and with regard to emptiness, becomes equal to God (FLN 297).

> The Creation is an act of love, and it is something that is going on perpetually. At every moment our existence is God's love for us. But God is only able to love himself. His love for us is love for himself by way of us. Therefore, He who gives us our being loves in us our consent not to be. If this consent is virtual, then he loves us virtually. Our existence is nothing else but his will that we should consent not to exist. He is forever begging from us the existence that he gives us. And he gives it us in order to beg it from us. (N 613–4) / God has given me my being in order that I may give it back to him. It is like one of those tests which resemble traps [...]. If I accept this gift, it has a bad and fatal effect. Its virtue becomes apparent through a refusal. (N 484–5)

It is the *will* in us that says "I," and this "I"-saying is the essence of sin, or voluntary evil. The will is what sins in the creature, for the will as such is sin. It is because we are born with a will that we are born in a state of sin, or voluntary evil, but by the same token it is precisely therein that we are born with the vocation to renounce our sin, which is to say, to abnegate our will. Sin is not an act but a *state* that necessarily produces acts of sin, and "original sin" is the symbol of this primordial state of sin prior to any act (N 192). We are born in a state of sin, and if at any time humanity was not in a state of sin, then it did not yet possess knowledge of the distinction between good and evil (N 234).

In that hypothetical case, humanity would have been, like the rest of nature, so purely "evil" (understood as gravity, otherness to God, separation from God) as to be innocent, for where evil is untouched by the dimmest knowledge of good, it can be nothing other than innocent. For there are all degrees of distance separating the creature from God, including a distance where the love of God is impossible: "Matter, plants, animals. Here, evil is so complete that it is self-annulling: there is no longer any evil: mirror of divine innocence" (N 616).

The thoroughgoing evil of nature, inasmuch as it is innocent of knowledge, cannot be other than what it is, as God has made it: bereft of knowledge of good, and therefore of evil. Yet because it is perfectly obedient, it is likewise perfectly innocent. Until a knowledge of good and evil is born in the creature there can be no such distinction, for all of nature is perfectly obedient as matter. In that respect, nature is "evil" (separated from God) in such a "good" manner (perfectly obediently) that it is good. Ignorance of good, and therefore of evil, is the vocation of all that is purely natural, untouched by the supernatural. There does not exist in nature a *will* to be other than God before such knowledge.

It is the human will in nature that changes this equation of evil and innocence. Human will, because it is granted the potential to decreate itself, to obey as spirit, to commit itself to the dominion of grace rather than gravity, is evil in a positive, non-innocent sense. It has the potential to renounce itself, negate itself, voluntarily abdicate the natural state in which it is created, and this potentiality is the actual image of God in the creature. For as God renounced his power and became a slave, chaining himself down by the limits of necessity

(N 191), we in turn are called to renounce our claim to existence and consent to be nothing in the divine image. Paradoxically, this likeness to God is precisely what makes the human being more distant from God than anything else in nature: "We are what is farthest removed from God, at the extreme distance whence it is yet not absolutely impossible to return to him. In our being God is torn asunder. We are God's crucifixion. My existence crucifies God" (N 564).

Here a perspectival qualification is called for: creation as such, the creation of matter, already tears God asunder, but does so in a way known only to God. Matter, plants and animals, lacking self-knowledge, are not conscious of their participation in crucifixion, yet their existence fully participates materially in the enactment of crucifixion. Ultimately, objectively, it is not human sin that separates God, it is *God* who separates and unites God for his own intradivine reasons.[1] "God testifies before God that he loves God" (FLN 241). Crucifixion is a reality in God, whether we consent to it or not, and our consent to decreation does not "undo" creation or eliminate crucifixion, but rather deepens and completes these acts as attestations of love. Separation and atoning reunion within the godhead is an intradivine drama, a supernatural event that does not depend on our creaturely initiative. The reconciliation of God with God is the work of the Holy Spirit, a divine work in which grace privileges us to take part when we give our consent.

Only through knowledge is it possible for the creature to participate *voluntarily* in creation, whether tending toward good or evil: indeed, this is what we do, moving in the direction of evil, already when we say "I." The will as such is the will to exist as a center that says "I" and claims being for itself. This means that our consciousness of evil is an implicit consciousness of crucifixion, and of our own will as active participant in creation–crucifixion. Once such consciousness arises, a fruit of the tree of knowledge of good and evil, the conscious creature has one of two choices: either to further crucify God by continuing to obey only as matter, in effect *voluntarily* dividing God from God, or to be crucified oneself, again *voluntarily*, in order that God be reunited with God in the soul.

This either/or decision was addressed in Chapter 4, the choice to obey as matter or to obey as spirit: to obey as created will in the form of evil or to obey as decreated consent in the form of love.

> What is creation from the point of view of God is sin from the point of view of the creature. God asked us "do you want to be created?" and we answered yes. He still asks us at every moment, and at every moment we answer yes. Except for a few whose soul is split in two; while nearly their whole soul answers yes, there is one point in it that wears itself out in beseeching: no, no, no! This point grows larger as it cries, and becomes a patch that eventually spreads throughout the soul. (FLN 211)

Because the world is created as the cross of Christ (IC 198) and creation *is* crucifixion, our will to be created is equivalent to a will to divide God from God; our renunciation of this will, on the other hand, is a willingness to be crucified ourselves. One or the other results from our answer to the question: Do you want to be created? Either we desire existence, making a claim to power, prestige, the right to say "I," and living in the illusion that we are something, or we consent to be nothing and take the way of the cross.

Our greatest good lies not in our creation but in our decreation; our creation is only virtually good inasmuch as it is the condition of decreation. Decreation can be regarded as the "transcendent completion of creation"; it is an annihilation in God that confers the fullness of being upon the annihilated creature, a fullness that is denied it as long as it goes on existing (N 471). We participate in the creation of the world negatively by decreating ourselves (N 309), which entails an abolition of the evil, the "original sin" of our created nature, lodged in our will.

As we have seen, God's abdication to necessity ensures that God does not mix up established orders; creation embodies this respect for established orders. God acts supernaturally within the sphere of the supernatural and naturally—in a sense not at all—within the sphere of nature. "He does not unmake creation; it is for creation to unmake itself" (N 243). Whereas God created because he was good, the creature let itself be created because it was evil; it can redeem itself only by persuading God, through prayer, to destroy it (FLN 123). "To abolish evil means to de-create; but that is something God is only able to do with our co-operation" (N 342).

One way Weil devises to speak of the generosity and sacrifice of God in creating us with the potential for decreation is by looking upon sin as a good. Just as "the possibility of evil is a good" (N 112), so sin is a good when it is considered from an impersonal point of view: "Sin in me says 'I' [. . .]. I sin. And yet, when considering sin, in the order of the world, under the aspect in which it is a good, it is not I" (N 126). This is to say, although "I"-saying is an illusion, a screen thrown between us and God, the effects of this illusion qua illusion are real. The reality of this illusion is a good because it furnishes us with the apparent self-possession requisite to give ourselves back to God. If not for this illusion, we would have nothing to renounce, for nothing whatever belongs to us, not even our wretchedness (N 128).

Our sin, our "I"-saying will, is the only thing that is truly ours, released into our possession by the Creator. Hence our death is the most precious thing that has been given to us, and it is the supreme impiety to make an improper use of it (N 103). Death is the one thing that is ours to give away; all else that we imagine belonging to us does so only through illusion. We give our death away freely, as a gift back to God, by consenting to die. Thus to answer *no* rather than *yes* to the question, "do you want to be created?" is the essential movement of decreation of the will.

Such a *no* to possessing existence is made possible only by an implicit *yes* to God's will, a *yes* to the wisdom and beauty of that will as love. Apart from this transcendent beauty—an infinitely greater good than any existent good—there would and could be no sense whatever in saying *no* to existence. Love alone can make us consent not to be God: "One must love like this, or else be like Lucifer; anything else is servility" (FLN 239). For it to be possible for us to answer *no* to our own Luciferian will, something transcendent must call to us from outside ourselves, from beyond everything we know and feed on by attachment, inviting us irresistibly to this act of renunciation. This is the work of grace; it creates the willingness to be purified by detachment, achieving a spiritual emptiness in which nothing but naked value survives—a good that is supremely real but nonexistent.

God waits for us in the void. Withdrawn and waiting "outside" the world, powerless on the cross within the world, God has the power to reward only those efforts that *cannot* be rewarded in the world, which is to say, those efforts carried out "for nothing" in the void. Yet we must not seek the void, for it would be tempting God to count on supernatural bread to fill it. Nor must we flee the void. These are the first and second temptations of Christ (N 160). Ours is to wait for God actively, attentively, by contemplating the real, putting off illusion, holding ourselves open to the "contact" of the supernatural, diminishing our will, opening a passageway for grace.

Grace Decreates the "I"

Until we are called by grace to decreation, we live out of the faulty perspective of our wills. The deepest problem with this is not, at its base, what is commonly described as egoism or self-love, but the fact that our creaturely perspective is inherently preferential: it favors particular states of affairs in relation to the conditions of our existence, our personal location, tastes, and attachments.[2] "What is generally named egoism is not love of self, it is a defect of perspective [...]. Finite creatures only apply the idea of legitimate order to the immediate neighbourhood of their hearts" (IC 133). Weil cites an example: from the perspective of such finite creatures in Europe, the massacre of 100,000 Chinese hardly alters the order of the world as they perceive it, whereas if a fellow worker receives a slightly higher raise in pay, the order of the world is turned upside down. This is not a consequence of thinking too highly of oneself; it is a product of being too enclosed in a particular viewpoint to be just in one's perception of the world, and therefore just in one's concerns and actions. "Man always devotes himself to an *order*. Only, except with the aid of supernatural illumination, this order is centred either in himself, or else in some particular being (who can be an abstraction) into whom he has transferred himself" (N 279). To escape from the errors of false perspective, all one can do is to carry one's heart beyond space, beyond the world, to God (IC 134).

The distortions of preferential perspective also cause human relationships to be fundamentally defined by attachment (necessity) rather than freedom (love). When a human being locates the center of the universe in another person or entity, this transference is always the effect of gravity, a "combination of mechanical forces" that subject the one who is dependent to the other with brutal results. This kind of gravity in the form of personal need defines all attachments of the will and its perspective: "Everyone disposes of others as he disposes of inert things, either in fact, if he has the power, or in thought" (IC 173).

Attachment, which is ruled by necessity, reigns over the desire to harm others as well. When I do harm to another, I receive something from him or her: what is gained is that I have enlarged myself, spread myself, increased the effective power of that which says "I" in me (N 181). Through doing harm, I have filled part of the void in myself by creating a new element of void in another person, although the vicious circle created by this transference of evil (N 624) means that the evil will have to be repaid. "It is the void that renders man capable of sin. All sins are attempts to fill voids" (N 149, FLN 160).

That void which is the root of sin is the nothingness, the radical poverty, the inherent misery of the creature covered over and denied: "Sin is nothing else but the failure to recognize human misery—it is unconscious misery and for that very reason guilty misery" (N 235). On the other hand, to become conscious of unconscious misery is to transform sin into misery confronted and consented to. To recognize and begin to inhabit one's radical poverty and misery is to approach God: "To become something divine, I have no need to get away from my misery, I have only to adhere to it. My very sins are a help to me, on condition that I know how to read in them the full extent of my misery. It is in the deepest depth of my misery that I touch God" (FLN 83). Adhering to my own misery means setting aside the illusions that fill the void, that make me feel that I am a center of power of being rather than a "nothingness" whose feeling of being something interferes with the true condition of things.

It must be recognized that nothing in the world is the centre of the world, that the centre of the world is outside the world, that nothing here below has the right to say *I*. One must renounce in favour of God, through love for Him and for the truth, this illusory power that He has accorded us, to think in the first person. He has accorded it to us that it may be possible for us to renounce it by love. (IC 174)

Only God has the right to say "I am." When we say "I" we arrogate a divine right unto ourselves. We are born with the original sin of desiring to be divine *as* creatures (N 216). Insofar as we are naturally prone to do so from birth, an imaginary divinity has been bestowed on us, and it is bestowed in order that we should strip ourselves of it as Christ did his real divinity (N 229). Saying "I" is the root of sin, the original sin through which we attempt to imitate God in his power rather than in his kenotic renunciation: "'Ye shall be as gods.' The sin consists in desiring to be as gods *otherwise* than through participation in God's divinity [...]. He emptied himself of his divinity. We should empty ourselves of the false divinity with which we were born" (N 216–7, 212–3).

The "I"-perspective must be removed from me. But how? Am I free to remove it by my own act? No, for "'I am free' is like a contradiction, for that which is not free in me says 'I'" (N 175). This is a liberation that can be effected only by undergoing a kind of death. While living, one must pass through death to the other side of the curtain. One accomplishes this not by transporting one's center into God's center, for this would be the work of one's own will and imagination, elevating oneself to the level of an imaginary God. "Some love God thus. Even though they should die as martyrs, theirs is not the veritable love of God" (IC 174–5). Rather, liberation is through true renunciation of the power to think of everything in the first person. This renunciation is effected in the form of *amor fati* (love of necessity, love of the world) and love of neighbor; through these we become centered in the true God, the kenotic God stripped of divinity.

Although full reality for God lies outside the world, "full reality for a man lies within this world, even should he happen to be perfect"

(N 374). This means that love is only real for human beings when it is directed toward particular objects that are real and concrete. For our love to transcend the errors of particular perspective while also remaining *real*, directed toward real rather than imaginary objects, Weil maintains that we must love by means of analogy and transference, as we have seen in Chapter 2: "In all departments of life, love is not real unless it is directed toward a particular object; it becomes universal without ceasing to be real only as a result of analogy and transference" (WG 184).

We must transfer the quality of our love for those things that are most real to us in the world unto things that are less real or unreal to us, and must do so on the basis of analogy. I can extend *real* love to a stranger only by transferring to him or her, by analogy, the reality I find embodied in a friend, and I must do this regardless of the stranger's actual qualities, simply because the stranger is no less real than my friend. To *see* the stranger as fully real is already to love him or her. "Among human beings, only the existence of those we love is fully recognized" (N 288 = WG 113), hence "belief in the existence of other human beings as such is *love*" (N 292 = WG 113). Not a preferential love of their individual qualities, but a recognition of their individual reality.

Decreation frees one to love all creatures equally, oneself included (WG 111), but now one loves the stranger as oneself and oneself as stranger. This is a matter of expanding and transforming one's perspective by analogical transference to the point where reality is evenly distributed in the universe. "If I were to think of everything that is limited as limited, there would no longer be anything in my thoughts which emanated from the 'I'. God and creation would then be in contact via me" (N 483).

Creation is "out of nothing" (*ex nihilo*) and we ourselves are, inasmuch as created, made of nothing. The nothing of which we are made is a nothingness formed out of God's abdication, a void created where there was God alone. Our existence therefore takes place in the space of void, and only when we consent to be nothing ourselves do we fully consent to the nothing that God has become for us in creation. Only then can we truly love God. Since everything that exists has existence as the token of God's withdrawal and renunciation, the thinking creature who registers this must feel and acknowledge, "I am God's abdication" (FLN 213).

Consent to God's abdication is the motivating power of the movement of decreation. The advent of creation from nothingness is retraced and revisited in decreation: when the creature is decreated, a rendezvous of creator with creature takes place in the void. Since the Creator and the decreated each consent to "become nothing" for the other, that nothing, the void, is the venue of their rapprochement, the place of reconciliation, where the creature's consent to become nothing rejoins the same in God. "Whoever humbles himself exalts himself. This is because the point of nothingness is the one where I am able to place myself in relation to God" (N 620). This dialectic of nothingness establishes what might be called a reciprocal nihilism between God and creature. The movement of God toward creation is a self-abnegation, a renunciation of godly power and being; reciprocally, every movement of the creature toward God is a relinquishment of creaturely power and being, or a movement toward that original ground of creation that is pure *nihil*.

But this apparent reciprocity is in a deeper respect nonreciprocal, inasmuch as not only creation but also decreation is effected by God. Decreation is a work of supernatural grace, and as such cannot truly be thought of as our reciprocation toward God, but rather as God's self-reciprocation in us: "The basis of the supernatural is asymmetry, non-reciprocal relations—'non-abelian' relations" (FLN 194). We can decreate ourselves only by asking to be decreated by God through the action of grace; never can we do so as the effect of our own will, for the patent reason that it is precisely the will that must be decreated and cease willing altogether.

Because decreation converts us into something radically other than what we are by nature—that is, it detaches us from existence and reconciles us with "nothingness" or the void—Weil suggests that inspiration, grace, and truth have to be regarded as *alien* to us, and here she evokes the authority of Paul (N 248). A rigorous and total judgment is at work in this process: we must expiate our creatureliness. To do so is not a natural act. It is never a natural act to seek out death and *"self-amputation to the quick"* (N 138). Grace alone can effect such self-amputation, which is a descent away from our natural existence into the nothingness of our foundation as creatures. "Grace is the law of descending movement. An ascending movement is natural, a descending one supernatural" (N 308).

We must not struggle against moral gravity by means of action, which would be willful, but by means of thought (N 419) or nonactive action. Because "I have not the principle of rising in me," I must be drawn upward by the thought of a veritable perfection (N 434). As soon as grace introduces this "point of eternity in the soul," there is nothing for us to *do* but guard and preserve it; it increases of its own accord like a seed (N 626). Grace is a nonactive action on the part of God (N 586); the seed of divine love grows of itself, and when protected and nurtured it grows exponentially (WG 133–4). This is the ground of ultimate hope: that our will, the seat of sin, can be undone by an exponentially increasing grace. "My misery is infinite with respect to my will, but it is finite with respect to grace. Thus it can exhaust itself, and perfection is possible" (N 249). Hope consists in knowing that the evil in oneself is finite and that the slightest orientation of the soul toward good, even if it endures only an instant, does away with a bit of that evil, for in the spiritual domain "every particle of Good infallibly produces Good" (N 304).

But as the calling unto good grows in us, so does our consciousness of evil. Every contact with pure good deepens our recognition of the distance brought about by the evil in ourselves, giving rise to a painful effort of assimilation (N 324). Yet even that pain is a suffering induced by hope, for suffering over evil (one's distance from good) expresses a desire to overcome that distance—and we overcome it precisely by decreating ourselves, becoming nothing, desiring to become nothing. Misery, suffering, pain—these generate the void in us that provokes us to desire the good above ourselves. Suffering is the unique grace that makes us love the good as that which we are not and can never be. Suffering makes us keenly aware of the void—the absence and poverty—in us, preparing us to receive what can only come from outside. "Grace fills, but it can only enter where there is a void waiting to receive it, a void for whose creation it is itself responsible" (N 198). The void attracts grace (NR 265).

Ordinarily, by nature, we seek a reward for what we invest, we expect to receive the equivalent of what we have given; but the economy of grace is of another order: "If, doing violence to this need [for reward], powerful as gravity, we leave a void, there takes place as it were an inrush of air, and a supernatural reward supervenes. It does not come if we receive any other wages; it is this void that causes it to come" (N 135). It is then that we can truly forgive debts and accept the forgiveness of our debts because we no longer seek "satisfaction" from creatures, or recompense for wasted energy, or retribution for harm. From God alone do we expect to receive this energy in the void, in the form of grace, and no longer from any creature (N 181)—no longer from another or ourselves. "To remit debts is to remain halted in the present, to acquire the feeling of eternity. Then, indeed, sins are remitted" (N 212).

Nothingness: The Humility of God

The descent of God in creation is imitated inversely by us in decreation: "Creation and de-creation, like centrifugal and centripetal force" (N 275). Just as God consents to surrender his power of being for the sake of an absolute other, so do we surrender our small power of being—or rather our illusion of power—for love of the one who surrendered himself absolutely for another. When God descends, he creates, crucifying himself on the cross of the world; when we descend, we decreate, crucifying ourselves in the image of God. This reciprocity, a mutual consent to crucifixion, is a dialectical one because of the negative relationship that obtains between God and the world (see Chapters 1 and 3): the world is the embodiment of God's absence; its existence exiles the Creator into nothingness. When we consent to be decreated, detaching ourselves from the desire to exist, we go to meet God in the nothingness that is the primordial ground of this sacrifice. Decreation is not a reversal or undoing of creation, but is far rather the culmination and completion of the act of creation as a crucifixion.[3]

Only when it arrives at this nothingness is love purified and perfected, the reason being that only there is it perfectly free as love and love alone, an utterly naked love, having given up every possession and given itself away with no possibility of reclamation. Thus love becomes purely and absolutely itself, manifesting its divinity. Love casts itself into the abyss as though nothingness were its desire, although it is not nothingness per se that love desires, but absolute self-manifestation as love. There, where every possession and attachment to the power of being has been cast away, love enacts itself, fulfills itself, redeems itself in self-fulfilling tautologies: "God creates God, God knows God, God loves God—and God commands God, who obeys him" (FLN 130). Love inclines and precipitates itself into the humility of nothingness, a nothingness that is the humility of God.

Nothingness, the void, makes actual the ultimate expression of humility. God has chosen this expression from the foundation of the world. God is the "absolute master" of nothingness because God has created and chosen nothingness as the means of giving himself over to the world and delivering himself into absolute nakedness. For this reason, we must meet him there and nowhere else. We must decreate ourselves—exile ourselves from created being, return to the primordial *nihil*, descending into nothingness—in order to have contact with him: "[God] has emancipated us in view of the fact that he has created us [. . .]. Our consent alone can, with time, bring about an inverse operation and convert us into something inert, something analogous to nothingness, where God is absolute master" (NR 277). Creation and decreation are reciprocal forms of crucifixion, or voluntary entrance into nothingness.

It is this kenotic descent into nothingness—into the *nihil* that is the ground of creation—that demonstrates the divinity and perfection of God. For this reason, when we desire good, when we seek God, we must venture into nothingness to find him. We have to *empty God of his divinity* in order to love him (N 283). We empty God of "God" to find him in the nothingness that is his humility. The true God is not the one we think of as "God"; he is the one dwelling in the poverty of nothingness, the "Lamb slain from the beginning" (N 246). And so we are called to pass through death, the ultimate humiliation, to find the God who is love, just as God passed through death on the cross to find himself—the God who is love. Just as the God who is power forsook himself to find the God who is love, we must forsake both ourselves and "God" in order to find the God who dwells in nothingness.

> When God is present to the sensibility, this is still a form of attachment; that is why it is necessary to pass through "My God, why hast thou forsaken me?" Extreme affliction removes God from the sensibility, as it does all other objects of attachment. Life alone remains present to the sensibility. If we can then accept death, it is the fullness of acceptance of death; it is the fullness of detachment. (N 223)

We must look for the secret of our kinship with God in our mortality (N 235). Death is the doorway. Not a literal death, but a spiritual living death, "a life pure as death" (N 384). Total humility means consent to death, and the saints are those who have really consented to death while they were still alive (FLN 353, 234). The way is not to kill ourselves, since any such effort would be an act of our will and therefore the perpetuation of sin, or voluntary evil; rather, it is God acting through truth and beauty that slays us, and the will cooperates only by negating itself, by being willing to die, to be killed. "The human creature has not created itself, and it is not for it to destroy itself. It can only consent to the destruction of itself that is brought about by God. The only good use for the will with which we are endowed is a negative one" (N 404).

By consenting to its own negation the will exercises its only genuine freedom, for "it is supernatural love that is free" (N 466). Imagining that God offered us boundless joy, power, and glory, it would not be in our power to refuse these gifts: "He chooses his gifts in such a way that we are free to refuse them. It is in our power, it is easy, to refuse the cross" (FLN 178). When the will exercises its freedom in consenting to negation, it consents to death and simultaneously to truth, which is "on the side of death" (N 161). The acceptance of death as the truth, of truth as on the side of death, is simply the full acceptance by the intelligence of the ineluctable ultimacy of humility: "Humility consists in the knowledge that one is nothing in so far as one is a human being, and, more generally, in so far as one is a creature. The intelligence has a great part to play here [. . .]. A rational creature is one that contains within itself the germ, the principle, the vocation of de-creation" (N 275).

Suicide is an act of will, whereas decreation—in diametric contrast—is an act of supernatural love responding to grace. Suicide is condemned as an "ersatz form of de-creation" (N 262). We cannot effect this death of the Pauline "old man" ourselves (N 78–9); we have got to be killed as an effect of grace, not will. "We must die—not commit suicide, die, be killed, not literally, but nearly so, feel through the fact of external things the chill of death" (N 61). Suffering and affliction communicate this chill of death, which, if it were not pressed upon us by necessity, we would never actually face or undergo.

Affliction presents the most extreme revelation of the creature's abject humility, and as such it extends the opportunity to the soul to share in the absolute nakedness of God. The humiliation of affliction, if faced without consolation, suffered without illusion, humbles the soul as nothing else can possibly do.

> To attain complete detachment, the soul must really suffer the equivalent of what Job experienced, or Christ on the cross (which was a veritable cross, with nails the reverse of symbolic). Affliction is not enough; it must be an affliction without consolation [. . .]. (Ineffable consolation then descends.) (N 211) / In this state the soul is lacerated, nailed to the two poles of creation: inert matter and God. This laceration is a copy, within a finite soul, of God's creative act. Perhaps it is necessary to pass through that in order to emerge from creation and return to the origin. (FLN 328)

What is this "return to the origin" if not a return into the *nihil* out of which all things were created? And what is the *nihil* but the actual godlessness of God—the place of abdication where God is bereft of himself, abandoned by himself?

In her complex conception of the *nihil* Weil conflates two powerful theological ideas of nothingness. A nothingness like that in Luria's creation *ex nihilo* is conjoined with a nothingness like the "desert" in Meister Eckhart, which is the innermost ground of the soul's reunion with God.[4] For Weil, however, this complex nothingness is not predominantly defined by creation, as for Luria, or by incarnation, as for Eckhart, but by crucifixion, as for Reformation theology in general. For all Weil's deep parallels with Eckhart, the divergence of her thinking from his is crucial: in Weil, the nothingness of God is not the *precreative* aboriginal ground of the Trinity as it is for Eckhart, but rather the *postcreative* ground in God of the crucifixion. The nothingness of God is that rending void in God that contains and manifests the supreme plenitude of divinity (N 149). Never, therefore, does Weil's thinking back-pedal away from the crucifixion or aspire to return to the precreative unity of God.

Both Weil and Eckhart insist that the soul must become as "free of all things" as God is (*Eckhart*, 201); for Weil, however, that freedom is achieved not by going back behind creation to the God beyond God, but by going *into the crucifixion*, the space of separation of God from God that is creation itself. Weil's theology thus implies a total commitment to the creation of the world as an actualization and manifestation of the true divinity of God. An Eckhartian union with God "beyond" or "before" creation would not bring the soul to that God who emptied himself on the cross. It is the God who emptied himself, Weil insists repeatedly, whom we must love and relate ourselves to (N 208, 248–9, 283–4, 411, 539, 541–2), not the precreative God who is an all-powerful ground and origin. Only when God abdicates the power and freedom he possesses as the precreative "God beyond God" does he fully realize himself as the God who is absolute love: the Crucified God. It is the cross of the world that renders God fully and truly God.

Heaven and Hell

As we have seen (Chapter 4), there are two nothingnesses for Weil—the nothingness of "heaven" and the nothingness of "hell"—and these two nothingnesses are the same nothingness of God differently regarded, or obversely valued, by the soul. "Heaven" is the nothingness of God consented to, whereas "hell" is that same nothingness refused. Both good and evil end in nothingness, but evil travels into nothingness by striving toward and imitating the power of God (which it can do only in illusion, not in reality), whereas good strives toward and imitates the love of God, which it can do in full reality by emptying itself.

> The soul's only choice is between travelling towards nothingness through more and more good or through more and more evil. The limit of both good and evil is nothingness. But it is not a matter of indifference whether one arrives at nothingness through good or through evil. On the contrary, it is the only thing that matters and everything else is indifferent. (FLN 310)

Everything else is indifferent; this "choice" governed by grace alone matters. All value in human existence is balanced on the question of whether one travels into the void saying *yes* or saying *no*. This is because it is precisely by saying *yes* with our faculty of consent that we share in transcendent value; our *yes* per se is our real participation in that value. To say *no* to the void is to cling to nontranscendent value on the way to a truly empty nothingness, a nothingness absolutely bereft of good, a "hell" of our own choosing.

Nothingness is our destiny as mortal creatures, we have no other. We must travel into nothingness, there is no alternative. But we do have the alternative in death of either merging into the nothingness of God or merging into a nothingness that is void of God. When we travel toward nothingness through increasing good, we are traveling toward the nothingness of God, for God's nothingness is the absoluteness of value (pure good) as it transcends existence; it is the fullness of being: "The fullness of being is identical with nothingness for the purposes of abstract thought; but not so when one is fleeing nothingness, and directing one's steps toward being. There is the nothingness from which we flee and the nothingness toward which we go" (N 232). Hence the need for *metaxu* to mediate the idea of transcendent good, of plenitude in the void, which prevents us from seizing hold of nothingness instead of full being (N 233).

Abstract thought cannot conceive the crucial difference between these two destinies—between disappearing into the absence of God versus disappearing into the presence of God—even though this difference is "the only thing that matters," to the point that it is "the only thing of unconditional importance" (FLN 310). Elaborate representations of heaven and hell (imaginative images, symbols, parables, and the like) have been needed to provide approximations of this difference that the imagination can grasp (FLN 142). But ultimately the two nothingnesses, heaven and hell, are the very same nothingness: heaven is the nothingness of God consented to and desired; hell is the nothingness of God refused, opposed by the will.

It is because God, the good, absolutely transcends worldly existence that God is necessarily a nothingness to the creature, and hence "negation is the passage into the eternal" (FLN 125). Hell is the nothingness of God met without love, without consent; it is an attachment of the will to its own condition of radical poverty, vacuousness, lovelessness, a refusal to transcend, an abject and irremediable rootedness in self-will. Souls who refuse consent because of their attachment to themselves and this world "just simply disappear," in a state of either intense suffering or unconsciousness, and this disappearance constitutes the infinite evil of "eternal death" represented by the notion of hell (N 468). "The perfect, infinite and eternal joy of God—it is this very thing that burns the lost soul. This joy is offered to the soul, but is declined by it, and this refusal constitutes hell [. . .]. Thus the souls of the damned are in Paradise, but for them Paradise is hell" (N 469).

The creature who continues to love purely in the void, on the other hand, desires the nothingness of God as a fulfillment greater than life, as a good beyond life and death, and is therein saved, for life itself is an ersatz form of salvation (N 269). Salvation is an unconditional consent to death, a *yes* in the soul consenting to dissolve into the transcendent nothingness of God. Weil thought it detrimental for us to attempt to picture a life after death, since belief in immortality tends to allay the pure bitterness and reality of death (N 468, 271), and our ignorance allows the imagination utter license when we think about it (FLN 177).

But eternal life *can* legitimately be visualized by us as "an annihilation that is light," wherein the infinite, eternal, and perfect joy of God enters into the finite soul and causes it to explode, to burst like a bubble (N 468). From our point of view, there is no difference between annihilation and eternal life, except light. If our joy is in God, not in ourselves, our annihilation into God is nothing else but eternal life; conversely, if our joy is in ourselves, not in God, our annihilation apart from God is none other than eternal death. Because hell is a final separation or alienation from God, only God could make such a self-absence or alienation possible, by his withdrawal. In this sense, the creation of the world was the act that founded a "Hell" as Weil uses the term (N 321), for creation is the advent of a reality that subsists by virtue of separation from God.

We have addressed the ambiguity of death (Chapter 2): death is the destiny of the limited being, but also the annihilation of the limited being (N 10). We long to be liberated from our limits as finite creatures, but as long as we seek to do so with a creaturely will and perspective, we willfully forestall the very possibility of such liberation. "I cannot bear to be less than God, but in that case I have got to be nothing; for all that I am is infinitely less than God. If I take away from myself all that I am, there remains. . ." (N 120, ellipsis in original). Paradoxically, letting go of the desire to possess all and to "be God" is the only way to fulfill that very desire. We have to "become universal" in order to be liberated from our creaturely limitation: "This irreducible 'I', which is the irreducible foundation of my suffering, must be made universal" (N 293).

We do this by passing through what might be called "death by love." We enter that which lies outside us by means of this death. We become other than ourselves, the purity of love detached from existence. We become God's own love for *what is* when "the divine values" pass into our soul:

> To implore a man is a desperate attempt to cause, by sheer intensity, one's own system of values to pass into the mind of

the other person. To implore God is the reverse; it is an attempt
to cause the divine values to pass into one's own soul. Far from
thinking with all the intensity of which one is capable on the
values to which one is attached, we have here an interior void.
One desires to become other than one is; one is thus turned
toward the outside. (N 188)

To be released from ourselves through this purification by void, this
death of the soul, is our one true freedom. We find God by having our
will to exist wrenched away, thus decreating our created nature. This
entails a consent to being nothing. "I have to love my nothingness,
love to be nothingness; to love with that part of the soul that lies on
the other side of the curtain" (N 262).[5]

But the part of the soul that is perceptible to consciousness is
unable to love nothingness and has a horror of it, which is why
acceptance of a void in oneself is a supernatural thing (N 135). The
violence of the void is indispensable for this entry into death; the final
detachment cannot occur without a wrenching imposed on the will
from outside. "There must first of all be a tearing asunder, something
of a desperate nature, so that a void may first of all be produced—
Void: dark night—" (N 135). When the laceration point is reached
and the void is produced, it registers on the soul as a total death, a
pure negation, an annihilating hell. "There is a period when the soul
is already detached from the world without being yet able to attach
itself to God: void, terrible anguish, dark night" (N 215). This night
is the moment of ultimate abandonment in which the soul discovers
that there is no God, no salvation, no hope, no life. There is only
death. Death is the truth. Everything that is, is crucifixion.

Yet by virtue of God's having passed into nothingness, God is
present in nothingness. This remains hidden from all except those
who pass to the other side themselves, traveling the dark night to its
ultimate conclusion. "The void is the supreme plenitude, but man has
not the right to know this. The proof lies in the fact that Christ himself,
for an instant, was completely without knowledge of it" (N 149). Such
trial by void effects a total detachment: not a literal but a spiritual
death. A literal death for this or that cause is not the same thing, and

may in fact be a debasement; indeed, it was easier to be faithful to Napoleon than to Christ, Weil asserts, because to die for Napoleon was to die for *something*, for a palpable and even "rational" cause, but to be faithful unto death for Christ is to be faithful in the void and to die for "nothing" (N 148). And yet this "nothing" makes all the difference; it is the only thing of unconditional importance (FLN 310).

This ultimate struggle has affinities with what Kierkegaard, in *Fear and Trembling*, calls the spiritual trial (*Anfoegtelse*), referring to the paradigmatic testing of the faith of Abraham, who is wholly isolated and alone with the psychic tensions of obeying the dreadful command of God to sacrifice Isaac: "What could be more complete as regards void?" (N 137). Both thinkers are concerned with an interior tension so authentically "spiritual" that it has no point of relief or support in any exterior correlate: *"Void, when there is nothing external to correspond to an internal tension"* (N 147). Confrontation with the void is not an outwardly visible struggle but an interior uprooting and transformation: the soul consents to be delivered into the nothingness in which God is absolute master and grace takes command. *"To know (in each thing) that there is a limit, and that one will not pass beyond it without supernatural aid* [...]. One has to go by oneself up to that limit. There one touches the void. ('God helps those who help themselves')" (N 136). We must not seek the void, but once we find ourselves in the void, we must seek that form of transference that transports us "outside space" (N 637). We must consent to the relinquishment of the I's appropriation; to have nothing, be nothing, and live by grace instead of will. Grace gives knowledge that all is essentially gift, nothing possession:

> Humility consists in knowing that in what we call "I" there is no source of energy by which we can rise [...]. Everything that is valuable in me, without exception, comes from somewhere outside myself, not as a gift but as a loan that has to be continually renewed. Everything that is in me, without exception, is absolutely valueless. Among the gifts that have come to me from elsewhere, everything that I appropriate to myself becomes immediately valueless. (N 180)

If God empties himself, who are we to possess?—we, who are formed out of nothing, granted existence, granted a will, and granted the freedom to renounce our will? We who are pure gift, originators of nothing? Destruction of the will is the dissolution of the appropriating "I" that takes possession of what is freely given rather than allowing it to abide as gift. The will is the center of possessiveness, and its energy is a vegetative, natural, gravitational energy. Expiatory and redemptive suffering together uproot the vegetative energy of the will, setting into motion a decreative process that "ransoms creation while unmaking it" (N 255). For decreation encompasses both expiatory and redemptive suffering: the former effects the negation of the will; the latter the crucifying contact with the void as the nothingness of God (N 342). Weil asserts that decreation is contrary to nature (N 276) precisely because apart from grace this counter-gravitational transformation is inexplicable: what creature would *willingly* unmake itself? This "will" comes from outside our will and converts our will to consent to it.

This descent into nothingness, a death on our part, is what Weil symbolizes as *resurrection:* "Resurrection. When we have felt the chill of death—unless we make haste to forget it, or it leaves us numbed—we pass on beyond, and this universe itself becomes a draught of immortality" (N 61). To undergo this dissolution of the will is to traverse death and to pass "beyond" while nonetheless remaining a part of the universe. Our decreation, which is our participation in the crucifixion of God, is at the same time our resurrection in God, for our vocation in this life is "to be like God, but God crucified" (N 213).

Transparency

Decreation effects detachment from every possession, every kind of having, and most comprehensively the "having" of existence, which is the very root of our wretchedness. "Being does not belong to man, only having. The being of man is situated behind the curtain, on the supernatural side [...]. The curtain is human misery: there was a curtain even for Christ" (N 127–8 = GG 38). The total detachment that is the effect of redemptive suffering delivers us from created existence as ourselves, as a creature that says "I," into a transcendent identity, the "I" of God, which is *all*; it is not an "I" (N 126). Through decreation we are freed to be other than ourselves—in effect, to be nothing other than God: "My 'I' is hidden for me (and for others); it is on the side of God, it is in God, it is God. To be proud is to forget that one is God" (N 127–8 = GG 38). To be thus equal to God, one has only to be without free will (FLN 236).

We dread and fear the tearing of the curtain that separates us from God, since our own death and dissolution is the only way across to this transcendent realization. It is not our existence in the flesh per se that forms the curtain but our manner of "having" the flesh. By nature we possess our flesh with a creaturely will, not as God does, who sustains our flesh with pure love and pure detachment at once, across a chasm of renunciation. We know that we cannot see God face-to-face without dying, and we do not want to die: "The flesh is not what keeps us away from God; it is the veil we place before us to screen ourselves from him" (N 623). God uses necessity as a veil to make our existence possible (N 402); we, from our side, cling to the veil of necessity, not realizing that it is not the veil that is desirable, but the good that lies behind the veil. In fact, what lies behind the veil is the only thing that is good, and apart from that ultimate good the veil is only a veil, concealing—revealing—an empty valuelessness.

Decreation dissolves the veil. It does so by dissolving not the flesh but the "having" of the flesh, which is a usurpation by the creaturely will or the "I." It is by saying "I" that we take possession of our creaturely will, and that possession itself is the "having" of the flesh.[6] Only decreation dissolves this "having" and makes us perfect as the heavenly Father is perfect, freeing us to love impartially in the way the sun sheds its light. "We must gather up our love in ourselves in order to spread it over all things. God alone loves all things, and he only loves himself" (N 206). It is not for us to love God, but for God to love himself through us as medium (N 363). Decreation converts the soul into a transparent pane that mediates and refracts God's love for God. "God only loves himself. He loves us—this only means that he desires, with our co-operation, to love himself through us" (N 280, 193, 613–4).

God is in silent dialogue with God, a dialogue of loving regard, and we are privileged by our intelligence to be caught in the middle, overhearing all. Our vocation is to be the decreated locus of God's regard for God: "The dogma of the Trinity is necessary so that there may not be dialogue between us and God, but between God and himself within us. So that we may be absent" (FLN 96). Weil maintains that love of self is the only love—because pure love by definition loves only love, which is itself. Because only God is absolute love, only God can love himself absolutely (WG 133). This means that there is no perfect love open to us, being radically less than God, other than to pray to become transparent so that God may love himself through us (N 193). "God is always absent from our love, as he is from the world; but he is secretly present in pure love [...]. The heavenly Father dwells only in secret" (FLN 275).

When our "I" ceases to exist, we remove the obstacle of ourselves and become the venue of exchange between God and God; even our prayer occurs without action on our part, though it takes place in us.[7] "We should pray εν τω κρυφαιω ["in secret," Matt. 6:18] even with regard to ourselves. It is not my 'I' that prays. If a prayer takes place within me, I must hardly be aware of it. I have no other Father than He εν τω κρυφαιω" (N 173). Once the "I" is eliminated, our body continues to exist in the world, but now it has become a lens refracting a universal love that we receive and communicate transparently, without blocking or distorting its path. We must become nothing not because it is good for *us*, but because it negates everything in us that stands in the way of a universal love and compassion: "For glass, there is nothing better than absolute transparency. For a human being there is nothing more than to be nothingness. Every value in a human being is really a negative value" (FLN 354).

This total detachment from the flesh while the flesh remains, this dissolution of the creaturely will while the creature remains, is what it means to cast off the flesh and become "spirit," for the spirit constitutes the "I" of the perfect human being, it is the decreated "I" (N 264): "By means of the disappearance of the individual 'I' the love of God for God passes through the soul of a man like the light through a piece of glass. That is what is meant by the presence of the Holy Spirit in the soul" (N 344). Decreation produces the effect that we no longer exist, but rather the spirit of God in us, making us into a vessel for descending grace, translating us into a reality unconditioned by the attachments of existence.

> St. John does not say: we shall be happy because we see God; but: we shall be like God, because we shall see Him as he is. We shall be pure good. We shall no longer exist. But in that nothingness which is at the limit of good we shall be more real than at any moment of our earthly life. Whereas the nothingness that is at the limit of evil is without reality. Reality and existence are two things, not one. (FLN 311)

Decreation of the soul is not the completion of our earthly task. On the contrary, our true earthly task only begins in earnest with decreation. Only now are we able to love creatures as God loves them. Only now, through our own virtual death, can we actually embody truth in the world—that truth which is on the side of death. Our vocation while on earth is not to *see* God but to *be* God by letting God take our place in the world and living out pure love for the world through obedience. "We must not desire to die in order that we may see God face to face, but to live while ceasing to exist in order that in a self which is no longer one's own self, God and his creation may find themselves face to face" (N 464, see 358). We are no longer there, God now occupies the space where we once stood and suffered as a will that says "I." It is now God who says "I" in us, who suffers to act in us, and we have nothing of our own to say or do. Decreation culminates in the perfection of obedience (WG 130), which is our docility to the spirit of God, our transparence as a medium of action.

Until we are decreated, we do active harm by blocking the communication of God's love directly to the world, like an unwelcome third party on a date:

> I am not the girl who is waiting for her lover, but the tiresome third party who is sitting with two lovers and has got to get up

and go away if they are to be really together [. . .]. My presence does infinite harm to those whom I love by maintaining in position the screen that I form between them and God, who loves to touch them, not only from the inside, through inspiration, but also from the outside, by means of the human beings who meet them on their way. (N 404)

The presence of the "I" does literally *infinite* harm inasmuch as it throws up a screen, a barrier to the grace of God's *infinite* love for finite things as such (N 482); whereas the withdrawal and disappearance of the "I" permits the infinitude of love to pass through, allowing God to have contact immediately with the world (N 378–9). For not only does God love himself by way of his creatures, but it is by way of his creatures that he loves creation (N 333). This makes our decreated existence an "indispensable intermediary" between God and the world, and if we refuse this role, we continue to form "part of the matter of the universe, through gravity" (N 207).

When the "I" disappears, it becomes an empty space through which God and creation contemplate one another (FLN 269): "If only I could manage to disappear, there would take place a perfect love union between God and the earth that I tread, the sea that I hear. . ." (N 403). Weil ponders whether it is necessary that the entire universe be our body for our perspective to become perfectly impartial (N 13, 60), so that we fully and perfectly attend to what God loves, that is, the entirety of the world, the incarnation. "Even though I die, the universe continues. That does not console me if I am anything other than the universe. If, however, the universe is, as it were, another body to my soul, my death ceases to have any more importance for me than that of a stranger. The same is true of my sufferings" (N 19).

To become universal is to see and identify with the value evenly distributed unto all things as loved by God—and, paradoxically, that value *is* itself the love of God present in all things. It is not the case that God loves all things in the universe because of their intrinsic value; rather, the things have value because God loves them to the extent of causing them to exist in his place, obliging him to be absent. To love with universal love is to love with the "transcendental 'I'" (N 251, 308): "It is a different being that has been engendered by God, a different 'I', which is hardly 'I', because it is the Son of God" (FLN 288). Thereafter the soul does not love like a creature with created love; rather, the love within it is divine, uncreated: it is the love of God for God that is passing through it (WG 133). Only a soul that has been killed, knowingly or not, by the love of God can really pay attention to the affliction of the afflicted (FLN 328). Then we do not go to the help of a neighbor *for* Christ but *through* Christ; we let the "I" disappear in such a way that Christ himself goes to the help of the neighbor via the intermediary formed by our body and soul (N 358).

One who has passed through this decreative conversion has a deeper love than ever for all that suffers the vicissitudes of finitude, including abandonment and affliction, but love in this case has become "a movement of God himself, a ray merged in the light of God" (WG 209).

> Our love should stretch as widely across all space, and should be as equally distributed in every portion of it, as is the very light of the sun [...]. Every existing thing is equally upheld in its existence by God's creative love. The friends of God should love him to the point of merging their love into his with regard to all things here below. (WG 97)

Such love has an anonymous and impersonal quality that is due to its universality. God loves not as we love, not as a person loves, but "as an emerald is green" (FLN 129). God is neither personal, as we are, nor impersonal, as a thing is, but is both at once in a higher transcendent sense (N 254, 173–4, 275, 126, WG 200). Perhaps though, Weil speculates, there is need to have a personal relationship with an impersonal God (N 173). The beauty of the world, she avers, proves that there is a God who is at the same time personal and impersonal—neither merely the one nor the other—and every perfect work of art has something essentially anonymous about it inasmuch as it imitates this anonymity of divine art (N 241): "Every time that a

man rises to a degree of excellence, which by participation makes
of him a divine being, we are aware of something impersonal and
anonymous about him" (WG 179). This is evident in all the
great works of art and thought, in the great deeds of saints and in
their words.

Given that the "I" of the personal will fades away in proportion as
a human being emulates God's impersonality, the image of a personal
God is a hindrance to such imitation (N 241, 174). This is a crucial
point at which atheism is a purification: one loves purely when one
loves anonymously and universally, not when one loves in the name
and image of a personal God. "One of the most exquisite pleasures of
human love—to serve the loved one without his knowing it—is only
possible, as regards the love of God, through atheism" (FLN 84). And
yet, ultimately, once our love is rendered sufficiently impersonal,
there is need to reclaim the personal dimension of God now
understood in a higher sense (WG 200). Weil affirms, just as my
wretchedness makes it so that I am "I," the wretchedness of the
universe makes it so that, *"in a sense*, God is 'I' (i.e. a person)" (N 126).
For the impersonal love of God suffers in particularity, suffers in *this*
and *that* condition, just as a person suffers.

Compassion

It is because of the impersonality and universality of God's love that,
paradoxically, he is able to be wholly present to personal suffering,
qua personal, as no mere person can be. "Only God, present in us, can
really think the human quality into the victims of affliction." Hence,
for God to be present in our love of neighbor, we have to bring a
personal love to the afflicted in their "inert, anonymous condition"
(WG 150, 151). Just as God loves finite things with an infinite love,
so God loves persons with a love that is impersonal in its *terminus a
quo* but personal, concrete, and individual in its *terminus ad quem*.

We deserve not only to be preferred but to be loved uniquely,
exclusively. But the thing in us which deserves that is the
uncreated part to the soul, which is identical with the Son of

God. When the self that is a composite of attributes has been destroyed and the uncreated part emerges, then "I no longer live in myself, but Christ lives in me" [. . .]. It is an impersonal love. (FLN 283)

Decreation of our "personality," our human personhood (*la personne*), is what makes it possible for us to imitate this impersonal *a quo* love of the person *ad quem*. Then it is not *we* who love the afflicted in God; it is God in us who loves them. "The sufferer and the other love each other, starting from God, through God, but not for the love of God; they love each other for the love of the one for the other" (WG 151). To love fellow human beings truly is to love them as God loves them, that is to say, "insofar as they are nothing" (FLN 77), having compassion for the wretchedness of their creatureliness as such. The love of God, which causes us to exist as nothing, infinitely distant from the good, also gives us the unique motive to love ourselves *although we are nothing*: "It is not because God loves us that we should love him. It is because God loves us that we should love ourselves. How could one love oneself without this motive?" (N 278). We have no intrinsic value but that God loves us, and we know that because we exist.

But until or unless we "see God" through some sort of direct mystical contact, authentic love of God is *realized* (made real) only through the medium of our love of creatures. Weil writes: "'Love God.' This can only mean the order of the world and one's neighbor, because, until he has come down and shown himself, we do not see God" (FLN 81). Just as the faith of a judge is seen not in her behavior at church, but in her behavior on the bench, so the soul's love of God shows up in that part of its behavior that is turned toward fellow creatures (FLN 146). To love God genuinely is to love what God loves, to love what God actually wills (which is why *amor fati* itself *is* love of God); it is not to love an abstract idea of God conceived apart from creatures. Weil goes so far as to affirm that love of neighbor as such *is* the anonymous love of God: "Whosoever loves his neighbour as himself, even if he denies the existence of God, loves God" (N 280).

Here we arrive at the crux of Weil's moral or ethical thinking. Like her aesthetic, which takes God as its starting point, all genuine ethics are fundamentally theological, which is to say, have a supernatural character (N 277). All love of God proves its authenticity by expressing itself as a pure love for creatures; conversely, all love of creatures, when pure, is a mediation to creatures of the love of the "anonymous" God. Weil reconciles the traditional contrast and apparent contradiction between love of God and love of creatures by insisting that it is one and the same movement of the heart:

> Praise to God and compassion for creatures. It is the same movement of the heart. But how is this possible, since the two are in obvious contradiction? To thank God because of his great glory, and to have pity for creatures because of their wretchedness. (FLN 102) / Supernatural love only touches creatures and is only directed toward God. He only loves creatures—what else have we to love but Him?—but he loves them as intermediaries. As intermediaries, he loves all creatures equally, oneself included [. . .]. The essence of created things is to be intermediaries. (N 496)

Although this passage seems to imply that created things are mere intermediaries between the love of God for God, elsewhere Weil can be found accenting the love of creatures as the *final* criterion and goal of our love for God. To wit: "The love of God is only an intermediary between the natural and the supernatural love of creatures" (FLN 144). To resolve this apparent equivocation on Weil's part it is necessary to recognize the genuine coincidence of the two-in-one movement of the mind and heart. Neither the one (love directed to creatures) nor the other (love directed to God) may be viewed as the uniquely decisive end apart from the other. Each movement of love is thoroughly imbued with the other. We must not prefer one movement over the other; rather we must unite them in the way we love, so that our love of creatures is purified by our love of God, and our love of God is held to its earthly criterion in the love of creatures. Pure love for creatures is not love for the "sake" of God, but love that

has "passed through God as through a fire" (N 616): it redescends from
God, purified and linked with the original generative love of God.

If to love oneself truly is to know that one is nothing and to love
being nothing in the image of the crucified God, then to love other
people truly is to love them as illusions for themselves of being
something—and this is the height of compassion and attention to the
other, according to Weil. Illusion qua illusion is real, and when we
love others in their full reality, we have compassion for their illusion,
which is part and parcel of their creaturely existence. "Other people
are illusions of existence for themselves. This way of regarding them
makes their existence not less but more real for me. For I see them as
they are related to themselves, and not to me" (FLN 97).

Decreation, by removing attachments of the will, simultaneously
removes the sole obstacle to compassion. Curiously, Weil speaks of
compassion as actually "natural" to human beings as soon as the
obstacle of the "I" is removed: "It is not compassion that is
supernatural, but the removal of that obstacle" (FLN 210, 318). The
fact that supernatural love for one's neighbor is even possible in itself
constitutes an experimental proof of the reality and goodness of God
(N 281). Compassion, as Weil defines it, is a conjunction of passible
and impassible, temporal and eternal elements. In order to feel
compassion for someone in affliction, she writes, the soul has to be
divided in two: "One part absolutely removed from all contamination
and all danger of contamination. The other part contaminated to the
point of identification. This tension is passion, compassion. The
Passion of Christ is this phenomenon in God" (FLN 97).

Finally all compassion for sufferers, including self-compassion for
one's own suffering, is in the image of the silent compassion of the
Father for the Son. Just as the only love is love's self-love, so the only
compassion is self-compassion: the compassion one feels for the afflicted
is identical to the compassion felt, in affliction, by the impassible part
of one's own soul for the part of it that suffers (FLN 94). The New
Testament commandment that we love our neighbor as ourselves
presupposes that we first love ourselves purely and rightly: that is,
as God loves us. All forms of love and compassion are supernatural
gifts descending from the impassible God into the kenotic passion

of God; so whenever we extend compassion to an afflicted stranger we imitate God's descending movement into suffering:

> God is he who bends over us, afflicted as we are, and reduced to the state of being nothing but a fragment of inert and bleeding flesh. Yet at the same time he is in some sort the victim of misfortune as well, the victim who appears to us as an inanimate body, incapable of thought, this nameless victim of whom nothing is known. The inanimate body is this created universe. The love we owe to God, this love that would be our crowning perfection if we were able to attain to it, is the divine model of both gratitude and compassion. (WG 214)

Compassion is much more than an imitation of God; it is itself an *act* of God, for God acts in us through the grace of compassion. The compassion of one human being for another participates sacramentally in the divine acts of sacrifice and redemption which, as we have seen (Chapter 3), coincide. Christ has redeemed the world to the extent to which such a thing can be done by a single man if he is the equal of God, and to that extent only; redemption is continued in all those who, either before or after his birth, have imitated Christ (N 383, 343). If God is present in the full extremity of evil through redemptive suffering, this maximal presence is not possible except through human cooperation, for "it depends on man that God should be able to traverse creation from end to end and pass to the furthest extremity, which is the extremity of evil" (N 343). Although God is negatively present to all of creation qua Father–Creator, and positively present in creation qua incarnate Son, his presence in creation qua Holy Spirit depends entirely on human decreative cooperation. Thus every movement of pure compassion in a human soul is a new descent of Christ upon earth to be crucified (FLN 97).

Action as Incarnation

Through decreation, energy that has served gravity is liberated for love, and every action taken is undertaken in obedience to God, for "with respect to God, love is no different from *obedience*" (N 265). In this way, energy that was formerly tied up in our will is liberated for use by our "transcendental I," which is essentially (though secretly) God in us. This is now a free energy capable of embracing the true relationships between things. Full attention is the key to this liberation: an attention "so full that the 'I' disappears—is required of me" (N 178–9). The energy that the transcendental "I" disposes is not its own species of energy, but rather a capability of regrading energy through the attention (N 251), refusing energy to gravity and converting it to the service of grace. This conversion process, although it entails a painful destruction of the "I," is essentially felicitous because the liberation and redirection of energy realizes a transcendent joy (N 378): "Pain liberates energy, and the utilization of this energy is joy" (N 558).

Having traversed death in order to reach God, the saint should "incarnate himself in his own body" in order to broadcast in the world, in daily life, the reflection of supernatural light (SNL 112). We approve God's creative abdication by showing that we are glad to be a creature, "a secondary cause, with the right to perform actions in this world," which is our one point of superiority over God (FLN 312). As we have observed already, God cannot feed the hungry, but we can. This is the unique privilege of an incarnate thinking being: once decreated, such a being can act not *for* God—since God must not be put in the dative (N 358, 625)—but *by* God. That is, one can act in God's place as a real and effective mediator of divine love and compassion where the Father, withdrawn from the world, is helpless to act. This makes sanctity a transmutation like the Eucharist (FLN 96) inasmuch as saintly action *incarnates* God in the world.

The decreated soul is not called to withdraw from the world and retire into God, but is "attracted from heaven down to earth not by gravity but by love, by wings raised to the second power" (N 323). This is a question of imitating God the Father in his abdication and descent, of which the complete fulfillment is the incarnation (FLN 154). True love of one's neighbor is an assimilation to this divine love that descends; even better than to love one's neighbor as oneself, Weil writes, is to love *all* creatures inclusively (N 284). In imitation of the descent of God, the soul descends in compassion toward all that is ruled by gravity, entrapped in the grip of evil. Being a free and voluntary descent into existence, this descent is governed by grace rather than gravity:

> For a man there is no other reality but that of earthly existence. Man ought to have come down, not from the sky where reside the gods, but from the world that lies on the other side of the sky, and by a movement in which gravitational force plays no part. Gravity makes us descend; wings make us rise; what wings raised to the second power can make us descend without gravity? (N 384)

When we descend on "wings raised to the second power" and undertake to act always in obedience to anonymous love, our actions make of us a living sacrifice, an incarnation of the spirit of God. Just as every movement of pure compassion in a soul is a new descent of Christ upon earth to be crucified (FLN 97), so every act of pure obedience is a new descent of God into nothingness, an act of generosity for love of another who is infinitely distant from himself, and yet himself. "How is it possible that the feeling should arise in a human soul that God desires a certain particular thing? It is a marvel as miraculous as the Incarnation. Or rather, it is itself the marvel of the Incarnation" (FLN 150). Even though we may be mistaken about God's will in particular circumstances, we can regard it as certain that God wishes us to do everything we believe to be in conformity with his will, according to Weil: "St. Francis thought he had received the order to carry stones to St. Damian, and while he was under this illusion, God wanted him to carry stones" (FLN 150).

This marvel consists in the presence of the "unconditioned in the conditioned," the unmoved causing movement in a certain direction, and this is the "nonactive action" that Weil so deeply embraced in the *Bhagavad Gita* and other spiritual traditions; that is, "acting not on behalf of a certain object, but as a result of a certain necessity" (N 124).[8] An effort without any particular end attached to it is an acceptance of the void, an acceptance of death; such efforts alone are pure, but they are humanly impossible: "We must renounce the energy that impulsions provide us with. Not only that, but we must expend energy directed against them. We then need an energy that comes from elsewhere" (N 202). Without this marvel we are entirely earthly beings, ruled by gravity; thus the great majority who have never experienced this marvel in themselves are "completely earthly beings" (FLN 150–1). Obedience is the only perfectly pure motive, the only one that does not in the slightest degree seek a reward (N 150), and therefore operates free of all gravity. A soul perpetually ruled by this obedience from birth to death is God become man, enacting unto perfection the movement of divine incarnation (FLN 150).

The obedience that incarnates God in the world is a marvel because it responds to particular conditions and needs but in total absence of particular incentives, for all particular incentives are errors, and only energy that is not derived from any incentive is good (N 237). Obedience to God, which makes God the unique object of all the soul's desire, in fact means obeying an unknowable object, for "I do not know what God's command will be tomorrow" (FLN 136). So to act is like obeying "nothing," Weil posits, for the good is a nothingness, and a just action effects an obedience to a good that is so transcendent as to be a "nothingness" from the point of view of existence: "Obedience to God, that is to say, [. . .] to nothing. This is at the same time impossible and necessary—in other words it is supernatural" (N 237).

The presence in our soul of this "nothingness"—transcendent good—actually weights the values by which we act, impelling us to obey more or less automatically, just as does the *pondus amoris* of Augustine (*Confessions* 13.9). In effect, thereby, this "nothingness" has a real and demonstrable impact in the world:

> Our soul is a pair of scales. The direction of the energy in our actions is the pointer of the scales, marking such and such a figure. But the scales are false. When God, the true God, occupies all the place due to him in a soul, then the scales have become true. God does not say what figure the pointer should show, but because He is there, the pointer is accurate.

(FLN 151) / Action is the pointer of the balance. One must not
touch the pointer, but the weights. (N 294, see 418)

If any adjustment is called for, the change must be made in our
relationship to the good, in the weighting of our love, not directly to
our course of action per se. If we are in right relationship to the good,
our action will be just as a result of the fact that "the absolutely
obedient soul is in a perfect order" (N 242). God is not the figure
marked by the pointer, but that by which the pointer marks accurate
figures; God is not what is manifested by the Word, but that by
which the Word is manifested; God is the *subject* of the act of love, not
the effect or the object (FLN 151). "One does not testify so well for
God by speaking about Him as by expressing, either in actions or
words, the new aspect assumed by the creation after the soul has
experienced the Creator" (FLN 144)—that is, the kenotic Creator
stripped of divinity. To die for God is not a proof of faith in God,
but to die for an "unknown and repulsive convict who is a victim of
injustice"—that is a proof of faith in God (FLN 144). In the former
case, one may be dying for an idolatrous illusion; in the latter case,
one is dying for what cannot possibly *appear* to have ultimate value,
thus the authentic universality of one's love is tested. In the case
of universal love, the weights of the balance register infinite value
wherever good or desire for good is hiddenly or virtually present,
whereas human partiality—which continually expresses preferential
"taste" and gravitates toward prestige—actively opposes this.

The crucial practical problem for Weil's ethics, centered on the
"earthly criterion," is the transposition of motives. Her problem is
"how to transfer to the high motives the energy contained in the low
ones?" (N 122). Any task completed in a certain way may become an
exercise for strengthening one's patience and capacity for obedience.
Weil regards this as a problem of "human mechanics," involving
issues of compensation and transference of suffering. Rather than
supplying elevated objectives for what are essentially low tendencies
(for example, the desire to excel over other people), one should seek to
attach elevated tendencies to low objectives (N 123), such as
persisting in one's effort to solve a difficult mathematical problem

with a view to the love of God (N 445, 449, 597); this is the focus of her essay, "Reflections on the Right Use of School Studies with a View to the Love of God" (WG 105–16).

In the practice of such transpositions of energy, action itself may help to generate or increase a motive. The energy we invest in helping or praying for others actually increases the rationale and precedent to invest more: "We must love our enemies, because they exist. We must [. . .] do them good *in order to* love them" (N 267). Virtuous action in a sense "creates" the transcendent here below by incarnating it; virtue then becomes in every respect analogous to artistic creation: "That poem is good which one writes while keeping the attention orientated toward the inexpressible, *qua* inexpressible" (N 417). Weil notes the analogousness between habit and grace when the latter is understood in the physical sense of the word as bodily or aesthetic grace (N 171); there is need to make a disciplined outward habit of virtue in order to incarnate "grace" in action. For "God allows us to convey our love towards him in two ways, through beauty or in the void" (FLN 139), and here the primary form of beauty she has in mind is that of the just person, the saint, the divinely inspired genius.

Yet Weil is a realist concerning action in a world in which good and evil everywhere condition one another. Action must contend with the double-sidedness of mixed good-and-evil. One part of obedience is *acceptance of gravity* in the guise of necessity, another part is *responsivity to grace* by way of "nonactive" action. She distinguishes three realms or domains of obedience (N 259): (1) The domain of that which does not in any way depend on us. Here we should love all things absolutely, as a whole and in detail, as love becomes transcendent when one reads the object loved through and beyond horrible things. (2) The domain of the will. Here we must carry out unfalteringly and without delay whatever appears to us to be manifestly our duty; or, if our duty is not manifest, we must follow "arbitrary but fixed rules" in order to avoid having a will of our own. (3) The domain of that which, without belonging to the domain of the will, is not entirely independent of ourselves. This is the domain in which attention plays a role in calling down and responding to grace. Here we must carry out only those acts we are irresistibly impelled to do—cannot stop ourselves from doing—by the requirements and constraints that grace places on the soul. This includes all "good works" that we feel genuinely inspired to carry out while our thoughts are turned in the direction of obedience (N 150, 239, 436).

In all three areas, actions and decisions grounded in the will are to be replaced by obedience to the will of God. This means that one's actions are in a sense "dictated" from outside of all particular perspective. This does not mean that we cease to do evil; it does mean, however, that whatever evil we cannot absorb by converting it into suffering will be transmitted through us mechanically, according to necessity, and will not originate with us.

> To imitate divine Love, no force must ever be exercised. Being creatures of the flesh and caught in necessity, we can be constrained by a strict obligation to transmit the violence of the mechanism of which we are a wheel; for example as leaders over subordinates, as soldiers over enemies. It is often very difficult, painful, and agonizing to determine just how far strict obligation goes. But it is simple to take as a rule with regard to others, and even with regard to oneself, in the wielding of stress, never to go even so much as a millimetre beyond strict obligation. (IC 120)

Here Weil's logic is informed by the nonactive action of the *Bhagavad Gita* as the only "innocent" way of incarnating oneself and participating in the good-and-evil mixture that is the world. We cannot put an end to evil or cease to participate in it as long as we live; we can only suffer it without harboring any illusion as to its nature and transmit it (when we have no choice) as a "wheel" effecting the workings of a higher will that is not our own. Thus obedience to God in the form of *amor fati* is the means of performing nonactive action. For by acting only on unconditioned or "eternal" motives, wherein God comes down and acts in place of oneself, obedience "transports action into eternity" (FLN 149).

All action is incarnational—whether originating in gravity or grace—but Weil held that manual labor was a particularly privileged locus of action because of its unique sacrificial–sacramental character. One cannot work effectively without obeying with one's body the order of the world and the ineluctable conditions it imposes, which makes labor an implicit consent to the order of the universe (FLN 358). Work, as a methodical submission to necessity, requires continual abandonment of one's personal will (N 597, NR 302), and this is an obedience unto death (N 78–9). The direct engagement of the laborer's body with the demands of necessity is the primary reason for this: "He who is aching in every limb, worn out by the effort of a day of work, that is to say a day when he has been subject to matter, bears the reality of the universe in his flesh like a thorn" (WG 170).

When we work we make ourselves obedient as matter, yet we are not simply matter (as matter itself is); we are "spirit" investing itself in matter in the image of God investing himself in the Eucharist (N 201) and in all matter inclusively (N 322). Work is spirit incarnating itself, expending its energy in order to give birth to the fruits of labor. As creation is God's own material obedience to the will of God, so work is our obedience in imitation of that descent into matter: "Labour is an imitation of creation" (N 269). This unique status of labor leads Weil to aver that all other human activities are inferior to physical labor in spiritual significance, and that any well-ordered society should honor labor as its "spiritual core" (NR 302). Indeed, she felt that the contemporary age had a particular vocation to found a new type of civilization around the spirituality of labor, and she saw presentiments of such a vocation in scattered passages of modern writers (including Rousseau, Shelley, Proudhon, Marx, and others). Weil considered such thoughts concerning labor to be the truly original thoughts of her time—the only thoughts not borrowed from the Greeks, among whom "labor was held to be servile" (NR 297).

Weil focuses on labor because she senses that it can be the key to reconciling mundane or "profane" activity in the modern secular world with sacred symbolism, and such a mutual penetration of the religious and the profane would constitute the essence of a Christian civilization (NR 299). Indeed, Weil sees in Catholic tradition the potential for turning labor into a spiritual exercise, but for that to happen it must be admitted that labor is a form of suffering (N 170, 79). Happily, this form of suffering is not only expiatory but also redemptive, as it shares in the cross. Weil views labor in a biblical light as a "ransom" from original sin, a participation in the redemption (N 170), but only when viewed as a *descending* movement is labor an imitation of creation (N 269), hence it is more properly thought of as imitating the creation qua crucifixion: "Work, as such, is not an imitation of Creation, but of the Passion" (N 372). Labor as a perpetual sacramental performance participates in a cycle of reciprocal consumption and communion with God: God turns himself into matter for humanity, and the individual, being decreated through labor, turns him- or herself into matter to be consumed by God: "Man eats God and is eaten by God" (N 329, 99).

Every particular action can only bring about an effect that calls for further action. One labors to eat, then eats to labor again. To realize this brings on the "dark night" of disgust for work (N 301). But this disgust is useful in that it forces us to see there is no end to the cycle of means leading to further means. Work makes us experience in a distressing way "the phenomenon of finality being shot back and forth like a ball" (N 496). Because all actions can only be means, not ends in themselves, seeking to grasp the nature of work makes us recognize that the truth lies in the cycle: "It is just when man sees himself as a squirrel revolving in a cage that, provided he doesn't lie to himself, he is close to salvation" (N 496). The essential value of any action is not the effects it brings about, but the adverbial quality of the doing: what matters ultimately is not the fruit, but being a good tree.

To recognize the cyclical futility of action is the first movement toward a transcendental perspective on action; for, paradoxically, "what is purely a means is an ersatz form of the absolute end because of its ubiquity" (N 599). Time is an image of eternity and also an ersatz expression of eternity (N 244). Precisely because work can only be a means in time, its endlessness is an image of eternity. Labor that is done with a view to giving oneself over eucharistically, like God, into matter and the futility of the cycle, irrespective of the fruits, is a labor that consents to the nothingness, the end-lessness of existence. One does not labor "in order to"; one labors because one must do something, because one is in time.[9] The best solution is to do something in time *timelessly*, which is to say, *endlessly*, because this is the closest imitation, within time, of eternity. Hence nothing in the world can make up for the loss of joy in one's work (NR 81), for to feel this joy is to embody a patience and quiescence in the very midst of action: it is the patience that transmutes time into eternity (FLN 101).

To live and work continually inspired by a consciousness of end-lessness is to convert all labor and indeed all action into sacred ceremony. Already as a young pupil of Alain, Weil wrote: "By the continual presence of the Spirit in us, each of our movements is ceremony" (OC 1.71). Nonactive action reconciles two contradictory levels: it undertakes to achieve a specific end as the temporal conditions of necessity require, and it also always simultaneously sacralizes time, incarnating eternity in the moment. Ceremony is an imitation of the order of the world and of the sacred silence of things (FLN 130). We should, Weil insists, turn everything—occupations, events, public functions, and the like—into intermediaries leading toward God in this way. "Each thing must be wrought upon to bring about a change so that it may be made transparent to the light" (N 328). Labor understood as sacrifice, sacrament, and ceremony has the power to transpose time into patience, a patience borne in us by God. Indeed, only God can truly bear being subjected to time, and it is ceremony that allows us to feel that.

CHAPTER 6

CONCLUSION:
WEIL'S THEOLOGICAL COHERENCE

The apparent absence of God in this world is the actual reality
of God [...]. This world, in so far as it is completely empty of
God, is God himself. Necessity, in so far as it is absolutely other
than Good, is Good itself. That is why any form of consolation
in affliction draws us away from love and truth. (N 424)

Given the interpretive difficulties that confront any reader of Weil, as
well as the wide-ranging eclectic influences that shaped her religious
thinking, commentators have tended to treat her religious thought as
in effect *sui generis*. Efforts to situate her in relation to traditions of
thought that nourished her theological vision have been partial,
fragmentary, and sometimes tendentious, accenting one stream of
influence—Platonic, "Gnostic" or "Manichaean," Cartesian, Kantian,
Spinozist—at the expense of others that are not treated or even
mentioned. To my knowledge, no balanced and comprehensive effort
to evaluate Weil's religious outlook vis-à-vis her background
influences has been ventured to date. As a consequence her location or
position as a religious thinker remains unanchored, tentative, still
largely undefined even among dedicated interpreters. This status—
better than being pigeonholed—cannot be all bad, but neither is it
entirely good. Surely some of the obscurities that surround Weil's
formative sources can be more definitely illumined?

One reason for her unanchored status may be that Weil herself tended to read texts ahistorically, as though all important ideas are "timeless," transcending historical context, and therefore her writings encourage this attitude toward her. A second and deeper reason is that any argument concerning her theological identity must be based on a comprehensive reconstruction of her religious reflections, predominantly those recorded in her late notebooks, drawing forth their logical structure and overall coherence. As the present study has attempted just that, it may provide a basis for helping to situate Weil's religious philosophy—however original it is in its unique gestalt—within the broader context of modern European religious thought. The following discussion points to productive directions for further exploration with the intention of provoking—not definitively settling—a more critically focused consideration of the matter.

Background Theological Influences

In the vein of *sui generis* interpretation, mentioned above, commentators who remark on the "Gnostic" aspect of Weil's thought tend to apply that epithet in a decontextualized manner, without attempting to account for it by searching out its most likely cultural-historical sources.[1] Clearly, whatever "Gnostic" likenesses Weil may appear to exhibit, they do not stem directly from the Gnostic systems of the first three centuries CE; not only is such a claim unconvincingly anachronistic, but as McLellan notes, Weil's specific knowledge of Gnosticism seems to have been sparse (*Utopian Pessimist*, 195). But neither are they grounded in the inspiration of medieval Catharism, as others have suggested.[2] Weil was indeed attracted to Catharism—or to what she imagined Catharism to be—but taking it as the key to her thought can only mislead. Any resemblance of Weil's thought to Cathar dualism is both incidental and superficial: incidental, because the predominance of the good–evil opposition was patent in her writings for several years before her overt interest in Catharism emerged; superficial, because the polar oppositions in Weil are essentially *dialectical* not dualistic. This is to say, all the oppositions central to Weil's thought—good–evil, gravity–grace, necessity–supernatural good—are maximized dialectically precisely in order that they be reconciled in a transcendent harmony. The telos of the opposition is fulfilled only in the transcendent union of the opposites: evil is transfigured as manifesting transcendent good; "pitiless" necessity is embraced as the providence of a merciful God. A more antidualist thinking can hardly be imagined.

In 1941 Weil read a monograph on Catharism by Déodat Roché and wrote him an appreciative letter in which she admitted to "knowing little about them" (SL 129), and this is not mere modesty. Weil's biographer Simone Pétrement proposes that Weil espied in Roché's account "a Christianity in which the Greek, Platonic element would be accentuated and the heritage of the Old Testament would be lessened" (SWL 395–6). Thomas Nevin agrees, pointing out that Roché's description of this movement as a form of Christian Platonism gave Weil something to seize on in her Marcionite-like desire to supplant the Judaic foundations of Christianity with a purely Hellenic inspiration (*Simone Weil*, 269). Weil was persuaded by Roché's treatment that Catharism was a form of Christian Pythagoreanism or Platonism, and this confirmed in her mind that it was the "last living expression in Europe of pre-Roman antiquity" (SL 130). What Weil found miraculous about Catharism was that in it "the highest thought" was incarnated in a whole human environment, steeped in the surrounding society, and not limited to a closed circle of disciples, making it a genuine religion rather than a philosophy (SL 131).

This does seem to be the basis of Weil's attraction: she pictured Catharism as a pure Platonic-Christian religion untainted by either of what she considered the two principal sources of corruption in Christianity: the "terrible violence" of Yahweh the God of Israel and the unfettered power-lust of imperial Rome (SL 130, N 505). The dualism of the Cathars was approved by Weil as evidence of their spiritual purity, not as an expression of doctrinal truth. Alain Birou has argued that "no one today would make of Catharism a Christian Platonism, nor a Pythagoreanism," and moreover, the cultural unity that Weil attributed to Catharism was not specifically Cathar but was a quality of Occitan civilization, and this unity was partially rooted—ironically—in the integration effected by Roman governance while it was part of the Empire.[3]

Much more to the point, it is in the powerful light of her own religious thought that Weil could never have embraced Cathar doctrine, which Birou summarizes as "essentially defined by a *dualism of Principles*: the Principle of Good, creator of the world of spirits, and the Principle of Evil, a co-eternal son turned rebel or a fallen angel, creator of the material world" (343). The relation between good and evil in Weil's thinking, Birou points out, is not at all of this order: for her there is a supreme good, identified with a God who alone is transcendent, the original source of the good and evil of creation; the material world is not evil in itself, and its evil is neither absolute nor irredeemable (344). In summary, then, to account for the superficially Gnostic-resembling dimension of Weil's religious outlook, it is logical to seek its ground in modern theological developments in France that trace back to the Pauline– Augustinian heritage, which constitute Weil's immediate context as a religious thinker.

As Weil was reared and educated entirely in France, Roman Catholicism was the only form of established Christianity she was culturally acquainted with in any significant degree. Rarely does she even refer to Protestantism or its key figures, which simply are not part of her experiential horizon (with the exception of a four-month stay in New York City in 1942 during which she visited African-American churches in Harlem). Her limited knowledge of Catholicism was acquired through personal exposure living in a Catholic culture, in the context of a secular upbringing, rather than through in-depth study of its theology or doctrinal history. And yet Weil has been interpreted by sundry scholars, including Maria Fuerth Sulzbach, as a quasi-Protestant.[4] The latter commented on Weil in 1951: "Though she lacks any deeper knowledge of theology, her interpretation of Christianity coincides much more with the eschatological and paradoxical form of Protestantism than with the Roman Catholic tradition" (350).

Sulzbach points to a wealth of elements in Weil's thought that coincide with Protestantism: her certitude of faith, her accent on the will of God, the fact that she does not believe supernatural good supplements the natural good, and the fact that natural theology, which is a vital dimension of Roman Catholic dogma, hardly exists for her (though this claim is qualified below). She goes on to note that Weil's ideas "frequently coincide with much contemporary dialectical Protestantism," alluding to the then-dominant Neo-orthodox theology of Karl Barth, Emil Brunner, and others. Sulzbach concludes that Weil's credo agrees with the "essence of all Protestantism, that 'without grace there is no possibility of faith, and without faith no possibility of salvation'" (352). At a loss to account for this, Sulzbach resorts to calling Weil a "primitive Christian"—an interpretation in the *sui generis* vein.

How to account for this resemblance to Protestantism in a secular Jewish thinker who came of age intellectually within a Catholic environment and was little exposed to or concerned with Protestant theology and culture? Sulzbach is keen in her observations, but misled in pointing to Protestantism, which hardly existed within Weil's horizon of thought. Rather, the missing link between Weil and the indirect but potent influence of Protestant—specifically Calvinist—theology within France may be found in the Jansenist movement.

The intellectual-spiritual legacy of Jansenism *and* its original root sources pervaded the cultural environment in which Weil was educated. Parisian thinking in the late medieval period was strongly Ockhamist, and this theology, which ruled the intellectual world from 1450 to 1550, made a rigorous distinction between the natural and supernatural spheres.[5] In the religious dimension, Ockhamist nominalism accented the incomprehensible majesty of God, while in philosophy its tenor was skeptical to a degree unprecedented in the history of Christian thinking. It was the "hard intellectuality" of this late Scholasticism that produced Calvin, and it was Calvinism reabsorbed into French-Catholic culture, much altered in the process, that produced the neo-Augustinian theology of Jansenism, notwithstanding that certain aspects of Jansenism can be characterized as "anti-Calvinist."[6] One cannot overlook, moreover, the crucial impact of both religious movements—Calvinism and Jansenism—on the thinking of Descartes. Jansenism and Cartesianism developed hand-in-hand in France. Though by no means can they be identified with one another, their mutual influence and points of affinity cannot be denied, as Descartes and Pascal exerted considerable influence on each other's development. Cornelio Fabro remarks on Pascal's sense of the loss of God: that nature is such as to point everywhere to a God who has been lost, both within man and outside of man.[7] Descartes's rationalism was itself a negative theology imbued with this sense: it shrouded God's essence in silence, or as the early Weil put it, "the view that Descartes had of God was of a God who is completely transcendent, whom one does not meet in the world, which is pure matter" (LP 181).

In his interpretation of Jansenism, the philosopher Leszek Kolakowski points out that the "Gnostic temptation" in modern Western thought was curiously reinforced by the advent of Cartesianism.[8] Descartes's thoroughgoing dualism of *cogitatio* and *extensio*—the basis of the modern mind–body dualism—has its genealogical source in the age-old Pauline–Augustinian dichotomy of *sarx* and *pneuma*, flesh and spirit. But what is radically new and "modern" in Descartes is the stark godlessness of the realm of matter, or *extensio*, and this starkly modern element is due to the powerful intervening impact of late medieval nominalism. The world, for Descartes, is an alien, inanimate, mechanical place, subject to exact scientific calculation but empty of vital soul or spirit.

> Human reality, defined in terms of *cogitatio* alone, was opposed by Descartes to the material universe that was governed inflexibly by a few mechanical laws; the world became soulless and godless, having no final causes, no moral qualities, and no mystery, transparent to the eye of a scientist, whereas human existence, in metaphysical terms, became bodyless. Thus we had to confront two areas of reality, severed from, and alien to, each other, naturally incommunicable. (*God Owes Us Nothing*, 88–9)

If Kolakowski's interpretation is well founded, the quasi-Gnostic dichotomy of spirit and matter in mid-seventeenth century Jansenism was patterned not directly on the Manichaean residuum in Augustinian thought, but rather on the highly modernized neo-Augustinian, neo-Manichaean aspect of Cartesian thought.

Weil does not ally herself with Jansenism, and in fact barely mentions it in her writings except negatively, yet André Devaux affirms that Weil "openly proclaimed that Pascal constituted part of her most fundamental intellectual and spiritual heritage."[9] Certainly Weil was a deep reader of Pascal and Racine, both key figures in the broader intellectual history of Jansenism, and both her mentor Alain (the philosopher Émile-Auguste Chartier) and her thesis adviser Léon Brunschvicg focused their scholarly work on key French thinkers steeped in Jansenist ideas, including Descartes, who was an utterly crucial influence on Weil. The inference is unavoidable that the general and diffuse cultural and intellectual influence of this historical movement profoundly shaped Weil's religious sensibility, as it did so many other prominent twentieth-century French writers and thinkers who were her contemporaries—Georges Bernanos, Jean-Paul Sartre, François Mauriac, Henry de Montherlant—even if this influence was largely indirect, subliminal, even atmospheric.

To cite specifics, Weil and the Jansenists share a rigorous distinction between the spheres of nature and grace; a sense of the transcendent "hiddenness" of God and the radical graciousness of faith; the notion that reason must recognize the super-rationality of faith; the conviction that all genuine morality depends on supernatural grace, that very few are numbered among the elect, and that recognition of our creaturely misery is our only hope; a solitaire spirituality, ascetic self-discipline, and devout obedience to conscience; a strong accent on education and the proper training and use of individual judgment; philosophical skepticism combined with an attraction to Cartesian (as against Aristotelian) thought; radical detachment from the world; suspicion of "worldly" social dynamics and of the political order as a necessary evil; passive resistance to the authoritarianism historically embodied in the Church (what the Jansenist luminary Antoine Arnauld called the "heresy of domination"); a desire for total reform of established Catholic Christianity; a profound veneration for the holy sacraments; and most of all a radical theocentrism—that is to say, the sense that everything at every moment must be directed toward God and that "whatever is not so directed is, in a strange sense, unreal" (Kolakowski, *God Owes Us Nothing*, 99).

Let us be mindful that three centuries before Weil recorded her meditations on the absence of God, Pascal wrote of a *délaissement universel*, a universal abandonment by God.[10] Weil scholar Henry Leroy Finch remarks on her attitude of *"cosmic alienation,"* the all-pervading sense of the "far-awayness or absence of God," that is to say, the feeling of "separation from our source, our home and destination, by the vast gulf of the physical world," the supreme symbol of this being the "vastness of cosmic space and time"; he then proceeds to misidentify the ground of this sensibility—as many have before him—tracing it to ancient Gnosticism and Manichaeanism by way of medieval Albigensianism (Catharism), claiming that it is "something not known to the Greeks, Hebrews, and Christians" (*Simone Weil and the Intellect of Grace*, 26–7). But a deeply convincing case can be made, quite to the contrary, that precisely such a cosmic alienation is keenly known to Pascal as an early modern Christian experiencing the abyss of the two infinities (*Pensées*, frag. 230) and the loss of God in that abyss.

The proposal here is not the anachronistic one that Weil "is" a Jansenist, but that a pervasive residual Jansenism in twentieth-century France—rather than Gnosticism, Catharism, Platonism, Kantianism, Hegelianism, or any other intellectual tradition—is the *primary* background influence informing the basic structure of Weil's religious thinking, most specifically her dialectical reflections on nature and grace, God and the world. To argue this conclusively would require a thorough historical-theological examination. The purpose at hand here is more limited: simply to indicate this productive direction for positioning Weil's religious thought in modern European intellectual history. A fond hope may also be held out that the term "Gnostic" used with reference to Weil will be carefully grounded in textual evidence and interpretive context, or dropped as a bad penny.

Dialectic of Nature and Grace

Weil forcefully declares, as we have seen, that "supernatural good is not a sort of supplement to natural good," but rather, in all the crucial problems of human existence, "the only choice is between supernatural good on the one hand and evil on the other" (SE 23 = SWR 327), for the only true good is supernatural good (N 410). This Protestant-sounding dichotomy of nature and grace— or in Weil's terms, necessity and the good—penetrates every corner of her religious thought. But for Weil, as for the seventeenth-century Jansenists—who were themselves commonly charged with being crypto-Protestants—the "nature" awaiting dialectical transformation by grace is conceived not as Scholastic philosophy pictured it, nor as Luther or Calvin did, but rather as Cartesian science imaged it: a material universe "governed inflexibly by a few mechanical laws," "soulless and godless," with no final causes and no moral qualities (Kolakowski, *God Owes Us Nothing*, 88). Nature is precisely such a Cartesian realm in Weil's thought.

Yet Weil's idea of nature is patterned more on Spinoza's transformation of Cartesian thought than on Descartes himself. Weil's resonance with Spinoza lies in the shared influence of Descartes *and* ancient Stoicism on their theological thinking. Her attraction to Spinoza has nothing to do with his absolute monism, which she does not accept, but has everything to do with the essentially Stoic tenor of his natural and ethical philosophy. Weil adheres to Spinoza's Stoic regard for necessity as issuing from God, a God who is to be loved precisely through knowledge of and reverence for *necessity*. Spinoza famously asserted that to arrive at enjoyment of the knowledge of the union of mind with the whole of nature is the "highest good" of a human being.[11] In a strikingly parallel statement, Weil avers that "the savant's true aim is the union of his own mind with the mysterious wisdom eternally inscribed in the universe" (NR 262). To attain this unitive knowledge is salvation and sanctification simultaneously.

This Stoic ideal is nowhere to be found in Descartes, although it borrows in whole cloth the Cartesian view of the world as *extensio*.

Since Spinoza denies that the world is created and that God has a will, the world's necessity is understood to be the immediate expression of God's essential nature; whereas for Weil necessity issues in a wholly voluntarist fashion from the will of God, mediately through his Word in the act of creation—a position closer in this respect to Descartes. Notwithstanding this essential difference, Weil and Spinoza converge in their "ethical" regard for necessity. To understand the true nature of necessity *is* to know God, and to succeed in loving necessity is to attain the highest human fulfillment possible.

Recognition of necessity—"consent" to it in Weil's language—alone makes a human being free. Both Weil and Spinoza affirm that every other notion of freedom is illusory. Human consciousness *feels* that it is free in pursuing this or that action, but to explain this Spinoza employs the well-known example of the falling stone: if a stone were conscious of its own action in falling, it would imagine that it "continues in motion for no other reason than that it so wishes"; so, similarly, "men are conscious of their desire and unaware of the causes by which they are determined."[12] We have seen (in Chapter 4) that Weil works with this metaphor from the other direction: a human being who turns away from God, though he may believe that he can decide and choose, simply gives himself up to the law of gravity: he is "only a thing, a stone that falls" (WG 128, IC 193). Wherever the virtue of supernatural light is absent, Weil argues, everything is "obedient to mechanical laws as blind and as exact as the laws of gravitation" (WG 128). Human beings who are not animated by pure charity, a gift of grace, are merely wheels in the mechanism of the order of the world, like inert matter (WG 157). Even their belief in their own free choice—the *liberum arbitrium*—is simply a phenomenon as rigorously determined as the refraction of light (IC 194).[13]

If nature, or the realm of necessity, is a mechanistic order, so in a correlative manner is the action of grace. The clearest brief summary of Weil's theology of grace is found in her last major writing, *The Need for Roots*, which reads: "Grace descends from God upon all beings; what becomes of it depends on what they are; there where it really penetrates, the fruit it bears is the result of a process similar to a mechanism" (NR 263). Such supernatural mechanisms, Weil continues, are at least as dependable as is the law of gravity (*la loi de la chute des corps*); they provide "the conditions necessary for producing pure good as such" (NR 264). A rigorous mechanism governs spiritual things, but it is a hidden one, such that real desire for pure good "compels" (*contraint*) grace to descend. If this does not occur, either the desire is not real or is too weak, or the good desired is not a pure good, but an imperfect one. But, if we exercise a sort of compulsion (*une espèce de contrainte*) upon God, she insists, it can only be a question of a mechanism instituted by God (N 249).

The mechanism of grace, like that of gravity, is a matter of *necessitation*; but in the case of grace, the principle that necessitates is good rather than evil, supernatural love and attention rather than will. Weil declares that we have to be "indifferent" to both good and evil, but while remaining indifferent, and bringing the light of the attention to bear equally on each, good prevails "as a result of an automatic mechanism." This, according to Weil, represents the essential form of grace: "A divine inspiration operates infallibly, irresistibly, if one does not turn the attention away from it, if one does not reject it. There is no need to make a choice in its favour; all that is necessary is not to refuse to recognize its existence" (N 303).

Here the question arises whether "free will" is at work in her stipulation that one must not turn one's attention away from divine inspiration, not reject or refuse it. Weil speaks of such refusal in a number of places, most notably in this passage: "One is called; one either comes running up, or one doesn't [. . .]. One enters or one doesn't enter into eternity, as the case may be, according to whether one has consented or refused" (NR 265). Elsewhere she remarks on the lack of free will in those who give themselves up to necessity, becoming like tiles blown off a roof by the wind: the only fault of such people is the "initial choice" by which they became such tiles (WG 128). The central issue becomes for Weil, as it was for Augustine, the question of the *initium salutis*, that is, whether the very first step or movement of the individual toward salvation comes from human will (nature) or from the grace of God.

Certainly Weil's statement that "grace descends from God upon all beings; what becomes of it depends on what they are" seems to indicate the universality of sufficient grace, in traditional theological terms. But what is the role of the will? Can our will block or resist interior grace in Weil's view, as it cannot in the strictly predestinarian Jansenist view? A nuanced answer is called for. We must deduce from Weil's other statements on grace that our "not refusing" is itself a gift of grace, not of nature. Weil makes clear that there is no other kind of freedom than supernatural freedom (N 464, 205). "To be free, for us, is to desire to obey God. All other liberty is false" (IC 186). Only when we act under the "constraint" of grace do we act without "I"-centeredness, without will, thereby transcending evil, for "all absolutely pure goodness lies completely outside the range of the will" (N 436 = GG 45). The creature's natural will is decreated and dissolved by the operation of a purely good will.

> When we think on God with attention and love, he rewards us by exercising upon the soul a constraint that is exactly proportional to that attention and love. (Here we have the spiritual equivalent of automatism.) [...] We must only carry out that which we are irresistibly impelled to do by this constraint. The rest belongs to the domain of evil, and whatever we do there, we can only do evil. (N 259)

Yet it is only when we "think on God with attention and love"—a condition we apparently cooperate in—that he rewards us with the mechanism of grace. Supernatural freedom is a question of directing the attention properly to set the "irresistible" mechanism in motion. Since in essence this purity of attention *is* supernatural love (an inspired, not a natural gift), the "decision" to pay attention rather than to refuse it is already an act of consent conditioned by prevenient grace.[14]

Even if the *initium salutis* (first step or turn toward salvation) is wholly conditioned by the grace of God, we do nonetheless contribute something. Grace alone is not sufficient, for God is only able to effect our decreation with our cooperation (N 342). We cannot positively contribute to "saving" ourselves; grace achieves that wholly without our will by enabling the necessary attention and love, for supernatural love is that in us which answers to the will of God with obedience (N 303). All we own that we can give to God is our consent, and "this consent comes from God" (FLN 206). The one thing our will *can* positively do is damn us, for "Hell is an evil choice" (N 343). When grace calls, we can disobey (WG 72); we have been given the capacity to refuse to obey as spirit, and to obey only as matter in response to gravity. In Weil's thought, the will does cooperate in salvation (N 340), but the mode of its cooperation is strictly negative: the sole contribution of nature is the *self-negation of the will* in response to prevenient grace. Nature's contribution is simply not to say no, not to refuse, which is in effect to deny itself and consent to die, in order to receive that which is wholly ulterior to itself: supernatural grace.

Grace does everything except extinguish the will, that part of our nature that has the responsibility to consent or refuse. The one and only free act that is possible for the will is voluntary death: consent to the destruction of the "I" (N 337). The will does not and cannot positively contribute to salvation, yet neither is it wholly abrogated by grace alone, for it has the capacity to consent to "die" or "be nothing"—which is simply to live in constant faithfulness to the truth of death (NR 249, N 161), the true relationship of finite things to the good that transcends them. God, who gives us being, loves in us our consent not to be, because mortality is the truth of our condition, and our existence is nothing else but his will that we should consent not to exist for as long as we do exist (N 613–4, FLN 123), living a life as pure as death.

God Beyond Good and Evil

Like many European intellectuals who were her contemporaries, Weil cherished a glowingly idealized picture of the golden age of ancient Greece.[15] Her image of the entire ancient world was of a "continuous civilization" imbued with one unifying inspiration. It was her conviction that the ancient Stoics "only reproduced in their language" the ideas of Orphism, Pythagoras, Socrates, Plato, and others (SL 125). Incredibly enough, Weil saw a unifying inspiration in ancient mystery religions, the pre-Platonic philosophers, Plato, the Stoics, the Christian gospels, the Gnostics and Manichaeans, and Spinoza in his Stoic aspect as well: the quest to overcome dualism through the harmony of opposites (SL 130); here Weil clearly misreads Gnosticism, Manichaeanism, and Catharism as aimed toward a unifying transcendent harmony, abrogating their essential dualism. Weil thought that the "miracle of Greece"—which she believed was given its definitive philosophic expression in Plato—was based in the intellectual discoveries of the Pythagoreans, whose essential genius consisted of having recognized the "feeling of equilibrium" (SE 147) as a principle of salvation:

> In the eyes of the Greeks, the very principle of the soul's salvation was measure, balance, proportion, harmony; because desire is always unmeasured and boundless. Therefore, to conceive the universe as an equilibrium and a harmony is to make it like a mirror of salvation. In relations between men, also, the good consists in abolishing the uncontrolled and unlimited; that is what justice is. (SL 125)

Thus to conceive the universe in all its apparent chaos and injustice as an equilibrium and a harmony is to make it into a "mirror of salvation" in that it abolishes the uncontrolled and unlimited, replacing it with a cosmic image of justice (SL 125). The Pythagoreans' key idea, Weil thought, is that the good is always defined by the union of opposites (N 447 = GG 100, SL 137). Harmony or proportion is achieved through the unity of contraries qua contraries. Such harmony is impossible if the contraries are either brought together forcibly, inappropriately, or unduly mixed; rather, the genuine point of unity has to be found. This is achieved by an intellectual-spiritual effort of contemplation: one must contemplate the object in question, whatever it may be, without either seeking consolation or resisting suffering, until one arrives at the secret point where the contraries converge into one and the same thing (SE 51).

A genuine contradiction, as we have seen (Chapter 1), cannot be reconciled, harmonized, or transcended either by "mixing" the contraries or suppressing either element of the contradiction. This principle applies *a fortiori* in the case of the most fundamental dichotomy of all: the one that pertains between necessity and the good. Supernatural harmony is realized only by maximizing the dialectical power of the opposition until the duality is as acute as possible: "There are two things come to us from outside, necessity and good; and they come to us together" (N 515); "it is through knowing what a difference there is between them that their unity can be grasped" (N 480).

Weil takes this point concerning transcendent good, which she gathers from her interpretation of Pythagoreanism and Plato, and applies it to her Christian theology of creation, crucifixion, and redemption. The opposition between necessity and the good originates when God abdicates to necessity, therein becoming the author of evil. But how is it thinkable that pure good should author evil? "God is the author of all; God is only the author of good: we cannot escape from this dilemma" (N 207). The supernatural "solution" to this insoluble contradiction is redemptive suffering (IC 142). It is through redemptive suffering, as we have seen, that God is present in extreme evil (N 343) while remaining purely good. God is "trapped by evil" when he contemplates what he has created, and subjected to the passion (FLN 329).

In redemptive suffering, evil comes to possess the utmost maximum of "evilness" possible. It is the radical goodness of redemptive suffering that maximizes the evil of evil for, as opposites, good and evil define and intensify one another. This is the point at which Weil's theology reaches its dialectical pitch: because God is pure good, God's absence is the divine form of presence that corresponds to evil (N 343); hence, the apparent absence of God in this world is the actual reality of God, and "necessity, in so far as it is absolutely other than Good, is Good itself" (N 424).

The desire to escape from duality is the sign of love in us (IC 110, see N 442), but we must "escape" in the right way: not by denying the contradiction but by grasping and consenting to the union of the contradictories. Grace alone, in the form of supernatural love, makes this transcendence possible: it harmonizes necessity and the good by grasping their unity, allowing us to pass beyond our captivity to the opposition of good and evil:

> Mysticism means passing beyond the sphere where good and evil are in opposition, and this is achieved by the union of the soul with the absolute good. Absolute good is different from the good that is the opposite and correlative of evil, although it is its pattern and its source. This union is an operation that is real and effective [...]. The transformation is the opposite of what took place when men followed the devil. (SE 214)

Love of good taken to the point of mystical union with God, beyond the sphere where good and evil are in opposition, is the means of overcoming the effects of the fall; it is itself redemption. We avail ourselves of this redemption by loving necessity along with its concomitant evil, even while hating the evil per se and preventing it wherever we have a strict obligation to do so.

We are called to love not evil but *necessity*, the principle that necessitates the existence of evil, and this love of necessity is an unconditional consent to suffer evil, just as creation is God's unconditional consent to suffer evil. Only through the medium of the notion of necessity, which excludes all representable forms of good, can we contemplate *everything* with love (N 271), including all the evil we cannot prevent. To love necessity is to love the non-good: that which is alien to God, separated from him by an infinite distance, yet willed by God as a revelation of love:

> There are two objects for us to love. First, that which is worthy of love but which, in our sense of the word existence, does not exist. That is God. And second, that which exists, but in which there is nothing it is possible to love. That is necessity. We must love both. (FLN 324)

Precisely because Weil proclaimed the highest reverence for Plato (SL 131), we must not fail to recognize that hers is a reverse or inverted Platonism, for *only through loving the non-good do we attain to genuine love of transcendent good.* Her thoroughly Christianized interpretation of Plato overlooks the abyss of difference that actually obtains between Plato's good and Weil's God, with respect to the latter's love for imperfect, finite creatures and the whole idea of a good that elects to descend and suffer evil in order to redeem it (everything that the creature suffers, God suffers too, N 191). As Gregory Vlastos points out, in Plato we see the polar opposite of the ideal that has molded the image of the deity in Hebraic and Christian traditions: the latter is a being whose perfection empowers it to love the imperfect. For Plato, by contrast, the individual cannot be as lovable as the Idea; the Idea alone is to be loved for its own sake; the individual, in the uniqueness and integrity of his or her individuality, will never be the object of love, and were we free of mortal deficiency we would have no reason to love anyone or anything except the Idea: seen face-to-face, it would absorb all our love.[16]

Weil's dialectical theology posits that creatures can know and love absolute good *only* through the intermediary of evil, and that is why not only the *possibility* of evil is a good (N 112), but the *actuality* of evil is a good, and this is the respect in which we must "love evil" (N 493), which is to say, consent to it as emanating from the will of God (N 505). "What we now hate, we shall manage to be able to love" (N 21), and this is how we relate ourselves to the good that lies "beyond good and evil" (N 20). If it is good that there should be necessity (N 254), it follows in all rigor that it is good that there should be evil. Good is revealed in evil as such, or evil would have nothing to be evil in relation to. The more powerful the sense of evil, the more powerful the good that is implied. We cannot know good any other way than through its deprivation in the form of evil. "The existence of evil here below, far from disproving the reality of God, is the very thing that reveals him in his truth" (WG 145). We can love the God who is voluntarily absent only by loving the absence of good: necessity. God can never be perfectly present to us, but he can be almost perfectly absent from us in extreme affliction, hence "for us, on earth, this is the only possibility of perfection" (SNL 177). We love God by loving that which reveals the good by depriving us of the good.

Hence we do not truly love God unless we love necessity, because God reveals the true infinitude of his goodness through necessity. In a correlative sense, we cannot manage to love necessity until we love absolute good as its source and author. This is why the opposition between necessity and the good has to be heightened to the furthest extreme. By participating in the extremes we reenact the "reasons" of incarnation and crucifixion and consent to them: "In order to find the One, we have to exhaust duality, go to the very extreme of duality. This means crucifixion" (N 436).

Love of necessity thus becomes the touchstone of love of God, and consent to evil (the evil we are not obligated to prevent) is in turn the touchstone of consent to necessity. Evil is the test of all the rest: "When we love God through evil as such, it is really God whom we love. We have to love God through evil as such: [. . .] to love God as the author of the evil we are actually hating" (GG 75 = N 340, 505). God is a good that transcends the opposition of good and evil, which means that God is not "good" in our common sense of the word. "Good" commonly indicates the opposite of evil, and the two notions, "good" and "evil," are defined by the relativities of our valuative regard. Transcendent good is essentially other than evil, but it is also essentially other than good considered on the level of evil and measured against it as one opposite against another; there is an infinite difference between transcendent good and "this good of the penal code order." "Above, there is a good that, in a sense, bears more resemblance to evil than to this low form of good" (N 127).

The essential truth of good and evil is that they are not reciprocally related, for "if good is the union of opposites, evil is not the opposite of good" (N 451). While evil is the contrary of relative good, pure good is not the contrary of anything (FLN 138, 318). And even though evil is contrary to good, good finds a supernatural use for it. The supernatural use for evil is as a means of increasing supernatural good. This is why good and evil are not reciprocally related: there is no evil use for supernatural good, but there is a supernaturally good use for evil. Good has no alternative but to love when faced with evil, to reply to evil with love, and therein the existence of evil actually "creates" good, that good which transcends the opposition. As mystery compels the virtue of faith to be supernatural, so does evil the virtue of charity (N 341 = GG 75).

Weil employs the analogy of reading to explain how evil is transfigured into good. The opposition of good and evil, like that of light and shadow, derives from our perception, our way of seeing; it is a perspectival reading. A radically alternate perspective may collapse the contraries into a unity (N 78, 81–2). When supernatural love rather than natural will is the reader, what is read is no longer evil but a transfigured reading: "Passage from evil to good, like when you turn a book over onto its other side" (N 109). A conversion of perspective by grace overcomes our dichotomizing, conditional, good-versus-evil valuations of the world, supplanting these with a "position of indifference" (N 224) that is folly to the world because it is wholly detached from all temporal security and advantage; in it the world is overcome (FLN 144).

What this alternate way of reading reveals is the supernatural goodness of evil. Necessity, the root of all evil, is thus seen to be the actual incarnation of the good: *"In order that Good may pass into existence, Good must be able to be the cause of what is already entirely caused by Necessity"* (N 99). When supernatural love contemplates stark necessity, necessity ceases to be an evil because it is the incarnation of God (N 480, 493). The change—the transfiguration—is not in the thing read but in the manner of reading, with the eyes of supernatural love. Weil makes clear that a concerted struggle of mind and *body* is needed to carry off such a radical transformation of our capacity to read; even if the new reading is a gift of illumination, a sustained effort is required to incorporate it fully into our being (N 23).

Although many would consider it a formidable challenge to reconcile Spinoza, the purest monist who ever lived, with Plato, the most influential dualistic thinker of the Western world, Weil is strangely able to draw them together without a sense of conflict (see, for example, SL 87). This is because of the peculiar way in which she reads each, accenting selected aspects while diminishing others. By drawing out the transcendental workings of intellect in Spinoza's realism, and by refiguring Plato's idealism within a Christian scheme of creation–incarnation–crucifixion, she manages to interpret both Spinoza and Plato as forms of what can only be called a *transcendental realism*.

Reality is transcendent, Weil writes, "this is Plato's fundamental idea" (N 480), and in a bold act of interpretation (or misprision?), Weil takes the very same idea as Spinoza's fundamental idea. This is to say, the immanent reality we encounter in the world is the mode of revelation of the transcendent, the eternal. Necessity, the order of the world, is the incarnate expression of God, or ultimate perfection: "Necessity, in so far as it is absolutely other than Good, is Good itself" (N 424). The crucial accent in Weil is on finding the transcendent embedded or actually incarnated in the real as real. Incarnation makes the transcendent immanent. The world *is* the transcendent, if only we become able to recognize it, and this depends on purifying our relationship to the real so that we "read" it correctly. In effect, we must learn to read the reality of the world as God himself—not pantheistically, but dialectically. To read the world directly as God himself is pantheism, but to read the world as God crucified, voluntarily emptied of himself, is to read it dialectically.

This brings us to the crux of Weil's religious thought: in order for us to have faith in providence as ultimately good (rather than evil or dualistically good-and-evil), we must "make" God the author of all evil, because only when evil has its origin in transcendent good is it redeemable. Hence Weil's insistence that "a definite choice must be made in favour of a real hell rather than of an imaginary paradise" (N 321). Counterintuitive though it may sound, *only when God is responsible for evil can all of reality be seen as an expression of supernatural love.*

This is what the cross means to Weil: it symbolizes the transfiguration of evil under the aspect of providence as wholly redeemable by love:

Faith in Providence consists in being certain that the universe in its totality is in conformity to the will of God [. . .]; that in this universe good outweighs evil. Here it can only be a question of the universe in its totality, for in its individual aspects there is, unfortunately, no room for doubting that evil is present. Thus the object of this certitude is an eternal and universal dispensation constituting the foundation of an invariable order in the world. (NR 271)

The good that comprises the unity of the opposites is a supernatural harmony symbolized in the cross: it signifies at once, dialectically, the abdication of God, the absolute good, which delivers the world into evil, and the redemption of the world, which reclaims evil for absolute good, so that "the Passion constitutes at the same time Redemption" (N 539).

A less Gnostic theology can hardly be imagined, given that the furthest extreme of evil is maximized in order that it be wholly reclaimed for providential good. Here we also encounter one of the most significant contradictions in Weil's thought: that she writes of the world as an alien place of pilgrimage, yet also as our homeland, our native country, the beloved fatherland of every soul (SL 140). There appears to be a contest in Weil's thought between her Platonic–Augustinian side and her Stoic side. How can it be that "the being of man is situated behind the curtain, on the supernatural side" (N 127), and yet "full reality for a man lies within this world, even should he happen to be perfect" (N 374)? On the one hand, our true home is outside the universe, with God, in "the world [lying] on the other side of the sky" (N 384), and on the other hand, "this place of the soul's exile is precisely its fatherland, if only it knew how to recognize it" (SL 125).

The human soul as Weil envisions it is exiled in time and space, which thrusts it into a crucifying contradiction and robs it of its unity. All methods of spiritual purification are techniques for freeing it from the crucifying effects of time—not by removing it from time but by allowing it to live in time *sub specie aeternitatis*. The purpose is "that it may come to feel almost at home in its place of exile" (SL 124). In order to see the universe as a home, thought aspires to conceive the world as analogous to a work of art, to architecture, or dance, or music; it needs to find harmony within the limitless multiplicity of the world, to grasp the proportions that govern it (SL 125).

Necessity is the master idea, not itself a force, that subjects natural forces to proportion and also accommodates the "supernatural mechanism" of grace as it is manifested in space and time. Hence we must love the mechanisms of necessity—both gravity and grace—as the governing hand of providence in order to love this real world in which we live as our home. "Gravity," along with all its evil, is seen to be a natural grace inasmuch as it is pure obedience to the God who has "emptied himself" (*s'est vidé*) on the cross (FLN 120, 140, N 216–7, 283–4). To be able to read the universe as an equilibrium and harmony is to recognize it as both crucifixion and redemption, making it into a mirror of salvation (SL 125). The abyss of infinite distance between God and the world, the eternal and the temporal, is seen to constitute their paradoxical unity. God and world are dialectically united, bound indivisibly together by the transcendent harmony of the crucifixion.

Weil's Anonymous Christianity

In Weil's religious thinking, pure love of the world—*amor fati*—is *implicit* love of the incarnation and crucifixion of God. This makes her theology a non-Protestant *theologia crucis* (theology of the cross) with a decisively Catholic intensive concern with the order of the world: the universe is sacralized as the cross of God and, commutatively, the cross is secularized as the universe. The incarnation–crucifixion reveals a truth about the eternal God that has been equally true throughout history, including pre-Christian and non-Western history, which has been grasped implicitly by "friends of God" through contact with the order of the world and intimated in revelations previous to and apart from Christian revelation (see IC passim).

Weil considered historical Christianity as "fallen" as any historical religion and, if anything, fallen with less excuse given the "perfect paradigm of Christ" in its possession. She was mindful of the atrophy and decay of Christianity in the modern world, which was caused, she thought, by its having cut itself off for too long from the sole source of genuine inspiration: the supernatural good. Nonetheless, she proposes, given that we in fact live in an age of incredulity, why neglect the purificatory use of incredulity (N 239)? There are two forms of atheism, she posits, one of which is simply a denial of God, and the other of which is a purification of the notion of God (N 126). Weil hoped that modern incredulity itself could lead to a purer, more universal and anonymous form of faith.

If a new Christianity should prove impossible, she thought, then there is need for a new religion altogether: "either a Christianity so modified as to have become a different thing; or something else" (FLN 299, WG 98–9). She perceived a historic crisis looming not only in wartime Europe but in the wider postcolonial world of late modernity, and she believed that in all recorded history "there has never been a period in which souls have been in such peril as they are today in every part of the globe" (WG 76). Surviving on an "insufficient spiritual diet" since the Enlightenment, she believed this spiritual deficiency was leading humanity onto the darkest paths (SL 129–31).

Weil sought to respond to this universal peril by reaching for a religious outlook that would extend a pure universality of regard: "We are living in times that have no precedent, and in our present situation universality, which could formerly be implicit, has to be fully explicit" (WG 98). This would mean abjuring in the name of a truly catholic and truly "incarnated" Christianity precisely any sort of attachment to Roman Catholic Christianity, for Weil felt that Christianity is "catholic by right, but not in fact" (WG 75–6). She sought the outlines of a new fully universal religion: a transformed Christianity that would be catholic in an unreserved sense, "not bound by so much as a thread to any created thing, unless it be to creation in its totality" (WG 98). Only the universe as a whole is a proper object of loyalty, since indeed, "only the universe is true" (FLN 122). No partiality is permissible in the exercise of love. For our love to be as impartial and universal as God's, we must love anonymously, without attachment to names and identities, or distinctions between secular and religious, or East and West, or so-called First and Third Worlds. We must aspire toward a universal destiny in which the entire world receives our nonprejudicial allegiance and is embraced as our home.

Weil is a religious universalist in the specific sense that the universal criterion of the cross is, in one way or another, implicit in all true religion, Christian and non-Christian alike: "The religions that have a conception of this renunciation, this voluntary distance, this voluntary effacement of God, his apparent absence and secret presence here below, these religions are true religion, the translation into different languages of the great Revelation" (WG 145–6). But in general, she asserts, the relative value of the various religions is a very difficult thing to discern, perhaps even quite impossible, for a religion is known only from inside (WG 182–3). We must have given *all* our attention, *all* our faith, *all* our love to a particular religion in order to think of any other religion that is not our own with the supreme degree of attention, faith, and love that is proper to it (WG 184, 228, N 344).

In a sense, Weil's universalism can be characterized as a religious pragmatism; that is, religious conceptions prove their value by their effectiveness in bringing about an attitude of *amor fati*—perfect humility, obedience, longing for justice, and action that is consistent with the ineluctable truth of finitude and death. Diverse symbols and teachings may be effective in support of this practical good, and all religious conceptions that advance it are authentic forms of faith in her eyes. Weil's pragmatism permits her to accept any faith as divinely inspired that advances justice, which she understands to be identical with the love of one's neighbor (*agape*) taught in the Christian gospels (WG 65). There is no such thing as merely human justice; all justice, wherever it is real, is divine, and "the Passion is the actual existence of perfect justice without any real admixture" (N 375). Therefore any faith that fosters justice is divinely inspired. Everything in Weil's religious thought is concerned, in Augustinian fashion, with the proper ordering of action by a proper weighting of loves. The Christian is not the one who confesses Christ's name but the one who feeds and clothes the stranger anonymously in the spirit of Christ. To obey Christ is not to act *for* Christ but to act by virtue of the compassion of Christ operative within as a commandment to love (N 230, 436, GG 45). In action, it is not the aim or consequences but the origin of the impulsion—the inspiration obeyed—that makes it pure.

She therefore acknowledges the authenticity of any religion that has the principle of pure *amor fati* at its core, and she saw evidence of this (correctly or not) in most of the major religions. The great religions and wisdom traditions, as Weil sees them, celebrate the order of the world as universal obedience to divine will (NR 285–94). Any religion that loves the order of the world purely loves God purely, and "if there exists another thinking species, there will always be the same God for it, only another Word" (N 233). Weil admits no essential difference between Christian love and pure *amor fati*; such a genuine Stoical love is as commonly found outside Christianity as inside, just as it is as commonly deficient within Christianity as outside. "Not to believe in God, but to love the universe, always, even in the throes of anguish, as a home—there lies the road toward faith by way of atheism" (N 469).

For Weil, the desired movement of faith is from explicit Christian naming toward an anonymous, universal, catholic love, a love that has been articulated through a multiplicity of names and symbols in human history. The key value of the name of God is that it points to a reality purely beyond all finite conceptions and namings, to a universal love that is essentially anonymous *because* it is universal. She credits non-Christian and secular traditions—those of Greece, Egypt, ancient India, ancient China, and pure reflections of beauty in art and science—with having delivered her "captive to Christ" (WG 94–5, see 160) as much as explicitly Christian ones.

Historical reality, structured by space and time, is the only reality we can know because matter is the condition of existence. The alienness of matter and time to God can only be overcome if God is found to be already "hidden" in time, absolutely yet secretly present. This movement of God into the world is not a profanation of the sacred but rather a sacralization of the profane or "God-less" secular world. Exactly such a sacralization of the secular mind and spirit (*l'esprit laïque*; NR 241, 229) is what Weil's religious thinking has in view. It proposes that Christianity leave its Roman, "Christian," and Western limitations behind, transforming itself into "a new religion"

(FLN 299) by letting go its too explicit naming of God, its confession of Christ in name only (without doing his will), the institutional confines of the Church, and all provincial and sectarian manifestations of the faith. Only then will Christianity become heir to the catholic truth it has celebrated all along: the incarnation of God in time, and the universal redemption of time that implies.

Although the world is to be loved with all possible loyalty, Weil's *amor fati* cannot be characterized as a cosmic piety, for the world itself is but a sign or metaphor of something more ultimately sacred (N 480), a memento (*souvenir*) for us of some beloved being (IC 183). We are called to love the world not because it is inherently lovable—for the most part it is not, being shot through with evil—but because it is the language of God, the expression of the *Logos*, or rather it is an *embodiment* of God: an incarnation that is identical to crucifixion. We are called to grasp not only the *Logos* but more purely the *alogos* truth: the silence of God that reverberates when suffering thought is stilled by the flood of revelation and when transcendent joy soars over pain. Divine love is what one touches in the depth of affliction, Weil writes, a love that is the intangible essence of joy, "like Christ's resurrection through crucifixion"; it is not a consolation, it leaves pain intact (SL 142).

The ultimate good—God—is not a "good beyond being" dissociated from evil in Weil's thinking. On the contrary, God is a good whose abdication brings evil into existence—tragedies, crimes, horrors—and who abides within every corner of the material universe in accordance with necessity in order to imbue evil with redemptive manifestation. What we call evil exists as a consequence of love—a love that is neither commensurate nor rational, but avowedly a madness (*folie*). Redemption occurs *on* the cross, not *from* the cross; the cross remains, crucifying God and us. The Lamb is slain from the foundations, eternally, irreversibly: "The Word—*purely* powerful, *purely* passive—has done everything from the beginning; the Lamb slain from the beginning" (N 246).

Weil's dialectical reading of reality adumbrates a negative sacramentalism (Chapter 3) in which our role—to be decreated—far from reversing or undoing the crucifixion, *completes* it by responding to the madness of unconditional love with similarly unconditional consent. Evil remains in place but is transfigured by a supernatural reading, for faith is above all the conviction that the good is one (NR 252), so that finally, ultimately, nothing lies outside it. God's Wisdom (*Logos*) and the brute force reigning in the world are one and the same thing, dialectically viewed: "It is one and the same thing, which with respect to God is eternal Wisdom; with respect to the universe, perfect obedience; with respect to our love, beauty; with respect to our intelligence, balance of necessary relations; with respect to our flesh, brute force" (NR 295).

Isaiah proclaims, "*Vere tu es Deus absconditus*" (45:15); the world both manifests and hides God (N 149). To love God through the void, in the midst of affliction, death, and tragedy, is to love the absolute good that is real—*truly* real—not imaginary. The sole reason for thinking that the universe is good, Weil writes, is that God, though eternally aware that evil would arise in it, willed eternally to create it, therefore "God is not proved by the goodness of the universe, but the goodness of the universe is proved by God; or rather, it is a matter of faith" (FLN 329). Faith consists in believing that reality is love and nothing else (FLN 260). This God, the providence of the world as it *really* is, good and evil at once, cannot be lost in any hell, abandonment, or void because it is hidden in all of them *ab origine* as a real, though negative, sacrificial presence (N 290). But extremely few souls—maybe one in a generation, she speculates (FLN 224)—are equal to this call of saintliness, putting away false imaginations and consenting to the God who *is*, who is *this* kind of impossible good, revealed most perfectly in the self-emptying void rather than in the plenitude of being, which we are naturally inclined to prefer.

NOTES

Introduction

1. Palle Yourgrau, *Simone Weil* (2011), 12. The majority of works that address Weil's thought have attempted to do so while also telling the story of her life. This is to attempt too much, and in trying to do it all, such studies inevitably give her thought short shrift, confined within the space of the chronological narrative. Given the challenging interpretive problems that exist, a comprehensive treatment of her thought requires undivided attention. Eric O. Springsted makes this point in *Christus Mediator* (1983), 1.

2. Weil's primary account of these religious experiences is the letter to Father J.-M. Perrin commonly identified as her "spiritual autobiography," available in *Waiting for God* and *The Simone Weil Reader*; additional context is provided in SWL 249, 307, 329f, 339f.

3. Weil's researches into pre-Christian and non-Christian religious traditions of the world are so extensive in her notebooks that the topic requires separate undivided attention. I have decided not to examine it here except when it unavoidably impinges on her Christian thinking.

4. The last quotation is from Raymond Rosenthal, "The Quality of Modern Life," *The New Leader* (April 13, 1964), 23; cited in Richard Rees, *Simone Weil: A Sketch for a Portrait* (1966), 94. The preceding phrases are from Springsted, *Christus Mediator*, vii; David McLellan, *Utopian Pessimist* (1990), 2; Rowan Williams, "The Necessary Non-Existence of God," in *Simone Weil's Philosophy of Culture*, ed. Richard Bell (1993), 53; Czeslaw Milosz, *The Land of Ulro* (1981), 256; Vetö's introduction, RM 2; Winch's introduction, LP 2.

5. Quoted from the first draft of Weil's 1940 letter to her brother André Weil, cited in Monique Broc-Lapayre, "Simone Weil et son refus de Nietzsche," *Cahiers Simone Weil* 3, no. 1 (March 1980), 20. In my opinion, a carefully qualified reconciliation of Weil's thinking with Nietzsche's may be more thinkable than

Broc-Lapayre allows, despite the invincible revulsion Weil felt for Nietzsche "even when he expresses things I think" (*même quand il exprime des choses que je pense*) (SL 122).

6. Erich Heller, *The Importance of Nietzsche* (1988), 67.

7. A phrase used by the poet T. S. Eliot in his 1952 introduction to Weil's *The Need for Roots* (1971), vii.

Chapter 1   Reality and Contradiction

1. Keiji Nishitani, *Religion and Nothingness* (1982), 5.

2. The classic study by Arthur O. Lovejoy that traces the evolution of this metaphysical tradition, *The Great Chain of Being*, was first published in 1936.

3. J. P. Little, "Simone Weil's concept of decreation," in *Simone Weil's Philosophy of Culture*, ed. Richard Bell (1993), 26.

4. Paradoxically, acceptance of death is most urgent for highly developed societies in which confidence in the power of advanced technologies has tended to erode the domain of death, allowing it to be systematically denied and repressed, rendered all but invisible (Phillipe Ariès, *The Hour of Our Death* [1981], 595).

5. Nishitani, so akin to Weil at this point, articulates this realization: "In the case of death, we do not face something that awaits us in some distant future, but something that we bring into the world with us at the moment we are born" (*Religion and Nothingness*, 4).

6. This is Weil's critique of the impulse to rebel against God in protest against human affliction in the manner of Ivan Karamazov in Dostoevsky's *The Brothers Karamazov*: "Ivan Karamazov: flight into unreality. But that does not constitute a movement of love. A child that is crying doesn't want you to think that he doesn't exist, or to forget that he does exist" (N 293, 283). "Revolt consists in averting one's eyes" (N 287). Ivan's rebellion is examined more fully in Chapter 3.

7. Spinoza's four kinds of knowledge are outlined in his *Treatise on the Emendation of the Intellect*, in *The Collected Works of Spinoza*, vol. 1, ed. Edwin Curley (1985), especially 12–13.

8. Weil writes of election and "the elect" only infrequently (FLN 109, 148, 159), but uses other terms to describe those who are transformed by grace, such as "the saints" and "the friends of God," whom she makes clear are very few (FLN 224). The mass of humanity is destined to obey not the call of grace but the force of gravity, not spiritual but natural impulsions, for "society is not a society of the elect" (N 148). Yet sanctity is the precious fruit for which the entire universe is needed, or in Weil's offbeat metaphor: "It is the whole cow that is milk-producing, although milk is only drawn from the teats. Similarly, it is the whole world that is the producer of sanctity" (N 553).

9. Weil's contemporary Jean Hyppolite posited that Kierkegaard and Hegel are not as divergent at this point as many interpreters make them out to be. He

argued that Hegel retains the notion of alienation even within his conception of the Absolute: "It is only in appearance that the Absolute transcends contradiction, that is, the movement of alienation. There is no synthesis for the Absolute apart from the presence of a permanent internal antithesis. Indeed, it is natural to think that Absolute Knowledge still contains alienation, along with a movement to transcend it" (Hyppolite, *Studies on Marx and Hegel*, ed. John O'Neill [1969], 86).

10. Spinoza's fourth kind of knowledge is outlined in his *Treatise on the Emendation of the Intellect* as the perception we have "when a thing is perceived through its essence alone, or through knowledge of its proximate cause" (*The Collected Works of Spinoza*, ed. Curley, 1.13), and again in his *Ethics*, available in the same volume.

11. As Weil was entirely enculturated in France, "the Church" (*l'Église*) in her writings virtually always refers to the Roman Catholic church; non-Catholic Christian churches did not affect or concern her except during her four-month sojourn in the United States near the end of her life in 1942 (SWL 478).

12. Michel Carrouges incorrectly characterizes Weil as having an "intense revulsion toward dogma" ("Religion et religions," *Le Monde nouveau-paru*, nos. 53–54 [1951], 223). Her revulsion is toward the Church's authoritarian manner of prescribing "belief" in dogma, not toward dogmatic formulae of faith per se. In a letter to Maurice Schumann, she professes total adherence to the mysteries of the Christian faith with the only kind of adherence that seems appropriate for mysteries: the adherence of love, not affirmation (SL 155).

Chapter 2   The Paradox of Desire

1. Weil is close to Hobbes in his realist definition of good, which reads: "And whatsoever is the object of any mans Appetite or Desire; that is it, which he for his part calleth *Good*: And the object of his Hate, and Aversion, *Evill* [. . .]. For these words of Good, Evill, and Contemptible, are ever used with relation to the person that useth them: There being nothing simply and absolutely so; nor any common Rule of Good and Evill, to be taken from the nature of the objects themselves" (*Leviathan* [1968], ed. C. B. Macpherson, 120). Where she breaks with Hobbes is in affirming an absolute good "outside" the world, transcendent to every relative good within the world. Spinoza, under the influence of Hobbes, states: "it is clear that we neither strive for, nor will, neither want, nor desire anything because we judge it to be good; on the contrary, we judge something to be good because we strive for it, will it, want it, and desire it" (*Ethics*, part 3, prop. 9, scholium; quoted from *The Collected Works of Spinoza*, vol. 1 [1985], 500).

2. Weil addresses this idea in a 1933 letter: "It is only the use of analogy that makes it possible for thought to be at the same time absolutely pure and absolutely concrete. Thought is only about particular objects; reasoning is only

about the universal [. . .]. The only way to resolve this contradiction would be by analogy" (SL 3).

3. Freud criticizes the Christian ideal of universal love of neighbor in *Civilization and Its Discontents*, ed. James Strachey (1961), 56–9, 90; a comparable scathing critique is a leitmotif of Nietzsche's work, notably in *Beyond Good and Evil* and *On the Genealogy of Morals*.

4. Immanuel Kant, *Groundwork of the Metaphysic of Morals* (1964), 128–31.

5. If desire for good is the sacred core of the creature, the question can be raised whether nonhuman creatures do not also in various degrees "desire the good," and therefore have a claim to the moral interest of human beings. This would bring theological support to philosophical arguments, such as the one made by Evelyn B. Pluhar, that any being "able to care about what happens to him or her" should be included in the realm of moral concern and accorded full moral significance (*Beyond Prejudice: The Moral Significance of Human and Nonhuman Animals* [1995], xvi). The present study concentrates on *human* relation to the good because that is Weil's focus, but the implications of her thinking admit of being pursued in this far more encompassing direction.

6. Weil's anthropology is especially Hobbesian in her well-known essay "Analysis of Oppression": "Power-seeking, owing to its essential incapacity to seize hold of its object, rules out all consideration of an end, and finally comes, through an inevitable reversal, to take the place of all ends" (OL 69 = SWR 138).

7. Freud, *Civilization and Its Discontents*, 65–6; he first explores this tension between instinctual drives in *Beyond the Pleasure Principle* (1920).

8. Weil's understanding of detachment should be distinguished from that of Buddhism, even if she herself did not observe a distinction. Béatrice Farron-Landry errs in claiming that Weil, under the influence of Buddhism, saw detachment as "above all the extinction of desire" ("Détachement, renoncement et origine du mal selon Simone Weil," *Cahiers Simone Weil* 2, no. 2 [June 1979], 72). Weil's notion of detachment preserves, purifies, and even intensifies desire, derived as it is from Plato and diverse Christian sources such as Augustine, Marguerite Porete, Meister Eckhart, John of the Cross, and Blaise Pascal, not from Buddhism.

9. Pierre Hadot remarks that this movement is essential to the progress of the soul in Neoplatonic spirituality: "We cannot attach ourselves to the Good and remain at the same time attached to something else beside it. From this point of view, the discarding of all form corresponds first of all to asceticism: the soul must detach itself from the body, the passions, and all memories of external objects. The soul must detach itself as well from all ideas and all intelligible forms" ("Neoplatonist Spirituality: I. Plotinus and Porphyry," *Classical Mediterranean Spirituality*, ed. A. H. Armstrong [1986], 245).

10. Emmanuel Gabellieri addresses Weil's Christian adaptation of the Platonic idea of *metaxu* in "Reconstructing Platonism: The Trinitarian Metaxology of Simone Weil," in *The Christian Platonism of Simone Weil*, ed. E. Jane Doering and Eric O. Springsted (2004), 133–58; see also Springsted, *Christus Mediator*. Because

substantial scholarly exposition of Weil's use of *metaxu* already exists, I do not emphasize it here.

11. Stéphane Mallarmé, "Hérésies artistiques: L'Art pour tous," quoted in Henry Weinfield, *Stéphane Mallarmé: Collected Poems* (1994), xii.

Chapter 3 God and the World

1. For example, Vetö, RM 166n8; Maurice Blanchot, "L'Affirmation," in *L'Entretien infini* (1969), 159, 169–72; W. Rabi, "La conception weilienne de la création: Rencontre avec la Kabbale juive," in *Simone Weil: Philosophe, historienne et mystique*, ed. Gilbert Kahn (1978); Richard A. Freund, "La tradition mystique juive et Simone Weil," *Cahiers Simone Weil* 10, no. 3 (September 1987): 289–95; Thomas R. Nevin, *Simone Weil: Portrait of a Self-Exiled Jew*, 249–50, 253; Dorothee Beyer, *Sinn und Genese des Begriffs "Décréation" bei Simone Weil* (1992).

2. See Nevin, *Simone Weil*, 249. Weil's wholesale condemnation of Judaism, which was based on a reductive preconception all too prevalent in the anti-Semitic France of her day, is the consequence of a regrettable and inexcusable—and singularly willful—blind spot in Weil, who was otherwise remarkably receptive toward the plurality of religious traditions. Emmanuel Levinas was one of the first to raise an articulate voice in protest against Weil's ignorant hostility in "Simone Weil against the Bible," in *Difficult Liberty* (1990).

3. Gershom Scholem, *Major Trends in Jewish Mysticism* (1941), 260–1.

4. Thomas Aquinas, *Summa Theologica* (1947), vol. 1, q. 45, art. 1, p. 233.

5. Arthur O. Lovejoy traces the paradox of the *felix culpa*, or fortunate fall: that Adam's fall into sin was fully expected and intended by God as "the *conditio sine qua non* both of a greater manifestation of the glory of God and of immeasurably greater benefits for man than could conceivably have been otherwise obtained" ("Milton and the Paradox of the Fortunate Fall," in *Critical Essays on Milton from ELH* [1969], 164–5).

6. Vetö perceives in Weil a quasi-Gnostic separation between Father and Son in order to "whitewash" God of any responsibility for evil ("Simone Weil and Suffering," *Thought* 40 [1965], 276, 279). He argues that "it is basically to exonerate divinity from all responsibility in the cruel mechanism of this world that she found herself led to posit God as Power separated from Love," establishing "a division within divinity between a mighty and impersonal God and a powerless God who is love" (RM 13–4, 157–8). Quite to the contrary, though, God is expressly *accused* of all evil, not whitewashed of it, since God the Father bears absolute responsibility for abdicating power and permitting the mechanical reign of necessity. The Father abdicates power just as fully as does the Son, which renders him *"God all-powerless"* in relation to the world (N 284). The Father is not "Power separated from Love" then, since power is renounced *within* the Father, who denies and empties himself by the act of creation ("[*Dieu*] s'est

vidé déjà dans cet acte de sa divinité {...}. Il s'est par l'acte créateur nié lui-même," OC 4.1.291). Christ imitates this abdication within the Father (FLN 154). Thus power is sacrificed for love by Father and Son mutually, and precisely this mutuality of will *is* the divine unity, thus there is no Gnostic-style separation between them. Infinite love (unity) triumphs over infinite separation (WG 127). Until the ultimate importance of this unity-across-separation is recognized, the core significance of Weil's trinitarian language remains obscure and indecipherable.

7. Very few commentators have grasped the crucial centrality of the "self-emptying God" to the deep structure of Weil's religious thinking; among them are Madeline Hamblin, "Simone Weil's Theology of Evil, Love and the Self-Emptying God," in *Mysticism, Nihilism, Feminism*, ed. Thomas Idinopulos and Josephine Knopp (1984), 39–56; and Louis Dupré, "Simone Weil and Platonism," in *The Christian Platonism of Simone Weil*, ed. Doering and Springsted, 15–16. Hamblin's first sentence declares that Weil's theological thinking "begins with her concept of a self-emptying or kenotic God," and within a few sentences she remarks on "God's colossal powerlessness in the universe" (39), displaying a rare grasp of Weil's most fundamental theological framework.

8. As a fantastic "solution" to the problem of evil, Ivan invents the Grand Inquisitor and his "great beast," a totalitarian religious authority that would displace all individual freedom. The Grand Inquisitor confesses that he stands for a lie, since his solution does not eliminate *evil* but only the agonizing burden of freedom—that is, the onus of responsibility for good and evil—converting it into a relationship of totalitarian authority and abject servitude. But we cannot univocally identify Ivan's own stance with either the Grand Inquisitor or with Christ as portrayed in his poem, since Ivan has authored both characters, and the confrontation between them, and we meet him in the existential throes of this imaginary confrontation.

Chapter 4   Necessity and Obedience

1. G. S. Kirk, J. E. Raven, and M. Schofield, *The Presocratic Philosophers*, 2nd ed. (1983), 118.

2. See Alain Goldschläger, *Simone Weil et Spinoza: Essai d'interprétation* (1982), 116–221.

3. Edwin Curley confirms that freedom is an illusion in Spinoza's system; "men believe themselves free only because they are aware of their actions and not aware of the causes by which their actions are determined" (*Behind the Geometrical Method* [1988], 81–2). David Cockburn argues that for both thinkers "the aim is not to *escape* determinism by one's circumstances, but to transform its character" ("Self, World and God in Spinoza and Weil," *Studies in World Christianity* [2001]: 182).

4. Weil is willing to speak figuratively of God's "will" as Spinoza is not. Spinoza denies that God has a will bearing any remote likeness to human will. If pressed, Simone Weil would finally agree on this point, as ultimately God's will and reality are simply identical. But because we are able to respond personally to God's love, it is in a sense personalized for us as voluntary. For us to know God as love, we must love him through both personal and impersonal aspects as a strategy for transcending the limits of both, and she faults Spinoza for not doing so, hence slipping into conceiving God as a thing (N 275). Weil resorts to paradoxical language to achieve this, writing of God as an "impersonal Person" (FLN 129). Personal and impersonal conceptions of God are addressed in Chapter 5.

5. According to Martin Andic, Weil did not find the term *amor fati* in any classical author, Greek or Roman, because they did not actually use it; rather, she found it in the writings of Friedrich Nietzsche—her arch adversary—though her development of the term differed from Nietzsche's (Martin Andic, "Amor Fati," unpublished paper presented at the American Weil Society colloquy, Chicago, April 1999).

Chapter 5   Grace and Decreation

1. Vetö proposes that the basic vision of Weil's entire philosophy rests on "a God suffering from being separated from himself by the obstacle of human autonomy" (RM 73, 5, 16–7), but this is true only from the limited standpoint of human subjective consciousness. There is far more to the story in an objective or ultimate sense, since God must actually be separated from God by all of creation in order to fulfill the intention that love go as far as it can go, an infinite distance, to become perfected. Existence (the world) and perfection (God) are incompatible on one plane and identical on another: "It is because there are these two planes that there is creation or manifestation" (N 142). Human subjectivity permits the most intimate possible participation in this universal cosmic manifestation, but is not the only locus of it; the entire universe is the locus.

2. Self-love (*amour propre*) that is self-aggrandizing and egoistic is not a genuine *love* at all but a knot of particular attachments centered in the will. Genuine self-love, if only we were capable of it, would render us perfect "as the heavenly Father is perfect" (Matt. 5:48). But no one loves himself (N 249): "If one could be an egotist, it would be very pleasant. It would be a proper rest. But one cannot, literally, be one." "It is impossible for me to regard myself as an end" (N 547). This is the human being's wretchedness and greatness (N 279 = GG 61).

3. This is to take exception to J. P. Little's interpretation: "It will be obvious that extinction of the self [in decreation] restores the original unity of God without creation," thereby allowing "the full existence of God once more" ("Simone Weil's Concept of Decreation," in *Simone Weil's Philosophy of Culture*, ed. Bell, 27). It is true that decreation removes an obstacle to God's unity, which is my

creaturely will or "I," but in decreation the creature consents to *co-enact* the crucifixion of God in creation, in that sense becoming both co-creator and co-crucified. In decreating ourselves, we participate in the divine creation of the world (N 309, FLN 328) by going into the void or *nihil*—the abdication of God—not the precreative unity of God. We must always remember that for Weil, "God not incarnate is not really God" (N 222). Divine love is only perfected when the creation of the world—the infinite distance—persists as a real distance.

4. The annihilated soul "wants nothing but its naked God, as he is in himself," and therefore "it wants to go into the simple ground, into the quiet desert, into which distinction never gazed" (*Meister Eckhart: The Essential Sermons* [1981], ed. Edmund Colledge and Bernard McGinn, 198; hereafter abbreviated as *Eckhart*). For expositions of Eckhart's idea that God is encountered in nothingness, see Bernard McGinn, "The God beyond God," *Journal of Religion* 61, no. 1 (January 1981): 1–18; Beverly Lanzetta, "Three Categories of Nothingness in Eckhart," *Journal of Religion* 72, no. 2 (April 1992): 248–68.

5. In *Meister Eckhart* the "poor man" who has annihilated himself, who wants nothing, knows nothing, and has nothing, has taken possession of the lowest place, and God *must* pour himself into this man or else he is not God (*Eckhart*, 199, 197).

6. At this point Weil's thinking closely parallels the doctrine of the will in the *Theologia Germanica*, the anonymous theological treatise that Martin Luther profoundly admired. For that author, the created will that is lodged in the creature is just as much God's will as what we term the eternal will; it is free by essential nature and what is free belongs to no one. When the creature "usurps" the created will, its precious unboundedness and unfettered nobility are destroyed. But as a human being comes to know the true situation, "he becomes poor and reduced to nothing as a self," and from then onward "God himself becomes the person" so that there is nothing that is not God in him and "nothing left in man of which he considers himself the proprietor"; thus "God is at work in man, living in him, knowing, empowering, loving, willing, doing, and resting" (anonymous, *The Theologia Germanica* [1980], 138, 140, 147). This treatise was composed in the Rhineland about half a century after Eckhart preached in his Sermon 52: "If a person really wants to have poverty, he ought to be as free of his own created will as he was when he did not exist," for then this person is so free of God and his works that he suffers God to work in him (*Eckhart*, 200, 202).

7. Hasidic prayer seeks a similar state in which the subject and object of prayer are one and the same, so that "one worships God with God," and to achieve this it is necessary to "consider yourself to be absolute nothingness" (Daniel C. Matt, "*Ayin*: The Concept of Nothingness in Jewish Mysticism," in *Essential Papers on Kabbalah* [1995], ed. Lawrence Fine, 89).

8. Vetö's chapter on "non-acting action" admirably articulates its interconnection with obedience: "The essential attitude of obedience is waiting, and when an

individual who is waiting receives an order, he or she carries it out without its involving any personal goal" (RM 137).

9. Samuel Beckett's *Waiting for Godot*, written in 1948, premiered in 1953, three years after Weil's *Attente de Dieu* (1950) appeared in France, embodies the full irony of the problem that there is "nothing to do" (*rien à faire*) while waiting for God and yet one must continually do something or other to fill the time.

Chapter 6   Conclusion: Weil's Theological Coherence

1. See Daniel O'Hearn, "The Gnosticism of Simone Weil," *Epochē: Journal of the History of Religions at UCLA* 12 (1984), 1–6; Henry Leroy Finch, *Simone Weil and the Intellect of Grace*, ed. Martin Andic (1999), 26–8; and Louis Dupré, "Simone Weil and Platonism," in *The Christian Platonism of Simone Weil*, ed. Doering and Springsted, 9–22. In this essay, Dupré posits that "Weil's Gnostic leanings can hardly be doubted and may in fact have been even more radical than ancient Christian Gnosticism was," for contrary to that ancient Gnosticism, "hers was shorn of any final triumph of good over evil" (21). The present exposition argues, contrary to this claim, that the crucifixion effects at once and simultaneously the advent of all evil *and* the final triumph of redemptive love over evil. It remains for the individual soul to realize through decreative *imitatio* the redemption that God has already "finished" (John 19:30; FLN 108), for God remains united to God across the infinite distance, and that *is* the final triumph of Good.

2. Czeslaw Milosz, for one, has written that "Simone Weil was, at least by temperament, an Albigensian, a Cathar; this is the key to her thought" (Czeslaw Milosz, "The Importance of Simone Weil," in *Emperor of the Earth: Modes of Eccentric Vision* [1977], 91, 115). See also Déodat Roché, "Catholicisme ou Catharisme de Simone Weil," *Cahiers d'études Cathares* 19 (1954), 169–82, and Curt Hohoff, "Christin ausserhalb der Kirche," *Merkur* 24 (1970), 234–43.

3. Alain Birou, "Simone Weil et le Catharisme," *Cahiers Simone Weil* 6, no. 4 (December 1983), 340–5, quotes on 341–2.

4. Maria Fuerth Sulzbach, "Simone Weil: Primitive Christian," *Theology Today* 8, no. 3 (October 1951): 345–53. Nevin similarly adverts to the "fundamental protestantism" of Weil's religious sensibility, with "its Pascalian need to examine and freely believe and its Cartesian autonomy reinforced by doubt" (*Simone Weil*, 273). It is highly telling that Nevin's points of reference are Pascal and Descartes rather than any Protestant thinker.

5. Friedrich Heer, *The Intellectual History of Europe*, trans. Jonathan Steinberg (1966), 315. A major study of the theological import of nominalist thought is Heiko A. Oberman, *The Harvest of Medieval Theology: Gabriel Biel and Late Medieval Nominalism* (1963).

6. Lucien Goldmann, *Le Dieu caché: Étude sur la vision tragique dans les "Pensées" de Pascal et dans le théâtre de Racine* (1959), 17; Walter E. Rex, *Pascal's Provincial Letters* (1977), 12–3, 73–4.

7. Cornelio Fabro, *God in Exile: Modern Atheism, a Study of the Internal Dynamic of Modern Atheism, from Its Roots in the Cartesian Cogito to the Present Day*, trans. Arthur Gibson (1968), 590; Fabro cites the original Brunschvicg edition of Pascal's *Pensées et opuscules* (1917), 536.

8. Leszek Kolakowski, *God Owes Us Nothing: A Brief Remark on Pascal's Religion and on the Spirit of Jansenism* (1995), 88.

9. André Devaux, "Simone Weil et Blaise Pascal," in *Simone Weil: La Soif de l'absolu,* ed. J. P. Little and A. Ughetto, *Sud Revue Littéraire* special issue (Marseilles, 1990), 76. Although Weil's allusions to Pascal in her writings are quite often negative, this cannot be equated with an absence of influence. Nearly all Weil's comments on Augustine are likewise negative, yet she is undeniably in certain key respects an Augustinian thinker. Her criticism of Pascal does not concern his understanding of nature and grace, but the whole premise of the wager and his "lack of probity" in his search for God (NR 249–50). The skeptical Cartesian side of Weil was repelled by the "will to believe" in Pascal, who sought consolation in religion when he should have rigorously sought truth.

10. *Pensées*, Br. 553, quoted in Jan Miel, *Pascal and Theology* (1969), 118.

11. Spinoza, *Treatise on the Emendation of the Intellect*, in *The Collected Works of Spinoza*, ed. Curley, 1:10–1.

12. Letter 58 to G. H. Schuller, in Baruch Spinoza, *The Ethics and Selected Letters* (1982), 250.

13. This nonexistence of free will or autonomy is little recognized among Weil scholars, who write of an "autonomous I" or "autonomous self" or "human autonomy" or "pure subject" in Weil (RM 16–8, 22, 35, 73, 167n20; J. P. Little, "Simone Weil's Concept of Decreation," in *Simone Weil's Philosophy of Culture,* ed. Bell, 27, 32, 36, 39, 51; McLellan, *Utopian Pessimist*, 199; Rowan Williams, "The Necessary Non-Existence of God," in *Simone Weil's Philosophy of Culture,* ed. Bell, 75; Louis Dupré, "Simone Weil and Platonism," 17). Although Weil does occasionally use the term "free will" (e.g., N 223, FLN 211, 212), we must recognize that ultimately there is no genuine autonomy for the later Weil because there is no positive free will—only a negative one, made efficacious by grace—and in this respect the later Weil is decisively non-Cartesian and non-Kantian. Human will per se is inherently heteronomous, for only that which is *not free* in me says "I" (N 175). Grace is the sole source of genuine freedom; the rest belongs to the kingdom of moral gravity.

14. At this point Nicolas Malebranche is a patent influence on Weil. For Malebranche human beings are free and responsible in the sense that they must "consent" to a motive; God inclines human beings through an Augustinian delectation toward the good or the general order (*volonté générale*), and one must feel this delight before consent is possible. But one can be motivated by delectation without being irresistibly or invincibly determined by it. Will, understood by Malebranche as consent to a motive, consists in passively permitting that motive to operate (*Treatise on Nature and Grace* [1992], 58–61).

A comprehensive treatment of Weil's background influences would need to address how Weil's view of providence parallels and differs from Malebranche's notion of *volonté générale*.

15. E. M. Butler traces this tendency among modern German writers in her 1935 study, *The Tyranny of Greece over Germany: A Study of the Influence Exercised by Greek Art and Poetry over the Great German Writers of the Eighteenth, Nineteenth and Twentieth Centuries* (1958). The figures Butler treats, except for Nietzsche and Spitteler, simply did not perceive the "dark background from which the Apolline art they worshipped sprang" (xi). Certainly Weil would have refused affinity with them, having written to her brother, "I will never admit that anyone in the nineteenth century understood anything at all about Greece" (SL 126). Yet her own idealizing tendency inclined her, for example, to a solemn and "heartbreaking" reading of the *Iliad*'s depiction of cruelty and death, whereas some scholars make the case that a grim humor is at work in the poem's treatment of battlefield slaughter that reflects a special Greek taste, their "picturesque and unsentimental ballet scenes" the ancient equivalent of silent movies (Emily Vermeule, *Aspects of Death in Early Greek Art and Poetry* [1979], 97, 96, 99, 85). This does not discount Weil's reading of the *Iliad* as a "poem of might," but it is also more a poem of entertainment than she seemed to be aware—a poem in a complex Greek way both tragic and comic.

16. Gregory Vlastos, *Platonic Studies* (1973), 31–4. Pierre Hadot argues that the same one-way street holds of Plotinus, father of Neoplatonism ("Neoplatonist Spirituality," in *Classical Mediterranean Spirituality*, ed. A. H. Armstrong [1986], 245).

SELECTED BIBLIOGRAPHY

Writings by Simone Weil

First and Last Notebooks. Translated by Richard Rees. Oxford: Oxford University Press, 1970.

Formative Writings, 1929–1941. Edited and translated by Dorothy Tuck McFarland and Wilhelmina Van Ness. Amherst: University of Massachusetts Press, 1987.

Gravity and Grace. Selections from Weil's Marseilles notebooks. Edited and with introduction and postscript by Gustave Thibon. Translated by Emma Crawford and Mario von der Ruhr. London: Routledge, 2002. First published as *La Pesanteur et la grâce*, Paris, 1947.

Intimations of Christianity among the Ancient Greeks. Translated by Elizabeth Chase Geissbühler. London: Routledge & Kegan Paul, 1957.

Lectures on Philosophy. Translated by Hugh Price. Cambridge: Cambridge University Press, 1978.

The Need for Roots. Translated by Arthur Wills. New York: Harper & Row, 1971.

The Notebooks of Simone Weil. 2 vols. Translated by Arthur Wills. London: Routledge & Kegan Paul, 1956.

Oeuvres complètes. 16 vols. Edited by André A. Devaux and Florence de Lussy. Paris: Gallimard, 1988–2006.

On Science, Necessity, and the Love of God. Translated by Richard Rees. London: Oxford University Press, 1968.

Oppression and Liberty. Translated by Arthur Wills and John Petrie. Amherst: University of Massachusetts Press, 1973.

Pensées sans ordre concernant l'amour de Dieu. Paris: Gallimard, 1962.

Selected Essays, 1934–1943. Edited and translated by Richard Rees. London: Oxford University Press, 1962.

Seventy Letters. Translated by Richard Rees. London: Oxford University Press, 1965.

The Simone Weil Reader. Edited by George A. Panichas. Mt. Kisko, NY: Moyer Bell, 1977.

Waiting for God. Translated by Emma Craufurd. Introduction by Leslie A. Fiedler. New York: Harper & Row, 1973.

Selected Works on Simone Weil

Allen, Diogenes, and Eric O. Springsted. *Spirit, Nature and Community: Issues in the Thought of Simone Weil.* Albany: State University of New York Press, 1994.

Andic, Martin. "Amor Fati." Unpublished paper presented at the American Weil Society colloquy, Chicago, April 1999.

———. "The Love of Truth." *Cahiers Simone Weil* 18, no. 4 (December 1995): 389–417.

———. "One Moment of Pure Attention Is Worth All the Good Works in the World." *Cahiers Simone Weil* 21, no. 4 (December 1998): 347–68.

Bell, Richard, ed. *Simone Weil's Philosophy of Culture.* Cambridge: Cambridge University Press, 1993.

Beyer, Dorothee. *Sinn und Genese des Begriffs "Décréation" bei Simone Weil.* Altenberge: Oros, 1992.

Birou, Alain. "Simone Weil et le Catharisme." *Cahiers Simone Weil* 6, no. 4 (December 1983): 340–5.

Blanchot, Maurice. "L'Affirmation (le désire, le malheur)." In *L'Entretien infini.* Paris: Gallimard, 1969.

Blumenthal, Gerda. "Simone Weil's Way of the Cross." *Thought* 27, no. 105 (Summer 1952): 225–34.

Broc-Lapayre, Monique. "Simone Weil et son refus de Nietzsche." *Cahiers Simone Weil* 3, no. 1 (March 1980): 19–32.

Cabaud, Jacques. *Simone Weil: A Fellowship in Love.* New York: Channel, 1964.

Carrouges, Michel. "Religion et religions," *Le Monde nouveau-paru*, nos. 53–54 (1951): 223–8.

Chaning-Pearce, Melville. "Christianity's Crucial Conflict: The Case of Simone Weil." *Hibbert Journal* 49 (1950–1): 333–40.

Chenavier, Robert. *Simone Weil: Attention to the Real.* Translated by Bernard E. Doering. Notre Dame, IN: University of Notre Dame, 2012.

———. *Simone Weil: Une philosophie du travail.* Paris: Cerf, 2001.

Cockburn, David. "Self, World and God in Spinoza and Weil." *Studies in World Christianity* (2001): 173–86.

Courtine-Denamy, Sylvie. *Simone Weil: La quête de racines célestes.* Paris: Cerf, 2009.

Daniélou, J. "Hellenisme, judaïsme, christianisme." In *Réponses aux questions de Simone Weil.* Preface by J.-M. Perrin. Paris: Aubier Montaigne, 1964.

Davy, Marie-Magdalene. *The Mysticism of Simone Weil.* 1951. Translated by Cynthia Rowland. Kila, MT: Kessinger, 2006.

———. *Simone Weil: Sa vie, son oeuvre avec un exposé de sa philosophie.* Paris: Presses Universitaires de France, 1966.

Debidour, Victor-Henry. *Simone Weil ou la transparence.* Paris: Plon, 1963.

Devaux, André. "Simone Weil et Blaise Pascal." In *Simone Weil: La Soif de l'absolu.* Edited by J. P. Little and A. Ughetto. *Sud Revue Littéraire* special issue, Marseilles (1990): 75–99.

Doering, E. Jane, and Eric O. Springsted, eds. *The Christian Platonism of Simone Weil.* South Bend, IN: University of Notre Dame Press, 2004.

Estelrich, Baromeu. "Simone Weil's Concept of Grace." *Modern Theology* 25, no. 2 (April 2009): 239–51.

Farron-Landry, Béatrice. "Détachement, renoncement et origine du mal selon Simone Weil," *Cahiers Simone Weil* 2, no. 2 (June 1979): 71–83.

Finch, Henry Leroy. *Simone Weil and the Intellect of Grace.* Edited by Martin Andic. New York: Continuum, 1999.

Freund, Richard A. "La Tradition mystique juive et Simone Weil." *Cahiers Simone Weil* 10, no. 3 (September 1987): 289–95.

Gabellieri, Emmanuel. *Être et don: L'Unité et l'enjeu de la pensée de Simone Weil.* Paris and Louvin: Peeters, 2003.

Goldschläger, Alain. *Simone Weil et Spinoza: Essai d'interprétation.* Sherbrooke, Québec: Éditions Naaman, 1982.

Idinopolus, Thomas, and Josephine Knopp, eds. *Mysticism, Nihilism, Feminism: New Critical Essays on the Theology of Simone Weil.* Johnson City, TN: Institute of Social Science and Arts, 1984.

Irwin, Alexander. *Saints of the Impossible: Bataille, Weil, and the Politics of the Sacred.* Minnesota: University of Minnesota Press, 2002.

Kahn, Gilbert, ed. *Simone Weil: Philosophe, historienne, et mystique.* Paris: Aubier Montaigne, 1978.

Kühn, Rolf. "La Décréation: Annotations sur un néologisme philosophique, religieux et littéraire." *Revue d'histoire et de philosophie religieuses* 65, no. 1 (1985): 45–52.

———. *Deuten als Entwerden: Eine Synthese des Werkes Simone Weils in hermeneutisch-religionsphilosophischer Sicht.* Fribourg im Breisgau: Herder, 1989.

Levinas, Emmanuel. "Simone Weil against the Bible." In *Difficult Liberty.* London: Athlone, 1990.

Little, J. P. "Simone Weil: Du vide-privation au vide-plénitude." *Cahiers Simone Weil* 10, no. 2 (June 1987): 181–99.

———. "Le Refus de l'idolatrie dans l'oeuvre de Simone Weil." *Cahiers Simone Weil* 2, no. 4 (December 1979): 197–212.

———. *Simone Weil: Waiting on Truth.* Oxford: Berg, 1988.

McCullough, Lissa. "Simone Weil's Phenomenology of the Body." *Comparative and Continental Philosophy* 4, no. 2 (2012): 195–218.

McLellan, David. *Utopian Pessimist: The Life and Thought of Simone Weil.* New York: Poseidon, 1990.

Meltzer, Françoise. "The Hands of Simone Weil." *Critical Inquiry* 27, no. 4 (summer 2001): 611–28.

Milosz, Czeslaw. "The importance of Simone Weil." In *Emperor of the Earth: Modes of Eccentric Vision.* Berkeley: University of California Press, 1977.

———. *The Land of Ulro.* Translated by Louis Iribarne. New York: Farrar, Straus, Giroux, 1981.

Narcy, Michel. *Simone Weil: Malheur et beauté du monde.* Paris: Éditions du Centurion, 1967.

Nava, Alexander. *The Mystical and Prophetic Thought of Simone Weil and Gustavo Gutiérrez.* Albany: State University of New York Press, 2001.

Nevin, Thomas R. *Simone Weil: Portrait of a Self-Exiled Jew.* Chapel Hill: University of North Carolina Press, 1991.

O'Hearn, Daniel. "The Gnosticism of Simone Weil." *Epochē: Journal of the History of Religions at UCLA* 12 (1984): 1–6.

Perrin, J.-M., and G. Thibon. *Simone Weil as We Knew Her.* Translated by Emma Craufurd. New York: Routledge, 2004.

Pétrement, Simone. *Simone Weil: A Life.* Translated by Raymond Rosenthal. New York: Pantheon, 1977.

Pirruccello, Ann. "'Gravity' in the Thought of Simone Weil." *Philosophy and Phenomenological Research* 57, no. 1 (March 97): 73–93.

———. "Interpreting Simone Weil: Presence and Absence in Attention." *Philosophy East and West* 45, no. 1 (January 1995): 61–72.

Rees, Richard. *Simone Weil: A Sketch for a Portrait.* Carbondale: Southern Illinois University Press, 1966.

Roché, Déodat. "Catholicisme ou Catharisme de Simone Weil." *Cahiers d'études Cathares* 19 (1954): 169–82.

Rozelle-Stone, Rebecca A., and Lucian Stone. *Simone Weil and Theology.* New York: Bloomsbury T & T Clark, 2013.

Rozelle-Stone, Rebecca A., and Lucian Stone, eds. *Relevance of the Radical: Simone Weil 100 Years Later.* London: T & T Clark, 2009.

von der Ruhr, Mario. *Simone Weil: An Apprenticeship in Attention.* London: Continuum, 2006.

Springsted, Eric O. *Christus Mediator: Platonic Mediation in the Thought of Simone Weil.* AAR Academy Series, vol. 41. Chico, CA: Scholars, 1983.

———. "Théorie weilienne et théorie platonicienne de la nécessité." *Cahiers Simone Weil* 4, no. 3 (September 1981): 149–67.

Sulzbach, Maria Fuerth. "Simone Weil: Primitive Christian." *Theology Today* 8, no. 3 (October 1951): 345–53.

Taubes, Susan A. "The Absent God." *Journal of Religion* 35, no. 1 (January 1955): 6–16.

Vetö, Miklos. *The Religious Metaphysics of Simone Weil.* Translated by Joan Dargan. Albany: State University of New York Press, 1994.

———. "Simone Weil and Suffering." *Thought* 40 (summer 1965): 275–86.

White, George Abbott. *Simone Weil: Interpretations of a Life.* Amherst: University of Massachusetts Press, 1981.

Winch, Peter. *Simone Weil: "The Just Balance."* Cambridge: Cambridge University Press, 1989.

Wolfteich, Claire. "Attention or Destruction: Simone Weil and the Paradox of the Eucharist." *Journal of Religion* 81, no. 3 (July 2001): 369–76.

Yourgrau, Palle. *Simone Weil.* Critical Lives series. London: Reaktion, 2011.

Other Works Cited

Anonymous. *The Theologia Germanica of Martin Luther.* Translated by Bengt Hoffman. New York: Paulist, 1980.

Aquinas, Thomas. *Summa Theologica.* Vol. 1. Translated by Fathers of the English Dominican Province. New York: Benzinger, 1947.

Ariès, Phillipe. *The Hour of Our Death.* Translated by Helen Weaver. New York: Knopf, 1981.

Armstrong, A. H. "The Divine Enhancement of Earthly Beauties." In *On Beauty.* Eranos Lectures, no. 6. Dallas: Spring, 1962.

Augustine. *Confessions.* Translated by R. S. Pine-Coffin. New York: Penguin, 1961.

Beckett, Samuel. *Waiting for Godot: A Tragicomedy in Two Acts.* New York: Grove, 1954.

Butler, E. M. *The Tyranny of Greece over Germany: A Study of the Influence Exercised by Greek Art and Poetry over the Great German Writers of the Eighteenth, Nineteenth and Twentieth Centuries.* Boston: Beacon, 1958.

Curley, Edwin. *Behind the Geometrical Method: A Reading of Spinoza's Ethics.* Princeton: Princeton University Press, 1988.

Dostoevsky, Fyodor. *The Brothers Karamazov.* 2 vols. Translated by David Magarshack. New York: Penguin, 1958.

Eckhart, Meister. *Meister Eckhart: The Essential Sermons, Commentaries, Treatises, and Defense.* Edited by Edmund Colledge and Bernard McGinn. New York: Paulist, 1981.

Fabro, Cornelio. *God in Exile: Modern Atheism, a Study of the Internal Dynamic of Modern Atheism, from Its Roots in the Cartesian Cogito to the Present Day.* Translated by Arthur Gibson. Westminster, MD: Newman, 1968.

Freud, Sigmund. *Civilization and Its Discontents.* Translated by James Strachey. New York: Norton, 1961.

Goldmann, Lucien. *Le Dieu caché: Étude sur la vision tragique dans les "Pensées" de Pascal et dans le théâtre de Racine.* Paris: Gallimard, 1959.

Hadot, Pierre. "Neoplatonist Spirituality: I. Plotinus and Porphyry." In *Classical Mediterranean Spirituality: Egyptian, Greek, Roman.* Edited by A. H. Armstrong. New York: Crossroad, 1986.

Heer, Friedrich. *The Intellectual History of Europe.* Translated by Jonathan Steinberg. London: Werdenfeld and Nicolson, 1966.

Heller, Erich. *The Importance of Nietzsche: Ten Essays.* Chicago: University of Chicago Press, 1988.

Hobbes, Thomas. *Leviathan.* Edited by C. B. Macpherson. New York: Penguin, 1968.

Hyppolite, Jean. *Studies on Marx and Hegel.* Translated by John O'Neill. New York: Basic, 1969.

Kant, Immanuel. *Groundwork of the Metaphysic of Morals.* Translated by H. J. Paton. New York: Harper & Row, 1964.

Kierkegaard, Søren. *Attack Upon Christendom.* 1854–55. Translated with an introduction and notes by Walter Lowrie. Introduction by Howard A. Johnson. Princeton: Princeton University Press, 1968.

———. *Fear and Trembling* and *Repetition.* Kierkegaard's Writings, vol. 6. Translated by Howard V. Hong and Edna H. Hong. Princeton: Princeton University Press, 1983.

———. *Practice in Christianity.* Kierkegaard's Writings, vol. 20. Edited and translated by Howard V. Hong and Edna H. Hong. Princeton: Princeton University Press, 1991.

Kirk, G. S., J. E. Raven, and M. Schofield. *The Presocratic Philosophers.* 2nd ed. Cambridge: Cambridge University Press, 1983.

Kolakowski, Leszek. *God Owes Us Nothing: A Brief Remark on Pascal's Religion and on the Spirit of Jansenism.* Chicago: University of Chicago Press, 1995.

Koyré, Alexandre. "Introduction to Descartes." In *Descartes: Philosophical Writings.* Translated by Elizabeth Anscombe and Peter Thomas Geach. London: Nelson, 1969.

Lanzetta, Beverly. "Three Categories of Nothingness in Eckhart." *The Journal of Religion* 72, no. 2 (April 1992): 248–68.

Liebes, Yehuda. "Myth vs. Symbol in the Zohar and in Lurianic Kabbalah." In *Essential Papers on Kabbalah.* Edited by Lawrence Fine. New York: New York University Press, 1995.

Lovejoy, Arthur O. *The Great Chain of Being: A Study of the History of an Idea.* New York: Harper & Brothers, 1960.

———. "Milton and the Paradox of the Fortunate Fall." In *Critical Essays on Milton from ELH.* Editor unknown. Baltimore: Johns Hopkins University Press, 1969.

Malebranche, Nicolas. *Treatise on Nature and Grace.* Translated by Patrick Riley. Oxford: Clarendon, 1992.

Mallarmé, Stéphane. *Stéphane Mallarmé: Collected Poems.* Translated by Henry Weinfield. Berkeley: University of California Press, 1994.

Matt, Daniel C. "*Ayin:* The Concept of Nothingness in Jewish Mysticism." In *Essential Papers on Kabbalah.* Edited by Lawrence Fine. New York: New York University Press, 1995.

———. "Varieties of Mystical Nothingness: Jewish, Christian, and Buddhist." *Studia Philonica Annual* 9 (1997): 316–31.

McGinn, Bernard. "The God beyond God: Theology and Mysticism in the Thought of Meister Eckhart." *Journal of Religion* 61, no. 1 (January 1981): 1–18.

Miel, Jan. *Pascal and Theology.* Baltimore: Johns Hopkins Press, 1969.

Nelli, René. *La Vie quotidienne des Cathares du Languedoc au XIIIe siècle.* Paris: Hachette, 1969.

Nietzsche, Friedrich. *Beyond Good and Evil: Prelude to a Philosophy of the Future.* Translated by Walter Kaufmann. New York: Vintage, 1966.

———. *On the Genealogy of Morals and Ecce Homo.* Translated by Walter Kaufmann and R. J. Hollingdale. New York: Vintage, 1967.

Nishitani, Keiji. *Religion and Nothingness.* Translated by Jan Van Bragt. Berkeley: University of California Press, 1982.

Novak, David. "Self-Contradiction of the Godhead in Kabbalistic Theology." In *Neoplatonism and Jewish Thought.* Edited by Lenn E. Goodman. Albany: State University of New York Press, 1992.

Oberman, Heiko A. *The Harvest of Medieval Theology: Gabriel Biel and Late Medieval Nominalism.* Cambridge, MA: Harvard University Press, 1963.

———. "Some Notes on the Theology of Nominalism with Attention to Its Relation to the Renaissance." *Harvard Theological Review* 53 (1960): 47–76.

Pluhar, Evelyn B. *Beyond Prejudice: The Moral Significance of Human and Nonhuman Animals.* Durham: Duke University Press, 1995.

Rex, Walter E. *Pascal's Provincial Letters: An Introduction.* London: Hodder and Stoughton, 1977.

Schelling, F. W. J. *The Ages of the World.* Translated by Jason M. Wirth. Albany: State University of New York Press, 2000.

Scholem, Gershom. *Major Trends in Jewish Mysticism.* New York: Schocken, 1941.

Sedgwick, Alexander. *Jansenism in Seventeenth Century France: Voices in the Wilderness.* Charlottesville: University Press of Virginia, 1977.

Shōtō, Hase. "The Structure of Faith: Nothingness-*qua*-Love." In *Religious Philosophy of Tanabe Hajime,* edited by Taitetsu Unno and James W. Heisig, 89–116. Berkeley: Asian Humanities Press, 1990.

Spinoza, Baruch. *The Collected Works of Spinoza.* Vol. 1. Edited and translated by Edwin Curley. Princeton: Princeton University Press, 1985.

———. *The Ethics and Selected Letters.* Translated by Samuel Shirley. Indianapolis: Hackett, 1982.

Vermeule, Emily. *Aspects of Death in Early Greek Art and Poetry.* Sather Classical Lectures, vol. 46. Berkeley: University of California Press, 1979.

Vlastos, Gregory. *Platonic Studies.* Princeton: Princeton University Press, 1973.

Wolfson, Elliot R. "Nihilating Nonground and the Temporal Sway of Becoming." *Angelaki: Journal of the Theoretical Humanities* 17, no. 3 (2012): 31–45.

———. *Nequddat ha-Reshimu*—The Trace of Transcendence and the Transcendence of Trace: The Paradox of *Simsum* in the RaShaB's Hemshekh Ayin Beit." *Kabbalah: Journal for the Study of Jewish Mystical Texts* 30 (2013): 75–120.

INDEX

Milton Keynes UK
Ingram Content Group UK Ltd.
UKHW020041280723
425932UK00012B/274